Illusions of Freedom

Illusions of Freedom

Thomas Merton and Jacques Ellul on Technology and the Human Condition

Jeffrey M. Shaw

PICKWICK *Publications* · Eugene, Oregon

ILLUSIONS OF FREEDOM
Thomas Merton and Jacques Ellul on Technology and the Human Condition

Pickwick Publications
An Imprint of Wipf and Stock Publishers
199 W. 8th Ave., Suite 3
Eugene, OR 97401

www.wipfandstock.com

ISBN 13: 978-1-62564-058-1

Cataloging-in-Publication data:

Shaw, Jeffrey M.

Illusions of freedom : Thomas Merton and Jacques Ellul on technology and the human condition / Jeffrey M. Shaw.

xiv + 194 pp. ; 23 cm—Includes bibliographical references.

ISBN 13: 978-1-62564-058-1

1. Technology—Religious aspects—History—20th century. 2. Ellul, Jacques, 1912–1994 3. Merton, Thomas, 1915–1968. I. Title.

T14 .S53 2014

Manufactured in the USA

For Robin, Kara, and Erin

Contents

Preface

Nearly every facet of daily life has seen some kind of change over the last few decades. A proliferation of gadgets, devices, and ways of incorporating these objects into daily routines has drastically altered our ways of doing work, interacting with each other, and defining who we are. This book does not have anything to say about any of the new devices or technologies that have appeared over the last few decades, or at any time in the past. Rather, it is an examination of a slightly different set of opinions on the impact that these technological advances have had on our human condition. It is an attempt to give two particular individuals their chance to be heard, and in doing so, to allow readers to reflect on ways of thinking about technology that heretofore, they may not have considered. One should not read this book thinking that the opinions expressed by either Thomas Merton or Jacques Ellul are "correct" or "incorrect." I have attempted only to compare their views on technology and its impact on freedom, and in doing so have hopefully allowed those who may not be familiar with either of these thinkers to investigate some of their other writing more thoroughly.

What impact does technology have on freedom in the thought of Thomas Merton and Jacques Ellul? Contemporary technology has the potential to hinder humanity's attainment of freedom in their opinion. Both thinkers offer unique perspectives on the impact that they believe technology has had on society in the twentieth century, and they both offer unconventional definitions of the concept of freedom. It is important to note at the beginning that neither Merton nor Ellul sought to provide definitive answers to the questions they posed, but rather to encourage others to begin thinking more broadly about the consequences of continued advances in technology. This book will hopefully encourage others to do just that, and to use the ideas that Merton and Ellul proposed not as answers to any particular question, but as avenues for further inquiry into the nature and meaning of life in contemporary society.

Examining the perspectives offered by Merton and Ellul on technol ogy and freedom allows those working within the disciplines of theology, literature, and the philosophy of technology to incorporate works by these two Christian thinkers within a variety of disciplines. Somewhat ironi cally, many readers may encounter this book online, or read it via e-book or on a Kindle—just a few of the marvels that contemporary technology has bestowed upon us. As one progresses through this book, it should be come apparent that neither Merton nor Ellul are leveling a critique against particular technological products (with the exception perhaps of nuclear weapons), but rather against the processes that compose what they believe to be an all-encompassing technological system. Of particular interest in developing this book is the assertion in the July 1998 edition of *lul Forum* that "for anyone who has read Ellul, the similarity of Merton's critique of technological civilization is startling and impressive. Virtually point for point, Merton and Ellul, writing about the same time, echo each other"[1] This study examines those mutual influences and addresses point-by-point a number of the similarities between Merton and Ellul regarding their critique of technology's role in contemporary society, and its impact on human freedom.

Situating Merton and Ellul within the ongoing philosophical debate over the role of technology in daily life and on the nature of freedom is another purpose behind this book. The chapters which follow identify similarities between their thinking and areas in which they found common intellectual ground. It is an attempt to fuse Merton's monastic response to the contemporary, technologically-focused world to Ellul's secular, albeit theologically-centered response. As one of the first comprehensive attempts to compare these two worldviews, this study represents a small but hope fully significant contribution to the field of Merton and Ellul scholarship.

In addition to their own ideas, the study identifies some of the com mon antecedents to their thought. Neither Merton nor Ellul developed their ideas concerning the impact of technology on the human condition in a vacuum. Having engaged with many of the intellectuals of their time, both thinkers either directly incorporated outside thinking into their own worldviews, or in some cases changed certain aspects of their thinking based on engagement with the ideas of others. Specifically, the study will address their intellectual engagement with Karl Barth, Søren Kierkegaard, Aldous Huxley, and Karl Marx.

1. Fasching, "In This Issue," 1.

Both Thomas Merton and to a lesser extent, Jacques Ellul, have had their lives recounted and their ideas presented in a number of works since their deaths, and this study will not attempt to provide a complete review of either author's entire body of work, nor a complete biographical account of their lives. Similarities between their upbringings will be identified, establishing the pattern through which the study will attempt to compare their thought on a point-by-point basis, noting similarities and differences throughout. Examining Merton and Ellul through theological, sociological, and political lenses allows a point-by-point comparison of a number of different ideas that directly relate to the impact that they believed technology has had on the human condition. This comparison identifies commonalities of thought and traces some of the antecedents to their thought. Merton the Roman Catholic and Ellul the Protestant offer remarkably similar conclusions regarding the impact that technology has had on the human condition. As Christians, they provide a distinctly Christocentric view of freedom, and it is against this unique view that the impact of technology and the idea of progress is evaluated. While many readers will not agree with the definition of freedom that both men present, some may find that their analysis of technology's impact on our human condition still resonates in the twenty first century. In other words, one does not have to subscribe to a Christocentric view of freedom to necessarily find points of agreement with the specifics of the critique that is presented in these pages. In summary, both Merton and Ellul are examples of men not only thinking about the impact that technology has had on human freedom as much as they are individuals firmly committed to living out the ideals that they spent their lives articulating.

Acknowledgments

This book owes its existence to many people who encouraged and supported me throughout the writing process. Originally a doctoral dissertation delivered in pursuit of a PhD in humanities at Salve Regina University, I would first like to thank the faculty at Salve and my classmates for their encouragement and friendship over the course of many long years of study in the program. I would like to especially thank my advisor and mentor, Timothy Demy, ThD, PhD, without whose oversight and guidance this project would never have been completed. Also on my committee were Dr. Dan Cowdin and Dr. Craig Condella, both of whom provided additional guidance, recommendations, and ideas. My thanks goes out to them and to everyone at Salve who helped me in this effort.

Others who provided valuable encouragement and support include Dr. Paul Pearson, the director and archivist of the Thomas Merton Center, Dr. Phillip M. Thompson, renowned Merton scholar and director of the Aquinas Center of Theology at Emory University, and Dr. David Gill, president of the International Jacques Ellul Society and the Mockler-Phillips Professor of Workplace Theology & Business Ethics at the Gordon Conwell Theological Seminary. I hope this book finds a place on their bookshelves, alongside their own contributions to both Merton and Ellul scholarship.

For permission to include excerpts of Jacques Ellul's poetry I would like to thank Didier Schillinger of Opales Publishing in Bordeaux, France. Also providing helpful Merton-related material was Albert Romkema, owner of one of the largest collection of Merton artifacts in existence. I would also like to thank two individuals at Wipf and Stock Publishers—Christian Amondson for his oversight of the project, and Jacob Martin for his guidance at the earliest stage of the editing process. The entire Wipf and Stock team provided timely and helpful assistance along the way.

Acknowledgments

Most importantly, my wife, Robin, and daughters, Kara and Erin, suf
fered through my many absences while I was writing this book. Robin's
suggestions and encouragement led to the publication of this dissertation
in its current form—without her help, it would not have seen the light of
day. It is therefore dedicated to them with, as always, my deepest gratitude
and affection.

1 Introduction

Technology has been a liberating force, which has for millions of people increased standards of living and longevity. Whether in the field of healthcare, nutrition, computers, weaponry, transportation, and education, various innovations and technological advancements have radically changed the way of life for many people on the planet over the last centuries, with very noticeable changes even just over the last decade or two. Millions, if not billions of people have benefited tremendously from the march of progress. Who would argue otherwise? Two twentieth-century figures have a different view of the impact that technology has had on the human condition. Thomas Merton and Jacques Ellul viewed technology differently than their contemporaries. In order to understand their particular points of view, one must first come to terms with their definitions of both technology and freedom. This introductory chapter will provided those definitions, as well as provide an overview of the chapters that outline the various perspectives that Merton and Ellul used to advance their argument that technology can and should be seen as a hindrance to humankind's attainment of freedom.

It should be noted that this book is not an attempt to label either Merton's or Ellul's particular point of view as "correct," or more accurate than other points of view that one might encounter in contemporary culture regarding technology. It is incumbent on the reader to discern the merits (or lack thereof) of the arguments presented herein. The intent is to compare the viewpoints that Merton and Ellul offer, identifying similarities, and occasionally differences, between their assertion that technology has had, and continues to have, a negative aspect. An additional objective is to provide scholars working in the fields of Merton and/or Ellul studies with avenues for further inquiry regarding the intellectual approaches that these two men brought to bear on this topic, as well as on other topics relating to the human condition in contemporary society. One final hope is that this book might compel the general reader to investigate both Merton and Ellul more closely, inviting new participants to the debate about our interaction with technology. Seven chapters support this discussion, focusing on three overarching perspectives through which Merton and Ellul formulated their thinking on technology. The first perspective will be the theological, fol lowed by the sociological, and finally the political, presenting a general trajectory from the transcendent to the immanent. Following the examina tion of their political perspective will be a chapter comparing their literary output.

Chapter 1 is the introduction, which provides the definitions of tech nology and freedom that Merton and Ellul employed in their writing. Read ers will note that these definitions are radically different from anything that might be encountered in popular culture, or encountered in the Western philosophical tradition in general. The similarity between their particular definitions of freedom is striking, and the chapters which follow illustrate the implications of their adherence to this definition.

Chapter 2 will provide an overview of both men's lives, although the intent is not to provide a simple biographical sketch. The objective will be to identify some common experiential sources for their worldviews as adults, specifically, their similar religious conversion experiences, and their up bringing in rural environments. The chapter will also address Ellul's theory of *technique* and explore both Ellul's and Merton's use of the dialectic as an intellectual device.

The third chapter will look at Merton and Ellul from a theological perspective, and begins with an overview of Karl Barth's (1886 thought and its impact on both men. Barth's thought regarding the nature of freedom is foundational to Ellul's entire body of work. Merton refines some of this own thinking on the subject of freedom through his engage ment with Barth's work. Critiques of the institutional church, referred to as the "visible church" as opposed to the "invisible church," are examined in this chapter, as both Merton and Ellul saw a disconnect between the individual practice of Christian faith and the institutional structures that purport to further such practice. They believe that the church has a specific role in helping humankind to identify the true self, and that technology has hindered the church in this regard. The true and false self are addressed in detail in chapter 4.

Chapter 4 examines the sociological perspective. Both Merton and Ellul were deeply influenced, but in different ways, by the Danish philosopher Søren Kierkegaard (1813–1855). English philosopher Aldous Huxley (1894–1963) also influenced various aspects of both men's thinking. This examination consists of another set of point-by-point Merton-Ellul comparisons beginning with their thinking on propaganda and the notion of the "mass man." The idea of self-transcendence in their thinking will also be addressed. Throughout Merton's writing, one finds references both implicitly and explicitly stated referring to the need to cast away the false self and seek the true self, allowing us to recognize and accept the gift of true freedom. Ellul does not emphasize the necessity to transcend the false self as emphatically as Merton does, but this idea is still one that he proposes as an essential step on the road to attaining freedom. Also discussed in this chapter will be technology's role in the furtherance of propaganda and the role that it plays in hindering self-transcendence, the City as the ultimate manifestation of *technique*, and their respective views on non-violence.

Chapter 5 will cover the political perspective. Karl Marx influenced both Merton and Ellul. This profound antecedent to their thought is addressed first, followed by a point-by-point comparison of Merton's and Ellul's views on the city—a phenomenon that they both see as the ultimate manifestation of human technology, and a major impediment to the discovery of the true self, a discovery which both men believe to be a first step on the road to achieving freedom. Another point of comparison is their similar approach to social work and Roman Catholic social teaching, which provides an example of the type of life that one might live upon accepting the gift of true freedom as defined in chapter 2. Although a Protestant, Ellul shares an affinity for the work and writing of Roman Catholic luminaries such as Dorothy Day (1897–1980) and Peter Maurin (1877–1949). Day and Maurin both profoundly influenced Merton. Ellul, although a member of the Protestant French Reformed Church and not a Roman Catholic, provided some of the intellectual framework for this movement although he did not participate in the movement directly.

Merton and Ellul often directed their societal critiques at both the capitalist societies of the West and the communist societies of the East. A section is devoted to this tendency in their writing. This chapter concludes with a look at their quest for a "third way" in politics. While this third way does not directly correlate into a prescription for achieving true freedom, it suggests that both men believe that one can evade the grip of propaganda and *technique* to various degrees, ultimately serving as a point of departure from which one can potentially overcome the false self.

The sixth chapter evaluates Merton and Ellul as poets and literary figures. Both men wrote poems that allowed them to express many of their ideas regarding the insidious effects of technology on the human condition. In addition to comparing their poetry, this chapter will also look at their engagement with the work of Albert Camus (1913–1960) and Eugène Ionesco (1909–1994). Also considered in this chapter will be an assessment of the status of language and the written word in both Merton's and Ellul's thinking. They identify the Revealed Word as the source of human freedom, and this chapter focuses on their thinking regarding the tension between word and image in contemporary society. The seventh chapter concludes the study, introducing some avenues for further inquiry.

Defining Technology

Both Merton and Ellul refer to technology throughout their writing. At times, their reference is to a particular technological product, such as the automobile, the television, or even to the simple tape recorder. However, for the most part, when referring to technology, it is the technological process—the rationality and efficiency that has culminated in the idea of progress—that is being questioned. Ellul expresses this idea as "*technique* wrote, "*Technique* refers to any complex of standardized means for attaining a predetermined result. Thus, it converts spontaneous and unreflective behavior into behavior that is deliberate and rationalized. The Technical Man is . . . committed to the never-ending search for "the one best way" to achieve any designated objective."[1] With this statement, Ellul presented his forceful thesis that contemporary society is a "civilization committed to the quest for continually improved means to carelessly examined ends." It is the predominant theme of much of Ellul's work—a theme with which Thomas Merton agrees. Despite their different faiths and the fact that they never met or corresponded directly with each other, "Ellul and Merton are strikingly similar in their perception of *technique* and of *technique's* hold on the world."[3] Speaking of technology, Merton wrote:

1. Ellul, *Technological Society*, vi.
2. Ibid.
3. Davenport, "Jacques Ellul and Thomas Merton on Technique," 10.

Technology. No! When it comes to taking sides, I am not with [those] who are open mouthed in awe at the "new holiness" of a technological cosmos in which man condescends to be God's collaborator, and improve everything for Him. Not that technology is per se impious. It is simply neutral and there is no greater nonsense than taking it for an ultimate value . . . We gain nothing by surrendering to technology as if it were a ritual, a worship, a liturgy (or talking of our liturgy as if it were an expression of the "sacred" supposedly now revealed in technological power). Where impiety is in the hypostatizing of mechanical power as something to do with the Incarnation, as its fulfillment, its epiphany. When it comes to taking sides I am with Ellul . . .[4]

Merton's agreement with Elul on this point is the framework for this book. *Technique's* deleterious impact on contemporary society will be the focal points for the chapters that follow.

It is also necessary to situate Thomas Merton and Jacques Ellul within the framework of the debate over technology and the human condition. Carl Mitcham, a leading contemporary thinker regarding the nature and philosophy of technology, believes that "technology, or the making and using of artifacts, is a largely unthinking activity."[5] This particular description of technology captures the essence of the word as it relates to this study. Technology not only refers to specific products but also to the largely unthinking processes that result in the manufacture of both the products themselves and the perceived needs that precede the appearance of the products. Mitcham also provides a link between technology and theology—a crucial idea that both Merton and Ellul spoke about at length:

Theology has generally concentrated on analyzing an apparently contingent or disconnected series of moral problems obviously engendered by technology (industrial alienation, nuclear weapons, the social justice of development, biomedical engineering, mass media, etc.) without either systematically relating such specific issues or grounding them in more fundamental reflections on the relationship between faith and technological reasoning.[6]

In other words, Merton and Ellul will approach the issue of technology through the theological lens, and in doing so will address nuclear weapons

---

4. Merton, *Dancing in the Waters of Life*, 166.
5. Mitcham, *Thinking through Technology*, 1.
6. Mitcham, "Technology as a Theological Problem," 3.

and social justice—issues which Mitcham raises in the above quote. Nuclear weapons are of course part of the environmental backdrop against which both men wrote—having done the bulk of their writing during the height of the Cold War. The social justice of development is emphasized as part of Merton's Roman Catholic social teaching, and the Protestant Ellul will engage this topic in his work. Both writers addressed mass media—Merton through his elaboration on the concept of the "mass man" and Ellul in his in-depth analysis of propaganda. Mitcham has thus introduced the problem confronting theology and theologians—how can one address these issues in a comprehensive Christian manner?

Many philosophers equate technology with machines. In particular, Lewis Mumford (1895–1990), an American urban planner and philosopher, did so in nearly all of his writing. According to Mumford, "the 'machine' may exist in other forms than as a physical object. The parts may not be metals but human beings; the organization may not be that embodied in the machine but an organizational chart; the source of power may not be electricity or the combustion of gas but muscle power or the pride of men; and the task may not be the manufacture of a product but the control of a nation."[7] Mumford not only equated technology with machines, but also with process, and more importantly, with the pursuit of power and control. This autonomous pursuit of power and control is similar to Ellul's theory of *technique*. However, Mumford dismissed Ellul as "a sociological fatalist," and so it is difficult to draw too many comparisons between Mumford and Ellul.[8] Others would dismiss Ellul as too pessimistic—offering no way out of for the individual seeking to escape the technological society. Even Merton would at times find Ellul's writing to be too pessimistic.

Merton's critique of technology originally centered on the actual products of modern technology rather than on any particular process. Once he entered the monastery, he had hoped to put himself out of the world's reach, but technology caught up with him. The abbot at that time, Dom James Fox, began a modernization project shortly after Merton entered the monastery at Gethsemane in Kentucky in December 1941. "The noisy tractors, replacing horses and wagons, annoyed a Merton who had come to the monastery seeking silence, and had suddenly found it becoming a place

---

7. Miller, "Effect of Technology," 6.

8. Mumford, *Myth of the Machine*, 290–91; quoted in Fasching, *Thought of Jacques Ellul*, viii.

of noise and distraction."[9] Merton came face to face with the distractions that he had specifically sought to escape. It would be another two decades before he would read anything written by Ellul and before he would begin to formulate his thought regarding the deleterious influence that technology had on society as a whole.

In the meantime, Merton would correspond with Lewis Mumford, and some of Mumford's ideas regarding the rapid pace of urbanization influenced Merton's thought on the impact of technology upon contemporary society. However, once Merton had considered the impact that technology and the idea of progress was beginning to have on society as well as on the Church, he would later proclaim, "I also think that the [Vatican] needs to rest on a deeper realization of the urgent problems posed by technology today. (The Constitution on Mass Media seems to have been totally innocent of any such awareness.) For one thing, the whole massive complex of technology, which reaches into every aspect of social life today, implies a huge organization of which no one is really in control, and which dictates its own solutions irrespective of human needs or even of reason."[10] In this passage, Merton clearly identified technology with a process and a phenomenon rather than simply pointing to some particular product or machine. He also mentioned the mass media, which will be covered in chapter 4. Pointing out the fact that no one actually controls technology's advance is another facet of this passage, placing Merton firmly in agreement with one of Ellul's central tenets regarding *technique*. Merton continued, "Technology now has reasons entirely its own which do not necessarily take into account the needs of man, and this huge inhuman mechanism, which the whole human race is now serving rather than commanding, seems quite probably geared for the systematic destruction of the natural world, quite apart from the question of the 'bomb' which, in fact, is only one rather acute symptom of the whole disease."[11] Merton equated actual products of technology with the technological process—a common tendency in much of his Cold War writing. However, he again demonstrated an affinity for Ellul's concept of *technique* through his assertion that the entire process is one that continues to operate outside of humankind's control. He concluded this lengthy discussion with the following:

9. Shannon, "Can One Be a Contemplative?," 12.

10. Merton, *Hidden Ground of Love*, 383–84.

11. Ibid.

I am not of course saying that technology is "bad," and that progress is something to be feared. But I am saying that behind the cloak of specious myths about technology and progress, there seems to be at work a vast uncontrolled power which is leading man where he does not want to go in spite of himself and in which the Church, it seems to me, ought to be somewhat aware of the intervention of the "principalities and powers" of which St. Paul speaks. I know this kind of language is not very popular today, but I think it is so important that it cannot be left out of account. For instance I think that the monumental work of Jacques Ellul on *La Technique* is something that cannot be ignored by the Church Fathers if they wish to see all the aspects of the crucial question of the Church and the world.[12]

These statements represent the pinnacle of Merton's thought regarding technology. It is informed by Ellul's theory of *technique* as well as by his own personal experiences in dealing with the Church hierarchy—experiences which will be covered in detail in chapter 3.

Responding to the question of whether or not he was against technology *per se*, as opposed to specific technological products, Merton wrote, "What I am questioning is the universal myth that technology infallibly makes everything in every way better for everybody. It does not."[13] He also stated that "there has never been such abject misery on earth as that which our technological society has produced along with the fantastic plenty for very few. What I am 'against' then is a complacent and naïve progressivism which pays no attention to anything but the fact that wonderful things can be and are done with machinery and with electronics."[14] These statements demonstrate that Merton's fully developed thought regarding technology was remarkably similar to Ellul's, although Merton would occasionally gravitate towards radical anti-technology statements while criticizing other facets of the social and political scene in the 1960s. For example, he remarked that "in our technological world we have wonderful methods for keeping people alive and wonderful methods for killing them off, and they both go together. We rush in and save lives from tropical diseases, then we come in with napalm and burn up the people we have saved. The net result is more murder, more suffering, more inhumanity. This I know is

12. Merton, *Hidden Ground of Love*, 383–84.
13. Merton, *Road to Joy*, 98.
14. Ibid., 99.

a caricature, but is it that far from the truth?"[15] He combined a critique of not only the products of advanced technology but also the mindset of efficiency and power exemplified in contemporary society. Like Ellul, he sought a way out, but unlike Ellul, he offers at least the statement, "What is my answer? I don't have one, except to suggest that technology could be used entirely differently. But the only way it ever will be is to get it free from this inescapable hang-up with profit and power, so that it will be used for people and not for money or politics."[16] Ellul would not concede that humans willfully wield technology, since *technique* maintains its own set of values that ensure its continued advance.

Like Ellul, Merton believed that an uncritical acceptance of the idea that technological progress offered a panacea to all of humankind's ills was dangerous and misguided. His thinking paralleled Ellul in this regard. Merton stated that "if technology helps to express the creative power of love, then all the better: it will give glory to God and have its own place in the Kingdom of God on earth. But technology by itself will never establish that Kingdom."[17] As Merton's thought on the topic coalesced, he repeatedly turned to Ellul, who had come to represent for Merton the leading thinker on technology. Merton stated that "the old structures, manifestly inadequate in some ways, are being taken away, and instead of being spiritually liberated, Christians are rushing to submit to much more tyrannical structures: the *absolute* dominion of technology-politics-business (or state capital) . . . Have you by any chance read the book of Jacques Ellul on the *Technological Society* (perhaps *La Technique* in French)? It is monumental, and one of the most important treatises on the subject."[18] Merton wondered how one could account for the dilemma posed by technology. Was contemporary society helpless to check the further spread of technology and the idea of progress? Seeking to discern some rationale for this phenomenon, and approaching the topic in a manner consistent with a viewpoint that either Merton or Ellul might have adopted, one might ask:

> Why would humanity accept a regime of "technique" that nurtured a coarsened view of social relationships? As the physicist Max Born noted, it was a triumph of the intellect instead of reason. The intellect distinguished between the possible and the impossible,

15. Ibid.

16. Ibid.

17. Ibid., 99–100.

18. Merton, *Hidden Ground of Love*, 468.

> while reason distinguished between the sensible and the senseless.
> Thus, manned space flight could simultaneously be a triumph of
> intellect and a failure of reason.[19]

The use of the word "technique" in this passage does not necessarily imply acceptance of Ellul's definition of the term, but according to Max Born, the combined play of intellect and reason serve to propel technology forward. Born, like Merton and Ellul, sought to explain how technology could prog ress on paths which seemed to be so far divergent from the interests of the greater part of humanity.

Throughout this study, the word "technology" will refer to either specific machines or tools, or to the intellectual process that leads to the creation of these types of products. In some cases, the idea of progress will be the focal point of both Merton's and Ellul's concern. Often, the study will address the idea that technology is a panacea with the potential to deliver greater freedom. This is a common perception, pervasive in twenty-first-century America. Albert Borgmann addresses it in his 2003 *Power Failure: Christianity in the Culture of Technology*, stating that "the full promise of technology has always been one of special liberty and prosperity. The prom ise inaugurated the modern era and has to this day animated our society's most coordinated and strenuous efforts. It comes to the fore in advertise ments, the public proclamations of our furtive aspirations."[20] Merton and Ellul agree with Borgmann that technology's promises have often turned out to be hidden perils. It is precisely this mindset and the acceptance of progress as the answer to our human problems that Merton and Ellul chal lenge in much of their work.

Defining Freedom

Often used interchangeably with the word "liberty," freedom for Ellul and Merton carries a different connotation than that usually associated with the term. For both Merton and Ellul, the notion of individual choice or the decision to act in a certain manner is not the type of freedom advocated by these two men. In Ellul's case, the choice that must be made in order to at tain true freedom is the choice to live out the will of God. Ellul proclaimed, "We know God fully only in Jesus Christ. Now Jesus Christ is free, and

---

19. Thompson, *Between Science and Religion*, 120.

20. Borgmann, *Power Failure*, 121.

this—but only this—enables us to speak with complete assurance of the freedom of God. The Gospels clearly show that Christ is the only free man. Free, he chose to keep the law. Free, he chose to live out the will of God. Free, he chose incarnation. Free, he chose to die."[21] This passage illustrates the relationship between "choice" and "freedom." One must choose to accept the will of God, and freedom is attainable once one makes this choice. Ellul is not referring to the many consumer choices available to us, or to lifestyle choices, or in choosing one television program over another. In deciding amongst these things, we do not exemplify our gift of freedom. According to Ellul:

> Freedom is not one element in the Christian life. It is not one of its forms. It does not express itself accidentally, or according to circumstances, or through encounters. In some circumstances temperance is the work of faith, in others faithfulness, in others strict justice, in others extreme clemency. Freedom, however, is not like this. It is not part or a fragmentary expression of the Christian life. It *is* the Christian life.[22]

For Thomas Merton, "the simplest definition of freedom is this: it means the ability to do the will of God."[23] This definition also presents freedom as grounded in a commitment to the Christian faith. Accepting the message that Jesus Christ freely chose to live his life in accordance with God's will is the first step on the road to freedom. This is what both Merton and Ellul mean when they refer to "freedom"—the choice to pattern one's life in this way. Many people would consider the type of freedom espoused by Merton and Ellul to be the very opposite of freedom as generally understood in contemporary culture. However, it is an acceptance of the Christian message and a commitment to live one's life in accordance with this message that defines freedom for these two men.

Merton recorded the following in his journal on October 21, 1950:

> The Church (Christ) is our liberator. Submission to her authority is *freedom*. Catholicity is freedom—*no* limitation on the spirit. Authority prohibits what limits and restricts the spirit of men . . . Holy Spirit must be permitted to "breathe where He will" in spiritual exercises and retreats . . . Churches not to be locked up outside time of public liturgical services. Freedom protected by

21. Ellul, *Ethics of Freedom*, 51.
22. Ibid., 104.
23. Merton, *New Seeds of Contemplation*, 201.

> protection of unity in spiritual life—error of those who had begun
> to create a division between public and private prayer, "morality
> and contemplation."[24]

Identifying freedom with an adherence to his Roman Catholic faith, Mer
ton firmly proclaimed that voluntary submission to divine authority is the
embodiment of freedom for humankind. Merton also derived some of his
thinking on the nature of freedom from St. Bernard, who "believed that
man is made solely for the purpose of loving God, but this love must be
expressed in freedom; the progress of the spiritual life must take place in
an atmosphere of liberty."[25] Freedom thus represents both the conscious
decision to live out one's life in search of God and in acting according to
His will.

In contemporary culture, freedom is not usually linked to choices
regarding the Gospel message. Regarding a theologically framed defini
tion of freedom, John F. Kilner, the director for the Center for Bioethics
and Human Dignity, proposes that this view of freedom is "fundamentally
different from the concept of autonomy commonly invoked in the public
sphere. Autonomy (literally 'self-law') suggests not only that people have
responsibility for making choices, but that the choices they make are right
by virtue of the fact that they made them."[26] Kilner's quotation above re
flects the commonly accepted notion of human autonomy and freedom,
ideas that provide the foundation for Western democratic values. He goes
on to explain that "a more biblical understanding of freedom rejects the
latter notion, insisting instead that there are standards of right and wrong
that are independent of people's own wishes and desires. People may make
wrong choices. God allows them the freedom to do so, but that does not
mean the choices are right."[27]

The dialectic between freedom and necessity is the core of all of Ellul's
thought.[28] Much of what he means by freedom can be understood only in
relation to the Fall—humankind's fall from grace in the Garden of Eden.

24. Merton, *Entering the Silence*, 436.

25. Adams, *Thomas Merton's Shared Contemplation*, 110.

26. Kilner, "Physician-Assisted Suicide;" cited in Demy and Stewart, *Suicide*
making this distinction between theologically grounded freedom in which life is lived
according to God's rule, and freedom as commonly construed in contemporary society,
Kilner specifically references Ellul's *Ethics of Freedom*.

27. Ibid.

28. Goddard, *Living the Word*, xx.

Ellul uses this intellectual construct to define freedom in greater detail in *To Will and To Do* (1969), in which he stated that before the Fall, man was

> free before God, which is to say that he could love God as well as cease to love him. He was free before God, but that freedom did not at all relate to some choice between doing and not doing, between a Yes and a No, after painstaking deliberation. To think in that manner about freedom shows clearly that we know nothing about it. We are distorting it, mutilating it, mummifying it. Freedom, precisely because it *is* freedom, cannot be defined in that way as an indetermination of choice.[29]

For Ellul, freedom is possibility, a constant process of action and virtue. Ellul scholar David Gill describes this freedom as "God's gift and response to man's hope."[30] On the other hand, as Ellul himself explains, "Freedom is first a power of possibility—a power to act and obey."[31] One chooses to accept the gift of freedom, or to reject it. This idea is also seen in Merton's conception of freedom.

Elaborating upon the idea that it is the necessities that hinder man's freedom, and that it is the necessities which we attempt to overcome by choosing freedom, David Gill stated, "Before the fall there was freedom; the fall brought chaos and confusion."[32] The Fall ushered in "necessity," which did not previously exist. Struggling against necessity, humankind grasps at freedom, which

> is not imposed on the reconciled . . . Freedom is arrested, rejected, undermined; Satan is still the "prince of this world." Though it is a crushing burden (and no cause for gloating), and Christians have failed miserably (again, no cause for gloating), it is nevertheless true, in Ellul's view, that Christians alone, in virtue of their conscious relationship to Jesus Christ, have the possibility of mediating freedom.[33]

As Canadian political philosopher George Grant (1918–1988) once wrote, "He [Ellul] does not write of necessity to scare men, but to make them free."[34] While Ellul and Merton both focus much of their writing on the

29. Ellul, *To Will and to Do*, 5.
30. Gill, "Jacques Ellul's Ethics," 6.
31. Ellul, *Ethics of Freedom*, 103.
32. Gill, *Word of God in the Ethics of Jacques Ellul*, 33.
33. Ibid., 47.
34. Grant, review of *Technological Society*, 416; quoted in Temple, "Jacques Ellul," 6.

idea of freedom, it is not merely a term to be defined or a concept to be grasped. It also plays an important role in Ellul's worldview *per se* interview in 1988, Ellul made the following statement concerning his theo logical methodology:

> I have sought to confront theological and biblical knowledge and sociological analysis without trying to come to any artificial or philosophical synthesis; instead I try to place the two face to face, in order to shed some light on what is real socially and real spiritu-ally. That is why I can say that the reply to each of my sociological analyses is found implicitly in a corresponding theological book, and inversely my theology is fed on socio-political experience. But I refuse to construct a *system* of thought, or to offer up some Christian or prefabricated socio-political solutions. I want only to provide Christians with the means of thinking out *for themselves* the meaning of their involvement in the modern world.[35]

For Ellul, freedom serves two purposes in his writing. The first is to de scribe man's condition before the Fall and the condition that man in the contemporary world still seeks, although attaining true freedom requires one to transcend the necessities (those things that humankind must do to survive), which have become a greater obstacle thanks to the technologi cal society and *technique*. The nature of the challenge posed by technology will provide the narrative for the following chapters. Second, the dialectical tension between freedom and necessity provides the foundation for Ellul's entire body of work.

In order for Christians to figure out their place in the modern world, as Ellul suggests, they must understand what it means to be free. Under standing *technique* and the necessities is essential to conceptualize freedom in the dialectical methodology that Ellul employs. He provides clarification in the introduction to *The Technological Society*:

> In my conception, freedom is not an immutable fact graven in the heart of man. It is not inherent in man or in society, and it is meaningless to write it into law. The mathematical, physical, sociological, and psychological sciences reveal nothing but neces-sities and determinisms, and freedom consists in overcoming and transcending these determinisms. Freedom is completely without meaning unless it is related to necessity, unless it represents vic-tory over necessity . . . We must look at it dialectically, and say that man is indeed determined, but that it is open to him to overcome

35. Gill, "Dialectic of Theology and Sociology," 1.

necessity, and that this *act* is freedom . . . He is most enslaved when
he thinks he is comfortably settled in freedom.[36]

For Ellul, freedom itself has a dialectical nature. It is not an act in and of
itself—a goal to obtain or a state of repose. It is a constant struggle against
the necessities. In order to transcend the necessities, of which *technique* is
one of the most visible manifestations, one must choose deliberately and
act accordingly. This conscious act is freedom. Those that do not seek to
transcend their determined condition choose not to be free.

Ellul's use of the dialectical method is apparent in his discussion of the
nature of freedom. He stated that "as we are always sinners and always righ-
teous, so we are always slaves and always freed."[37] However, this dialectical
emphasis has a tendency to cloud the true meaning of freedom in Ellul's
thought. Turning to Karl Barth, we can gain a more complete understanding of freedom in Ellul's worldview. Chapter 3 will further examine Ellul's
intellectual debt to Barth, but is necessary to illustrate the extent to which
Ellul's dialectical presentation of freedom is derived from Barth's work.
Having many times acknowledged his intellectual debt to Barth, the area
of freedom is one in which Ellul makes it clear that Barth does not go far
enough. Ellul stated that

> Barth, of course, has a great deal to say about freedom in his
> *Church Dogmatics*. In most cases, however, the reference is to God.
> Freedom is a freedom for God . . . But it is far too restricted. In
> these circumstances it is not surprising that for ordinary people
> in the church freedom has neither meaning nor content and poses
> no questions. It is a theme which has vanished from the Christian
> horizons.[38]

Again Ellul brings the dialectic into play by stating that freedom "poses no
questions" for ordinary people. What, then, is the question that it poses
for Christians, and how critical is it to understand what this question is
in order to fully grasp Ellul's definition of freedom? If, as Goddard states,
"The dialectic between freedom and necessity is the central and controlling
idea in all of Ellul's work," then it is essential to try and grasp this elusive
concept.[39] Freedom and the dialectical method are hallmarks of Ellul's writ-

---

36. Ellul, *Technological Society*, xxxii–xxxiii.
37. Ellul, *Ethics of Freedom*, 104.
38. Ibid., 105.
39. Goddard, *Living the Word*, 61.

ing and his thought. Ellul believed that "we live in permanent dialectical tension between the necessity of the world and the freedom of the Wholly Other."[40]

Therefore, for Ellul, freedom is the God-given gift to live life according to God's commandments. It is not simply the "right" to choose one thing over another, or the commonly construed ability to choose between types of products, merchandise, or lifestyle choices. Life, Liberty, and the Pursuit of Happiness is not the encapsulation of freedom in his thinking. Ellul's freedom is a radical acceptance of God's grace. It flows from his acceptance of the Word of God through his religious conversion (discussed in chapter 2), from his reading of Kierkegaard and Barth, and is expressed in dialectic against the necessity of *technique*.

Thomas Merton held a similar notion of freedom, but with some important differences. Throughout his writing, Merton discussed freedom both metaphorically and poetically. Having "left the world" when he entered the monastery in December 1941, many would consider Merton to have given up his freedom. Nevertheless, as he recalled in his autobiography, "Brother Matthew locked the gate behind me and I was enclosed in the four walls of my new freedom."[41] Clearly, his conception of freedom differed considerably from that which was commonly held by most people in mid-twentieth-century America. Referring to this notion of Merton giving up his freedom, Merton scholar Raymond Bailey observed:

> Most men spend their lives in a small corner of the world yearning for broader horizons, for open doors through which they may move to become "men of the world." Thomas Merton came as near to being born a cosmopolitan man as is possible, but his longing was for a solitary reservation in an out of the way place where he could put down roots . . . a place where he could breather fresh air, smell aromas untainted by asphalt, sewage, and the like . . . a place where he could see the sky, hear himself—and God—and as a result become a universal man. Behind walls as drab as those of any prison . . . he discovered freedom.[42]

This paragraph demonstrates some similarities with Ellul's thought, but there are some subtle differences as well. The idea that freedom is found outside of the bonds of society—a society determined by *technique*

40. Gill, "Dialectic of Theology and Sociology," 2.

41. Merton, *Seven Storey Mountain*, 372.

42. Bailey, *Thomas Merton on Mysticism*, 33.

under sway of the necessities—is prevalent. Other ideas that will be explored in this and later chapters relate to the notion of the city as a hindrance to the full expression of man's freedom, and the need to transcend the false self, which is imposed upon individuals by society. Contradictory to Ellul's notion of freedom is the element of choice inherent in Merton's decision to enter the monastery in pursuit of an objective that one could describe as an end in itself. Perhaps Ellul's notion of freedom as constant action, as constant struggle against the necessities, is lacking in this description of Merton's search for freedom, but that idea will be explored later in this chapter.

Illuminating even further Merton's conception of freedom is his statement, "Thus, once again, we see that Nirvana is not an escape from phenomena and from the everyday world with its problems and risks, but a realization of that Void and True Self which is the common ontological ground of both personal freedom and the objective, problematical world."[43] These ideas will be further refined in chapter 4 in the discussion on the centrality of self-transcendence as a means of achieving freedom.

More likely to use the term "liberty" than Ellul, Merton nevertheless presents a number of ideas similar to Ellul's notion of freedom. He referred to freedom frequently in *New Seeds of Contemplation* (1961), stating, "The mind that is the prisoner of conventional ideas, and the will that is the captive of its own desire cannot accept the seeds of an unfamiliar truth and a supernatural desire. For how can I receive the seeds of freedom if I am in love with slavery and how can I cherish the desire of God if I am filled with another and an opposite desire?"[44] This "slavery" to which Merton refers could be likened to Ellul's theory of *technique*, or to the necessities that Ellul describes at length throughout his writing. Ellul often referred to "the powers," which he described as "spiritual realities which are independent of human decision and whose power is not constituted by human decision."[45] Perhaps Merton was alluding to this notion of the powers as entities that captivate human behavior but are beyond human control. Of course, *technique* is another manifestation of the powers, as it is a force which acts on all of humankind, yet remains beyond our control. The "opposite desire" referred to by Merton can be seen as man refusing to participate in an act of transcendence over *technique*. Merton elaborated when he stated that

43. Merton, *Mystics and Zen Masters*, 285.

44. Merton, *New Seeds of Contemplation*, 16.

45. Goddard, "Ellul on Scripture and Idolatry," 6.

"God cannot plant His liberty in me because I am a prisoner and I do not even desire to be free."[46] Again there are differences here between the exact nature of freedom that Ellul described and Merton's rendering of freedom as an attribute directly given to us by God, but the overall impression is that without this freedom, man is embedded in the immanent and unable to appreciate the transcendent. Merton continued his description of God implanting freedom in us, illustrating the consequences of our refusal to accept it. He stated, "If these seeds would take root in my liberty, and if His will would grow from my freedom, I would become the love that He is . . ." If this freedom is accepted, "I would grow together with thousands and millions of other freedoms into the gold of one huge field praising God."

Chapter 2 will explain that Merton spent his young life prior to en tering the monastery as somewhat of a Bohemian, travelling frequently, and savoring the pleasures of the world. Prior to entering the monastery, "Merton was . . . free, in the world's sense."[49] Anyone who reads his autobi ography can conclude that in his early twenties, Merton was certainly free according to the accepted notions of freedom in Western culture. However, speaking of freedom, he wrote:

> Every moment and every event of every man's life on earth plants
> something in his soul. For just as the wind carries thousands of
> winged seeds, so each moment brings with it germs of spiritual
> vitality that come to rest imperceptibly in the minds and wills of
> men. Most of these unnumbered seeds perish and are lost, because
> men are not prepared to receive them: for such seeds as these can-
> not spring up anywhere except in the good soil of freedom . . . [50]

How does this observation compare with Ellul's view of freedom? Giving further indication that not only does ones' freedom originate with God, but the primary impediments to this freedom are similar to Ellul's notion of *technique*, Merton went on to say that "Pope John's message of freedom calls man, first of all, to liberate himself from the climate of confusion and desperation in which he finds himself because he passively accepts and

---

46. Merton, *New Seeds of Contemplation*, 16.

47. Ibid., 17.

48. Ibid.

49. Kline, "In the Company of Prophets?," 126.

50. Merton, *New Seeds of Contemplation*, 14.

follows a mindless determinism."[51] This "determinism" resembles Ellul's notion of *technique*.

Merton would not agree with Ellul's assertion that only Christians could discover true freedom, or that the inability to attain freedom was a problem only for contemporary Christians. Merton's ecumenism would distinguish him from certain types of exclusivist Christianity in this regard. He stated:

> Today more than ever, man in chains is seeking emancipation and liberty. His tragedy is that he seeks it by means that bring him into ever greater enslavement. But freedom is a spiritual thing. It is a sacred and religious reality. Its roots are not in man, but in God . . . In other words, for man to be free he must be delivered *from himself*. This means not that he must be delivered only from another like himself: for the tyranny of man over man is but the external expression of each man's enslavement to his own desires. For he who is the slave of his own desires necessarily exploits others in order to pay tribute to the tyrant within himself.[52]

How does the idea of *technique* relate to this phrase? As in Merton's earlier quotation in which he engaged the idea of slavery, is the "greater enslavement" to which Merton refers in this passage in some way comparable to the impact that Ellul ascribes to *technique*? While similarities and differences with Ellul have been noted, both Merton and Ellul would find common ground through their reading of and interpretation of the work of Karl Barth. According to Ellul, "Karl Barth has dealt very thoroughly with the matter [of freedom] at various points in the *Church Dogmatics*, and . . . I am in full accord with his presentation."[53] Chapter 3 will discuss Barth's influence on both Ellul and Merton and their notions of freedom.

---

51. Merton, *Seeds of Destruction*, 105.

52. Merton, *Inner Experience*, 153.

53. Ellul, *Ethics of Freedom*, 120.

2 Merton and Ellul—
     Comparative Worldviews

Thomas Merton and Jacques Ellul were contemporaries. Prolific authors and men who corresponded with a number of the leading intellectuals of the mid-twentieth century, one only finds cursory mention of Jacques Ellul in Merton's journals and there is no known direct correspondence between the two. Similarly, there is no mention of Thomas Merton in any of Ellul's work or in his correspondence. However, both men wrote pas sionately about the impact that technology was continuing to have on the human condition as the twentieth century progressed. This chapter will examine some of the salient life experiences that shaped their worldviews, tracing some of the similarities and differences in their upbringing and the resulting influence that these events had on their respective outlooks. A section defining the term *technique* and a discussion of the use of the dia lectic method conclude the chapter.

Thomas Merton was a Roman Catholic monk and a prolific author. His extensive writing addresses the idea of what it meant to be a Roman Catholic in twentieth-century America. Having authored more than sev enty books and hundreds of journal articles throughout the decades of the 1940s, 1950s, and 1960s, Merton's writing is familiar to many people. He is most famous for his autobiography, *The Seven Storey Mountain* which became an instant bestseller. The book is widely credited with hav ing compelled a number of young men to embark on the monastic life of solitude after the Second World War.[1] Merton's writing had an impact far outside the borders of the United States, and his life story has been de scribed as an "autobiography with a pattern and meaning valid for all of

1. Kramer, *Thomas Merton*, 12.

us."[2] Foreshadowing many of the themes that will be addressed in this study, Robert Inchausti notes that

> *The Seven Storey Mountain* resonated powerfully with those look-
> ing for a nonmaterialistic, nonscientific alternative to the ideolo-
> gies of the new super states. To meet the dangerous new power
> alignments of the postwar world, a new America had emerged—
> corporate, consolidated, internationally connected, and militarily
> ready, run by professional managers, social scientists, and experts.
> The most pressing question of the era was not how the country's
> unique democratic character was going to be preserved, but rather
> whose interests this new class of technocrats were going to serve.[3]

This quote introduces many of the challenges that beset post-war American society, challenges which Merton addressed throughout his life.

Jacques Ellul, a Frenchman who remains relatively unfamiliar to most Americans, shared these concerns. He is best known to Western readers in general as a philosopher and sociologist primarily concerned with the impact that technology has had on society collectively as well as on human beings individually.[4] Ellul first appeared in American intellectual circles with the publication of the English edition of *The Technological Society* (1964), a book which generated a small cadre of followers, many of whom would go on to study his writing in depth. However, he did not seek to convert anyone or to gather a group of like-minded disciples. Those who chose to examine what he had to say and to question their own assumptions about the impact of technology on the human condition believed that Ellul's work has not received adequate attention.[5] In order to determine how much of our attention Jacques Ellul's extensive corpus deserves, it is first necessary to define what exactly it is that he provides today's students, thinkers, and academics.

Neither Merton nor Ellul sought to acquire a large, loyal following. Ellul hoped to point others in the proper direction to help them discern for themselves what perils were hidden within the technological society. This task can be difficult as he is often considered too pessimistic and his writing can be verbose and his thought difficult to penetrate. A German reader once asked Ellul how, after having written *The Technological Society*, he could go

---

2. Massa, "Young Man Merton," 108.

3. Inchausti, *Thomas Merton's American Prophesy*, 42.

4. Kluver, "Contributions of Jacques Ellul's 'Propaganda'" 1.

5. Ellul, *Sources and Trajectories*, 1.

on living. Fortunately, that reader acquired a better understanding of Ellul's thought after spending ten years reading his work.[6] Many of the readers that go on to study Ellul in depth find that they are "never quite the same." In his work, Ellul is not offering solutions, nor does he believe that solutions to the human condition are to be found in the Bible. He wrote, "Christianity does not offer [solutions] for social, political, economic problems (or even for moral or spiritual problems!)"[8] He believed that through Scripture, God put questions to individuals to resolve and answer for themselves. Ellul believed that each individual must find his or her own solutions to the many pressing issues posed by life in contemporary society. Thus, for example, *The Ellul Forum*, a venue for those who study and appreciate Ellul's thought, explicitly states that it is not the Forum's intention to appeal to "true believers" or "Ellul groupies," but rather to serve as a starting point for a critical dialogue.

While Ellul employed the dialectical style to frame his entire body of work, readers should not go away with the impression that he has presented a neatly segmented and easy-to-digest line of reasoning. Rather, one should ask if either Merton or Ellul have presented what can be approached as a coherent whole that is open to easy analysis. Ellul scholar David Gill asked:

> To what extent is it even possible to find an overall synthesis, or even a dialectical "rhythm," in Ellul's life and work? It is a tempting project and a gigantic challenge . . . That is, he is perennially, vocationally, "contrary"—sometimes to his own earlier (or simultaneous!) thinking, always going against the stream, resisting any orthodoxy or power. Ellul creates a dialectic without a comfortable, predictable "rhythm"—sort of an a-rhythmic, anti-modern, anarchist, free verse, expression anchored only by an unquenchable thirst for the truth.[10]

It would be difficult enough from the above passage to try and distill a coherent sociological critique out of Ellul that could be compared to one of his contemporaries. However, when that contemporary is Thomas Merton, another individual that is difficult to categorize intellectually, the task becomes that much greater.

6. Vanderburg, "Iconoclasm of Ellul," 77.

7. Ibid.

8. Ellul, "Mirror of These Ten Years," 200.

9. Fasching, *Thought of Jacques Ellul*, 9.

10. Gill, review of Goddard's *Living the Word*, 20.

Thomas Merton did not present his body of work in any organized manner. He would have been opposed to any attempt to place him on a pedestal, which would have been "in direct contrast to everything for which he stood."[11] He worked in a number of diverse fields to include cultural studies, poetry, theology, liturgical studies, and art, all of which were the result of "his search for God [which] expressed itself in varied modes depending upon the situation in which he found himself."[12] Thus, categorizing Merton is difficult, because he evades the stereotypical label of philosopher or theologian, or even of ordinary monk. "It is a simple fact that Merton does not *fit* comfortably into any usual category of analysis. For this reason, he has never been easy to interpret, so that even his friends, in my opinion, have occasionally missed the mark."[13] Merton described himself "as a 'patchwork,' a 'bundle of questions and doubts and obsessions,' and a person with a 'complex self-contradictory temperament.' "[14] In addition, although Merton was a devout Catholic, "the stimulus for much of his writing came from those with whom he did not entirely agree: French existentialists, American Marxists, Buddhist philosophers, and Reformed theologians."[15] Ellul (as well as Karl Barth as will be seen in chapter 3) could be included in this group as he was a member of the French Reformed Church. Merton's engagement with Ellul's thought went far beyond a mere repetition of Ellul's ideas. Instead, "Merton went on to his own reflections, informed by, but not prisoner to, Ellul's point of view."[16]

A brief comparative biographical sketch is necessary for those who wish to engage with Merton and Ellul and to consider the implications of the many serious charges that these two men leveled against the contemporary technological society. This sketch will trace some of the similarities in their upbringing that have had the most impact on their fully developed worldviews. Of primary significance is that both Merton and Ellul were raised in non-religious households, they both had parents that were artists, and they were both exposed at an early age to open, rural, and natural environments that were untrammeled by technological intrusion in the form of urban development.

11. Finley, *Merton's Palace of Nowhere*, 8.

12. Kramer, *Thomas Merton*, 161.

13. Reardon, "Many-Storied Monastic," 52.

14. Thompson, *Between Science and Religion*, 112.

15. Adams, *Thomas Merton's Shared Contemplation*, 113.

16. Davenport, "Jacques Ellul and Thomas Merton," 10.

Thomas Merton — Biographical Sketch

Thomas Merton was born in Prades, France, on January 31, 1915. His name at birth was simply Tom—Tom Feverel Merton, since his mother disliked the name Thomas.[17] Of his birth, he wrote, "I came into the world . . . free by nature, in the image of God, I was nevertheless the prisoner of my own violence and my own selfishness, in the image of the world into which I was born."[18] He believed that from the beginning of his life, he was free, yet the world conspired to prevent him from realizing his freedom. He would spend his life searching for a way to find it.

His father, Owen Merton, was born in New Zealand. He met Ruth Jenkins, an American citizen, when they were both art students in France. They married, and soon after Tom was born, the family would leave war-torn France for Douglaston, New York, to live with Ruth's parents. Ruth (with her husband's support) had determined that their son would be an independent-minded person, and when he demonstrated his penchant for independence and his disdain for authority, "she may have been tempted to regret her training."[19] Looking back, Merton recalled his parents' art profession with pride, noting that "my father and mother were captives in that world, knowing they did not belong with it or in it, and yet unable to get away from it. They were in the world and not of it—not because they were saints, but in a different way: because they were artists. The integrity of an artist lifts a man above the level of the world without delivering him from it."[20] In this passage, he is not in hindsight describing only his parents. He also describes the type of life that he would eventually lead.

Owen Merton was not a particularly pious man, and aside from taking a position as the organist in the Episcopal Church in Douglaston, Long Island, he did not inculcate in his son any religious instruction. Religion was not a part of the Merton family life, even though his mother would occasionally attend Quaker meetings, but always alone.[21] Merton recalled that "churches and formal religion were things to which Mother attached not too much importance in the training of a modern child, and my guess is that she thought, if I were left to myself, I would grow up into a nice,

17. Furlong, *Merton*, 3.
18. Merton, *Seven Storey Mountain*, 3.
19. Pennington, *Thomas Merton*, 19.
20. Merton, *Seven Storey Mountain*, 3.
21. Furlong, *Merton*, 13.

quiet Deist of some sort, and never be perverted by superstition."[22] Despite this, his father would occasionally take him to the Episcopal Church, and Tom recalled attending services there with some delight. He admired the stained glass windows, the music, and the candles. He remembered that after leaving church, he had a "kind of comfortable and satisfied feeling that something had been done that needed to be done."[23]

Owen did not participate in World War One, although many of his fellow New Zealanders fought and died in France. He believed that war was "a monstrous interruption of reality" and that life consisted of the important pursuits of making friendships and developing and sustaining personal relationships."[24] Providing a glimpse into his particular worldview, Owen wrote:

> Sincerity gives one a clear vision, and one carries that out in work by means of *order*—and when I see a farm run well, no matter if the man's house is abominable, even if he drinks and overworks his hands or makes out some idea in work—I find this in doctors, sailors, in woodcutters and harvesters, and in everyone else. It is marked in businessmen (confound them). We shall never be satisfied with anyone less than Christ, however, and I think the reason is that as Van Gogh says, he was the greatest artist we have ever had, for he dealt with men, not with colors and brushes, he *almost created men*. If our pictures do not in some measure create the men who look at them, or perhaps better *recreate* them those pictures are not much good . . . Men like you and me *have* to paint sometime or other. I am certain it has grown to be a perfectly natural function with me. On the farm it used to make me feel absolutely sick with worry and strain till I could get to myself and go and draw for a little while. It seemed there was some essence in one's body which had to find its way out through one's fingers or not at all.[25]

This passage demonstrates some interesting ideas that may have influenced Tom later in life. Speaking of Christ is somewhat surprising as Tom grew up in a household in which religion was rarely a topic of conversation, but presenting the idea of Christ as the greatest artist allows us to see a possible formative element in his later thinking. However, it may have been the

22. Merton, *Seven Storey Mountain*, 6.

23. Furlong, *Merton*, 13.

24. Ibid., 9.

25. Ibid., 10.

institutionalized form of religion that Owen Merton kept at bay, not faith or belief itself. In addition, Owen's passion for art and for creating would be reflected in Tom as he would eventually come to demonstrate the same passion for contemplation, and for literary creation.

Ruth Merton died of stomach cancer when Tom was six years old. This event profoundly affected the young boy in many ways. Merton's re lationship with his mother was complex, as he recounted in his later years. It was the literal beginning of Tom's wanderings as Owen took him and his younger brother John Paul on many journeys, pursuing opportunities to paint in Bermuda, back to France, and subsequently to England. It was also the beginning of Thomas' spiritual journey, as this loss of his mother, whom had been his spiritual center, set him on a path to rediscover some solidity, some comfort and a firm foundation on which to build his life.[26]

Following his mother's death, Thomas travelled extensively with his father and younger brother. These travels exposed him to many places possessing natural beauty and charm. First visiting Provincetown on Cape Cod, he remembered the sand dunes, the sea, and the ships[27] Although ill while on Cape Cod, he recalled the natural beauty and the opportunity to spend a great deal of time outdoors and immersed in nature. Traveling next to Bermuda, he was able again to be close to nature and to a simple, hermit-like existence. Regarding Bermuda, he recalled vividly, and in a writers prose, "You could already see the small white houses, made of coral, cleaner than sugar, shining in the sun, and all around us the waters paled over the shallows and became the color of emeralds, where there was sand, or lavender where there were rocks below the surface."[28]

For Thomas Merton, his artistic and non-religious parents set him on a path that would culminate in his entering the monastery and becoming a literary figure and monk. *The Man in the Sycamore Tree* (1972) is Ed Rice's tribute to Merton—his close friend. In this book, Rice describes Merton's days at Columbia, his summers in Olean, New York, and his eventual move into the monastery at Gethsemani in Kentucky. Rice recounts that Mer ton's reading of Aldous Huxley's *Ends and Means* (1937) led him to delve deeper into mysticism and into Zen Buddhism in particular.[29] Rice also attributes two main themes to Merton's later life; the first being peace—

---

26. Ibid., 15. From this point on, Thomas will be used instead of Tom.

27. Furlong, *Merton*, 17.

28. Ibid.

29. Rice, *Man in the Sycamore Tree*, 13.

whether through an adherence to non-violence or racial justice, and the second being the pursuit of the interior life through contemplation.[30] Following the *way* of Zen Buddhism, Merton stressed that Western adherents to Buddhism, such as himself, were seeking an antidote to the "widespread dissatisfaction with the spiritual sterility of mass society, dominated by technology and propaganda, in which there is no room left for personal spontaneity."[31] This would be a path that Ellul did not follow, although he and Merton were trying to reach the same destination.

The events thus far that have shaped Thomas Merton's life included his lack of any religious instruction at home, the artistic parents that exposed him to art and the artist's outlook on life, his mother's death when he was six years old, and the life of travel and adventure that exposed him to nature and self-sufficiency. He would join the monastery and embark on the contemplative life, not to escape from the world, but as a "rejection of those illusions which we so often mistake for reality: the illusions of war . . . an uncontrolled technology, and power politics."[32] Merton's thoughts on these very topics will be covered in the following chapters.

JACQUES ELLUL—BIOGRAPHICAL SKETCH

Jacques Ellul was born on January 6, 1912, in Bordeaux, France. While Merton was born in France to a father from New Zealand and an American mother, Ellul was born in France to a father from Austria who was also a British citizen, and a Portuguese mother, although she was a French citizen. Ellul noted, "I owe my existence to an encounter between a Portuguese woman and an Austrian which took place in Bordeaux."[33] Merton and Ellul were thus both born in France to parents that were of neither the same nationality nor French by birth. Ellul would remain in France throughout his life, living through some of the "most pervasive propaganda periods," including the Spanish Civil War, the Nazi occupation of France, the liberation, the Algerian Civil War, and the Cold War.[34] These events would shape his worldview.

---

30. Ibid., 12.

31. Rice, *Man in the Sycamore Tree*, 13.

32. Adams, *Thomas Merton's Shared Contemplation*, 21.

33. Ellul and Troude-Chastenet, *Ellul on Politics*, 35.

34. Marlin, *Propaganda & the Ethics of Persuasion*, 31.

Jacques Ellul recalled that his mother's painting and vocation as an artist influenced his upbringing. He also recalled that he was raised in a "universe of honor and art that today would be labeled a fantasy world." In addition to painting, Ellul's mother steered her young son towards poetry—a gift that would stay with him for life as he would write his own poetry in later years. He stated, "My mother passed on her love of poetry to me. [She] always guided me towards the better poets. From the age of six or seven I have always had a taste for poetry. Poetry is the art form which pleases me the most and in which I find deep meaning."[36] While the penchant for art would have a greater influence over Merton's young life and his development than it would for Ellul, it was the lack of a religious upbringing that would be of the most consequence to both young men as they reached adulthood.

In young Jacques Ellul's case, his father was a skeptic and a follower of Voltaire. Ellul recalled that his father was a tolerant man, and that "he wouldn't let me have any religious instruction but he would let me read the Bible at home."[37] However, Ellul's mother was a devout Christian, but had vowed to her husband not to influence Jacques with any religious instruction. She was loyal to her husband and so never exposed Jacques to her beliefs. Having read the Bible when he was eighteen or nineteen, he went to her and said, "Do you know something, Mother? I believe in Jesus Christ and I have converted."[38] Reflecting on this incident, he said:

> I was not brought up in an especially Christian family, and had only a very remote knowledge of Christianity in my childhood. On the other hand, my family was rather poor and I spent all my youth in the midst of the people of the docks at Bordeaux. I began to earn my own living when I was sixteen and continued to do so while completing my university studies. When I was nineteen, I read, by chance, Marx's *Capital*. I was enthusiastic about it. It answered almost all the questions that I had been asking myself. I became "Marxist" and devoted a great deal of my time to the study of his writings. But I was disappointed with the Communists, who seemed to me to be very far from Marx, and I never entered the Party.[39]

35. Ellul, *In Season, Out of Season*, 8.

36. Ellul and Troude-Chastenet, *Ellul on Politics*, 49.

37. Ibid., 36.

38. Ibid., 41.

39. Holloway, *Introducing Jacques Ellul*, 5.

This short introduction to his own life tells us a great deal about Ellul. It is difficult to learn much about him from his own writing as he tends to offer little in the way of autobiographical information in any of his work, and thus, whenever he specifically addresses some aspect of his past, it should be closely examined. This study will rely on as much of Ellul's own reflections on his life as possible, while also looking at a number of secondary works to include dissertations on Ellul and his thought.

Ellul described his upbringing as one in which he lived in complete freedom, although in this case he is using the term "freedom" differently than he would in his later writing. He was free to explore, to wander around the countryside and the docks of Bordeaux. His father's aristocratic, formal and reserved demeanor was counter-balanced by his mother's very devout adherence to Christianity—however, as noted, she did not expose Jacques to the her own professed beliefs as her husband did not want the boy exposed to any "mythical" ideas.[40] Unlike in Merton's case, Ellul's father was not an artist; he was a businessman with a strong sense of honor and integrity. Ellul later recounted, "As he told me so many times, to be a man of honor does not involve simply making a point of honor, it means never letting your friends down, always being available to the poor, and always standing up to powerful forces."[41] Certainly, Ellul took this advice to heart as he would be a proponent of the poor and throughout his long life would speak truth to power. This mix of practical reason exhibited by his father and his mother's religious devotion would set the intellectual stage for the rest of Jacques Ellul's life.

While Ellul would consider himself to be a product of the great French "melting pot," he did not travel nearly as extensively as did Merton over the course of his life. Yet, this would not preclude Ellul from having a sense of "rootlessness," as he recounted that being a child of foreigners could explain "why I have never felt nationalistic. I love France very much, but I have roots everywhere. I feel just as much at home in Italy as in France, and I have strong Serbian roots."[42] But like Merton, he found his childhood to be one of complete freedom and independence, and he reveled in the natural environment that was to be found in the area around Bordeaux in the 1920s. He recalled that there were marshlands "which were partially drained into hundreds of small streams. These marshes and the extraor-

40. Ellul, *Perspectives on Our Age*, 2.

41. Ellul and Troude-Chastenet, *Ellul on Politics*, 36.

42. Ellul, *In Season, Out of Season*, 5.

dinary wild-life from the streams provided . . . untold discoveries and adventures."[43] He remembered these years as an "unfettered childhood" and he experienced a degree of freedom that he thought "few children to day could even imagine."[44] This natural beauty and freedom to roam the countryside was something that Merton also enjoyed, yet for Merton the opportunities presented themselves in many more locales. While their lives as children and teenagers present a number of similarities, such as both be ing raised by parents (or in Ellul's case, one of his parents) that were artists, their religious conversion and their time spent in the rural environment deserve closer attention.

SIMILAR RELIGIOUS CONVERSION EXPERIENCES

Both Merton and Ellul were shielded from religious instruction and from religious belief in general, either deliberately or passively, at a young age. They were left to themselves to discover whatever vestige of faith they could find. They would both undergo conversion experiences around their twen tieth year. For Merton, this would be a gradual process while for Ellul, it would be a dramatic event of which he rarely spoke.

Regarding his conversion experience, Merton stated:

> I was in my room. It was night. The light was on. Suddenly it seemed to me that Father, who had now been dead more than a year, was there with me. The sense of his presence was as vivid and as startling as if he had touched my arm or spoken to me. The whole thing passed in a flash, instantly, I was overwhelmed with a sudden and profound insight into the misery and corruption of my own soul, and I was pierced deeply with a light that made me realize something of the condition I was in, and I was filled with horror at what I saw, and my whole being rose up in revolt against what was within me, and my soul desired escape and liberation and freedom from all this with an intensity and an urgency unlike anything I had ever known before. And now I think for the first time in my whole life I really began to pray—praying not with my lips and my intellect and my imagination, but praying out of the very roots of my life and my being, and praying to God, the God that I had never known . . .[45]

43. Ellul and Troude-Chastenet, *Ellul on Politics*, 45.
44. Ibid.
45. Merton, *Seven Storey Mountain*, 123.

Many people describe having had religious conversion experiences. For Thomas Merton, this experience was one that he recorded in great detail in his autobiography. It resulted from an extensive inquiry into the increasingly meaningless nature of his life as a young man. Merton had slowly (and somewhat reluctantly at first) begun to read about Scholastic philosophy, such as *The Spirit of Medieval Philosophy* (1936) by Etienne Gilson (1884–1978). Later, while reading Gerard Manley Hopkins (1844–1889), Merton was overcome with an irresistible desire to become Roman Catholic. He recounted:

> "What are you waiting for?" said the voice within me . . . "Why are you sitting there? It is useless to hesitate any longer. Why don't you get up and go?" Suddenly I could bear it no longer . . . I went out into the street . . . towards Broadway in the light rain. And then everything inside me began to sing—to sing with peace, to sing with strength, and to sing with conviction . . . And then I saw Father Ford coming around the corner from Broadway . . . And I said: "Father, I want to become a Catholic."[46]

Ellul recounted a similarly dramatic experience. He did not enjoy discussing his conversion, and only did so in any of his writing when he was specifically asked to comment on the experience, and even then he did so reluctantly. He considered it to have been "brutal" but also acknowledged the life-changing impact, noting that

> when it did occur it was overwhelming I would even say violent. It happened during the summer holidays . . . I must have been seventeen at the time as I had just taken my final exams at school. I was alone in the house and translating Faust when suddenly, and I have no doubts on this at all, I knew myself to be in the presence of something so astounding, so overwhelming that entered into the very center of my being. That's all I can tell you.[47]

Having both become Christians, Merton and Ellul would formulate their technological critique and their views on human freedom through two distinct theological frameworks—Merton through Roman Catholicism and Ellul through the viewpoint of the French Reformed Church. Throughout this study, instances in which significant differences between the Catholic and the Protestant worldview are apparent will be noted. However it is in the similar conclusions that both men reach regarding the

46. Ibid., 236–37.

47. Ellul and Troude-Chastenet, *Ellul on Politics*, 52.

impact that technology has had on human freedom that the study will be most concerned.

Growing Up in Rural Environments

Merton and Ellul learned to appreciate the natural, rural world. Unspoiled by urbanization and largely unsettled, the areas in which they spent much of their time in their youth would leave an indelible impression as they grew older. Characterizing the time spent in rural environments as carefree and unstructured, these experiences led to an appreciation for "being" over "doing," and for an appreciation of nature and a general disdain of urban environments. A comparison of some of their views on the impact that technology and progress was beginning to have on the natural environ ment demonstrates a marked similarity in their outlook.

In January 1963, Merton wrote to environmental activist Rachel Car son concerning his thoughts on humanity's continued negative impact on the natural world. In this particular letter, he addressed not only environ mental degradation, but the idea that propaganda and advertising contrib uted to this problem. He wrote:

> We don't like the looks of a Japanese beetle. We let ourselves be convinced by a salesman that the beetle is a dire threat. It then becomes obvious that the thing to do is exterminate the beetle by any means whatever even if it means the extermination of many other beings which have not harmed us and which even bring joy into our lives: worse still, we will exterminate the beetle even if it means danger to our children and to our very selves. To make this seem "reasonable" we go to some lengths to produce arguments that our steps are really "harmless." I am afraid I do not relish the safety of the atomic age.[48]

Ellul expresses similar concerns regarding nature and man's changing attitudes towards nature which he insisted are due to the technological im perative's demands. Speaking about the desacralization of nature, he stated:

> What is now so awful in our society is that technology has de stroyed everything which people ever considered sacred. For ex ample, nature. People have voluntarily moved to an acceptance of technology as something sacred. That is really awful. In the past, the sacred things always derived from nature. Currently, nature

48. Bochen and Shannon, *Thomas Merton*, 207.

has been completely desecrated and we consider technology as something sacred. Think, for example, on the fuss whenever a demonstration is held. Everyone is then always very shocked if a car is set on fire. For then a sacred object is destroyed.[49]

The automobile as a symbol of technology's captivating influence over contemporary Americans is a metaphor that Merton employed as well. There is a sacred element inherent in this attachment to technology's most advanced and complex machines, very similar to that pointed out in the above passage from Ellul. On this topic, Merton wrote, "The attachment of the modern American to his automobile and the *symbolic* role played by his car, with its aggressive and lubric design, its useless power, its otiose gadgetry, its consumption of fuel, which is advertised as having almost supernatural power . . . that is where the study of American mythology should begin."[50] It is important to note that neither Ellul nor Merton are pointing out any particular shortcoming or negative repercussions of automobiles *per se*, rather they are criticizing the acceptance of the automobile as sacred object. It is the automobile that represents, in these particular passages, the entire panoply of advanced technological products and their pervasive influence which has contributed to the desacralization of nature and the sacralization of technology. It is also significant that Catholic author Simone Weil (1909–1943) presented the automobile as a metaphor for Western Civilization, "launched at full speed and driverless across broken country."[51] Again, the idea that technology has been both driver and vehicle for contemporary society's maladies is consistent with other social critics writing at the same time that both Merton and Ellul were presenting their own ideas on this topic.

It is as one of the many mechanical manifestations of *technique* that Ellul (and Merton) has portrayed the automobile in these passages. Ellul's use of the idea of *technique* to explain contemporary humankind's condition is prevalent throughout his work. He describes *technique* as "the rearranging of everything in terms of technical progress."[52] In order to evaluate Ellul's (and Merton's) case against contemporary society, and the impact that technology has had on freedom, it is essential to understand what Ellul means when he uses the term "*technique.*"

49. Van Boeckel, *Betrayal by Technology*, 1992.

50. Merton, *Conjectures of a Guilty Bystander*, 76.

51. Weil, *Oppression and Liberty*, 111.

52. Creegan, review of *Technological Bluff*, 2.

THE CONCEPT OF TECHNIQUE

Technique is one of the foundational terms that underlies Ellul's entire cor
pus. This word presents some difficulty, especially in that it is not presented
in the same manner as one would expect when using the term to address
the "technique" for accomplishing some given task. Ellul himself attempted
to provide some clarity, especially in light of the fact that his most impor
tant sociological work, *The Technological Society*, is actually a poor transla
tion of *Technique: The Wager of the Century*. Realizing that his magnum
opus had been mistranslated, Ellul felt it necessary to provide some insight
into what he actually meant when he referred to *technique*. He stated:

> When I use the French word *technique*, normally translated into
> English as *technology*, I do not mean exactly the same thing as the
> French word *technologie*, which is also translated into English as
> *technology*. We have to be meticulous about this simple point of
> vocabulary. I know that the two are habitually confused . . . Now
> when I speak of *technique* [English *technology*], I am speaking of
> the technological phenomenon, the reality of the technological . . .
> I know the difficulty of this semantic problem in English, for there
> is only one single word, *technology*, to designate both *la technique*
> (the concrete thing) and *la technologie* (the discourse, the teaching
> of the subject itself).[53]

For Ellul, what is taking place in contemporary society (specifically West
ern society, although *technique* is likely to prevail in all societies over time)
is that the natural milieu is being replaced by a technical milieu.[54] It is not
a case of human conquest of the natural world, or some plan rationally
designed to increase standards of living and the like; rather *technique*
ates under a set of conditions that Ellul thoroughly describes in *The Techno
logical Society*. He distinguished between machines and *technique*, and like
Merton, he is not anti-technology *per se*. Ellul is not opposed to "the society
of machines" but rather "the society of efficient *techniques*."[55] *Technique*
many aspects are all encompassing, "vague phenomena, which are signifi
cant only by their bulk and their general nature . . . but [which] eventually
give a certain negative style to human life" by distorting time and space,
and limiting access to nature.[56]

53. Ellul, *In Season, Out of Season*, 32–33.

54. Mitcham, *Thinking through Technology*, 60.

55. Fasching, *Thought of Jacques Ellul*, 15.

56. Creegan, review of *Technological Bluff*, 2–3.

Ellul stated unequivocally that he had attempted to synthesize all of human history through a Christian perspective.[57] This attempt occupied his intellectual undertaking between 1940 and 1955. Ellul explained that it was in this search to synthesize history through the Christian perspective that the need arose to explain exactly how the Christian perspective related to life in his age, and it was here that he became aware of the need to define technology more precisely.[58] This need would lead to the formulation of a concept that he would refer to as "*technique*." Ellul noted that he was neither for nor against *technique*.[59] Like an earthquake or an avalanche, he was simply describing what he sees, realizing that regardless of his own opinion on the matter, the phenomenon is here to stay.

Seven general characteristics are associated with the concept of *technique*. They are rationality, artificiality, self-directedness, self-supporting growth, indivisibility, universality, and as already mentioned, autonomy.[60] He further defined *technique* as "the totality of methods, rationally arrived at and having absolute efficiency in every field of human activity."[61] It is important to distinguish the idea of *technique* from technology itself. The products that result from advanced technology should be seen as only the most visible manifestation of *technique*. *Technique* pervaded, as Ellul clearly stated, every field of human endeavor, whether politics, medicine, or education. *Technique* is self-directing; constantly seeking "the one best way" to accomplish any given objective.[62] Rational calculation replaces any other possible reason for accomplishing any given task. It is automatism that propels *technique*—not human actions or decisions. This characteristic results in *technique* determining humankind's actions, and not vice-versa. According to Ellul, one of the most visible manifestations of *technique* is the immediate impact that it has had on daily life. He stated, "Never before has the human race as a whole had to exert such efforts in its daily labors as it does today as a result of its absorption into the monstrous technical mechanism—an undifferentiated but complex mechanism which makes it

---

57. Ellul, *In Season, Out of Season*, 173.

58. Ibid., 174.

59. Creegan, review of *Technological Bluff*, 2.

60. Ellul's definition of *technique* is presented in greater detail in *Technological Society*, vi–viii, x, xviii, xxv–xxvi, xxxvi, 13–18, 19. Only a cursory overview is presented in this study.

61. Ellul, *Technological Society*, xxv.

62. Ibid., 80.

impossible to turn a wheel without the sustained, persevering, and inten sive labor or millions of workers, whether in white collars or blue."[63]

Although there may be some differences in their emphasis, Merton agreed with Ellul's conclusions, and often noted that he was in agreement with the concept that *technique* posed a number of threats to contempo rary society. His extensive reading list of the early 1960s included Lewis Mumford, another philosopher of technology. Merton's "reading of Lewis Mumford and Jacques Ellul provided some depth and breadth to Merton's instinctive distrust of the frenetic activity characterizing the contemporary human condition."[64] In his journal, he noted his reaction to Ellul's overall concept that *technique* was the primary threat to contemporary society and to the human condition. He wrote, "Reading Jacques Ellul's book *The Tech nological Society*. Great, full of firecrackers. A fine provocative book and one that really makes sense . . . I wonder if all the Fathers [currently convened in Rome] are aware of all the implications of a technological society." would go on to review *The Technological Society* for the Catholic journal *Commonweal*:

> One of the most important books of this mid-century, this study in sociology is required reading for anyone who wants to seriously evaluate the relation of the Church with the contemporary world. Modern technology has produced a world in which means deter- mine ends and become ends in themselves. The world of *technique* "destroys, eliminates or subordinates the natural world and does not allow this world to restore itself or even to enter into a symbi- otic relationship with it." To assume that our massive technology is fully under the rational control of human intelligence orient- ing it towards a flowering and fulfillment of man is not only naive but perilous. Ellul does not say that it *cannot* be brought under such control. But he thinks the situation is desperate and that we have not yet begun to do anything serious about it. A frank, hard- hitting and doubtless controversial statement of our most crucial problem.[66]

In this particular review, Merton did not specify what exactly it was about the Church in the contemporary world that he found noteworthy in *Technological Society*. However, in *Mystics and Zen Masters*, Merton's

63. Ibid., 319.

64. Thompson, *Between Science and Religion*, 118.

65. Merton, *Dancing in the Water of Life*, 159–60.

66. Merton, review of *Technological Society*, 357.

critique of the Church in the mid-twentieth century is much easier to discern. He believed that an increasingly inflexible institutional hierarchy had compromised the faith. Many other facets of contemporary society that have also felt *technique*'s impact (in reality, *all* of society and every human pursuit is subject to *technique*'s demands) will be evaluated as this study proceeds.

Merton's critique of technology's impact on the human condition did not spring solely from reading *The Technological Society* or from reading Lewis Mumford. Having read Hannah Arendt's *The Human Condition* (1958), he refined his thinking on the relationship between man and technology. While it is sometimes difficult, as we have seen, to distinguish in Merton's writing between his opposition to the products of technology and the process of technological "progress," it is clear in his reflection on Arendt that his opposition is to the process itself. This line of thinking more clearly parallels Ellul. Merton noted in his journal that Arendt believed "being has been replaced by process. The process is everything. Modern man sees only how to fit without friction into productive processes and in this he finds 'happiness.'"[67] This thought is remarkably congruent with Ellul's observation on the effects of *technique* although there is one major difference. Merton asserted that man had chosen to fit himself into the process whereas Ellul would argue that *technique* molds man into the process unknowingly. For Ellul, *technique* determined its own path, whereas Merton seemed to imply that man had chosen to go along with the process willingly, yet without adequately reflecting on the price he had paid.

Despite this difference in approach, Ellul also emphasized "being" over "doing" at various points in his writing. He wrote, "Man always looks for a good which will determine a 'deed'—whereas in Jesus Christ it is always a matter of 'being.'"[68] He also noted, "When asked what to *do*, Paul answers by saying what we should *be*."[69] Ellul scholar David Gill cites these two passages in his discussion of Ellul's ethics, and in the same article, he added "while ethics will sketch out decision- and action-guidelines—indicatives if not imperatives—the heart of the matter in Christian ethics is to be brought into a stance of hope before God (to which God can give freedom) . . . In a Christian church deeply tainted by the modern scientific quest for abstract, universal laws followed by rational decision and effective action,

67. Merton, *Turning toward the World*, 11.

68. Ellul, *To Will and to Do*, 28.

69. Ellul, *Ethics of Freedom*, 309.

Ellul's call back to an ethics of stance and virtue, is a powerful antidote." Ellul's thinking, *technique* is solely concerned with doing, and with efficient processes. "Being" is not part of *technique*'s calculus. Both Merton and Ellul add to this ongoing discussion on the nature of being as opposed to doing.

A major thread that runs through all of Ellul's work is his concern with freedom. Individual freedom is the greatest good to Ellul, and quite simply, *technique* has become the greatest threat to freedom. The notion that freedom has been threatened or somehow curtailed by society's in creasingly technological nature is one that other philosophers have noted. British philosopher John Stuart Mill (1806–1873) observed technology's impact in the midst of the industrial revolution of the nineteenth century. He wrote:

> Take for instance the question how far mankind has gained by civilization. One man is forcibly struck by the multiplication of physical comforts; the advancement and diffusion of knowledge; the decay of superstition; the facilities of mutual intercourse; the softening of manners . . . the great works accomplished . . . and he becomes that very common character, the worshipper of "our enlightened age." Another fixes his attention, not upon the value of these advantages, but upon the high price which is paid for them; the relaxation of individual energy and courage, the loss of proud and self-relying independence; the slavery of so large a portion of mankind to artificial wants . . . the dull unexciting monotony of their lives, and the passionless insipidity, and absence of any marked individuality in their characters.[71]

This quote, from 1840, captures a great deal of the critique leveled by Merton and Ellul against twentieth-century society. Ellul further charac terized the impact that technology has had on the human condition, and not just on civilization itself, when he stated that, "regarding the human condition in this system, we have repeatedly witnessed the transformation of human beings by technology."[72] While Mill was specifically addressing his concerns in this quote to the effects of "civilization," it is clear that he is referring to one aspect of civilization in particular, and that aspect is the advance of certain modern technologies. There is an element of what El lul refers to as *technique* in the quote as well. It is interesting to note that

70. Gill, "Jacques Ellul's Ethics," 5.

71. Mill, "Coleridge (1840)," in *Collected Works*, n.p.

72. Ellul, *Perspectives on Our Age*, 85.

Mill's quotation was written slightly before Karl Marx wrote *Das Kapital* (1867). Ellul's acceptance of Karl Marx as a philosopher and a social critic had important implications for his later thinking. Ellul recalled that having read *Das Kapital* for the first time, "I discovered a global interpretation of the world, the explanation for this drama and misery and decadence that we had experienced. The excellence of Marx's thinking, in the domain of economic theory, convinced me . . . it was the first breakthrough giving me a general interpretation of the world, my first general education."[73] Marx's dialectical style had a tremendous influence on Ellul's entire corpus. Ellul effectively stripped Marx's dialectical method of any ideological overtones.[74] Having never joined the Communist Party, Ellul held the position that opposing the party line—any established party line—was one of the only ways to ensure that individual freedom maintained a foothold in his life. It was Ellul's objective to provide a text that would encompass the same essential truths regarding society and the human condition in the twentieth century as Marx's *Das Kapital* had done for the nineteenth century.[75] Ellul was convinced that had Marx lived in the twentieth century, "he would no longer study economics or the capitalist structures, he would study *Technique*."[76] Ellul would finally break with Marxist thought, as he recalled at age 70, "[I broke] with the kind of Marxism that claims to be the aim of and the key to everything. On the other hand, I totally agree with a Marxism that offers a method of interpretation . . . I can no longer say that Marxism represents the ultimate in science, the ultimate in truth . . . on the contrary, when Marxism becomes dogmatics it is actually a lie."[77] Interestingly, Ellul would reserve the same disdain for the dogmatics exhibited by the institutional Church—a topic that will be considered in chapter 3, while Marx's influence on both Merton and Ellul will be treated in chapter 5.

Ellul went on to note that the type of work to which humankind had been subjected, or more accurately, to which *technique* had subjected humankind, was characterized by an absence, rather than a presence. Traditionally, work absorbed man's efforts in such a way as to engage all of his faculties, the product of which could be seen as an extension of the worker. Work once produced a feeling of pride, of craftsmanship; it was

73. Ellul, *Sources and Trajectories*, 29.

74. Burke, "Jacques Ellul," 6.

75. Mitcham, *Thinking through Technology*, 57.

76. Ellul, *In Season, Out of Season*, 176.

77. Ellul, *Sources and Trajectories*, 30.

an exercise in which the producer "contemplated and recognized himself." Ellul did not believe these characteristics were to be found in the type of work available to those living in the twentieth century. He explained that in the modern world, although work may have become less fatiguing, espe cially in the field of agriculture, it still, however, demonstrated remarkable shortcomings when compared to the work of craftsmen and artisans of the past. He added that work had become "aimless, useless, a callous business, tied to a clock, an absurdity profoundly felt and resented by the worker whose labor no longer has anything in common with what was tradition ally called *work*."[79]

The concept of "necessity" is seen throughout Ellul's writing. Al though he thoroughly defined *technique*, he has been criticized for not explaining what he means when he uses the term "necessity." He described necessity's entrance into the world at the time of the rupture in the Garden of Eden, that "brought about by the fall, necessity is introduced into the world. Determinism, mechanism of history, scientific law, destiny, *ananke* whatever name is used to cover it up, whatever be the form in which man accepts it, necessity is always the same."[80] Necessity represents those things with which humankind must contend in order to survive. Basically, "neces sity is definable as what man must do because he cannot do otherwise." *Technique* is a manifestation of necessity which hinders our attainment of freedom. Along with *technique* and the idea of the necessities, one must also understand Ellul's (and to a much lesser extent, Merton's) use of the dialectic, especially as "the dialectic between freedom and necessity is the central and controlling idea in all of Ellul's work."[82]

DIALECTICAL APPROACH IN ELLUL AND MERTON

A form of systematic reasoning designed to reconcile opposed or contra dictory ideas, the dialectical process runs through Ellul's entire body of work, although Merton relies less on this philosophical device. According to Ellul:

78. Ellul, *Technological Society*, 320. For a more recent examination of this idea, see Crawford, *Shop Class as Soulcraft.*

79. Ellul, *Technological Society*, 320.

80. Ellul, *To Will and to Do*, 59.

81. Ellul, *Violence*, 128.

82. Clenendin, *Theological Method in Jacques Ellul*, 59.

> To discuss my own work may seem pretentious, and yet my books constitute a totality conceived as such. To the extent that I have arrived at the conviction that it is impossible to study modern society in its unity without a spiritual reference, and also that it is impossible to engage in theological study without reference to the world in which we live, I have found myself faced from the outset with the need to find the link between the two, and this link can be nothing other than the dialectical process.[83]

Ellul's use of the dialectic serves one very important function, which is quite simply to facilitate grasping the whole picture of reality. Ellul wrote, "The dialectician is the one who sees reality (Republic *VII*). Dialectic, then, is not just a way of reasoning by question and answer. It is an intellectual way of grasping reality, which embraces the positive and the negative, white and black."[84] Further explaining his employment of the dialectical method, he stated:

> I should perhaps explain the concept of dialectics. Dialectics, as a way of understanding reality, has become quite common, quite current in the Western world. This is due to the influence of Marxian thought . . . I would say very simply that, at bottom, dialectics is a procedure that does not exclude contraries, but includes them. We can't describe this too simplistically by saying that the positive and the negative combine; or that the thesis and the antithesis fuse into a synthesis; dialectics is something infinitely more supple and more profound.[85]

Following his religious conversion experience, Ellul became a member of the French Reformed Church. While by no means a member of the clergy, he has been described as a "lay ecclesiastic."[86] Having written fifty-eight books and contributed numerous other articles to various philosophical and religious journals, Ellul's work generally follows two very distinct lines of thought. First, Ellul was concerned with the Christian Revelation—the meaning of the revealed Word and the radical message of the gospel. This is his theological track. Second, he presented an enormous body of work on society and technology. This is his sociological track. Rarely do the two tracks—theological and sociological—intersect in any one book. Ellul

---

83. Ellul, *What I Believe*, 43.

84. Ibid., 31.

85. Ellul, *Perspectives on Our Age*, 7.

86. Menninger, "Ellul," 235.

believed that his entire life's work was best presented in the dialectical manner. Each book fit into a larger scheme which was to be taken as a whole. He also believed that as he continued to add to the corpus, he would clarify his message, but never would he actually resolve the argument and bring about some final synthesis to the dialectic between freedom and necessity. He stated:

> The writing I had undertaken in a tentative frame of mind assured a progressively better structure. The whole of it is a composition in counterpoint. Every sociological analysis of mine is answered (not in the sense of replying, but in that of noting the other dialectical pole) by a biblical or theological analysis. For example, to my book *The Political Illusion*, a study of politics as actually practiced in a modern state, corresponds to my *Politics of God, Politics of Man*, a biblical study of the Second Book of Kings. To my book on technology corresponds my theologically based study of the great city as the supreme achievement of man's technology.[87]

Ellul's theological and sociological tracks serve distinct purposes in presenting his worldview. Darrell Fasching summarizes the distinctions in *The Thought of Jacques Ellul* (1981). Fasching notes that in his sociological analysis, the paradox that Ellul "wishes to expose is . . . that the citizens of the technological society believe themselves free while they are not free but must conform to the demands of modern technology."[88] Likewise Ellul's theology posits that "the possibility of freedom in the technological society can occur on the basis of an apocalyptic hope in that which is 'other' than this society, namely, the 'Wholly Other.'"[89] The purpose of the dialectic was to help the reader confront the problems of the day rather than to solve the problems or to answer any specific question. He went on to explain his use of the dialectic, noting that "the only thing that will be of any use is not synthesis or adaptation, but confrontation; that is, bringing face-to-face two factors that are contradictory and irreconcilable and at the same time inseparable. For it is only out of the *decision* he makes when he experiences this contradiction—never out of adherence to an integrated system—that the Christian will arrive at a practical position."[90] Finally, the dialectical tension between freedom and necessity, the struggle against the forces of

87. Ellul, "Mirror of These Ten Years," 2.
88. Fasching, *Thought of Jacques Ellul*, 15.
89. Ibid., 65.
90. Ellul, "Mirror of These Ten Years," 2.

determinism which act against humankind, provides the very basis for freedom itself. Ellul stated, "We must not think of the problem in terms of a choice of being determined or being free. We must look at it dialectically, and say that man is indeed determined, but that it is open to him to overcome necessity, and that this *act* is freedom."[91] Dialectics thus not only provides the structural basis upon which Ellul presents his entire corpus, but also provides the parameters within which freedom is expressed.

Much like Ellul's corpus is based on the dialectic between freedom and necessity, Merton also presented a dialectic in his work, but to a degree that is far more subtle and much less pronounced than Ellul's dialectics. For Merton, there are multiple layers to the dialectic that he employed throughout his writing. The English poet William Blake (1757–1827) provided Merton with a model of a different type of dialectic, one focused on the "loving and fiery" elements of passion and mysticism rather than simply an intellectual argument such as Ellul employed.[92] However, Merton's dialectic is predominantly one that juxtaposes collectivity and community; his task was "to expose—in ourselves as well as in our society—the illusions that the collectivity lives by and to work for the building up of the community."[93] This is not necessarily the dialectic around which Merton patterned his entire worldview, but it was one that "has taken place within the context of an ever-escalating technology," and thus became Merton's concern as his writing began to focus on this technological threat in the 1960s.[94] Saint John of the Cross provided Merton with additional elements of his contemplative worldview with such intellectual constructs as *Todo y Nada*—the emphasis of "all and nothing" that characterizes Saint John's thinking on contemplation.[95]

Finally, Merton often wrote in a dialectical style without actually intending to provide a dialectic as formal as Ellul's. Explaining the appeals of a German priest condemned to death in Nazi Germany, Merton wrote, "In

91. Ellul, *Technological Society*, xxxiii.

92. Merton, *Literary Essays of Thomas Merton*, 6.

93. Pennington, *Toward an Integrated Humanity*, 182.

94. Ibid.

95. Merton, *Ascent to Truth*, 53. *Ascent to Truth* outlines Merton's attempt to explain St. John of the Cross to contemporary readers. Merton's debt to St. John's writing is outlined in part 2 of this book. Much of Merton's Catholicism can be discerned through his reflections on Christian mysticism in this work, as he explains the influence of St. John of the Cross, St. Thomas Aquinas, and St. Teresa of Avila on his particular Catholic worldview.

other words, Father Delp is reiterating the basic truth of Christian faith and Christian experience, St. Paul's realization of the paradox of man's helpless ness and God's grace, not as somehow opposed, fighting for primacy in man's life, but a single existential unity: Sinful man redeemed in Christ." Merton's use of the two contradictory elements of helplessness and redemp tion resolved in one existential unity resembles Ellul's dialectic of freedom and necessity. Regarding the community, which Merton juxtaposes against the collectivity in his dialectic, Merton stated, "It means seeing life as a long journey in the wilderness . . . a journey with an invisible Companion, toward a secure and promised fulfillment not for the individual believer alone but for the community of man to whom salvation has been prom ised in Jesus Christ."[97] Merton would not have been reluctant to employ a dialectical approach in his thinking as dialectics had always been a part of the monastic tradition, and was "the usual complement to grammar." Merton's Catholicism in this instance provided him with an intellectual tool similar to that which Ellul would derive from the Protestant tradition, specifically from the influence of Karl Barth as discussed in chapter

Describing *technique*, Gabriel Vahanian provides some insight into Ellul's thinking regarding community which in a sense mirrors Merton's dialectic view of community and collectivity. Vahanian wrote that "Ellul is always reminding us that *technique* doesn't mean tool or machine so much as it does a *milieu*, or an order which is replacing the orders of nature or history, a society which is less organic than organized, and, I may be bold to suggest, a charismatic communion rather than a so-called community."

Some similarities to Thomas Merton's methodology for understand ing the human condition can be seen in Ellul's reliance on the evaluation of direct, lived experience. Recounting the importance of the lived experience as a criterion for discerning the objective situation in which humans live in the here and now, Ellul stated:

> This reality ought to be grasped first of all on the human level . . .
> We must no longer think of "men" in the abstract, but of my neigh-
> bor Mario. It is in the concrete life of this man . . . that I see the real
> repercussions of the machine, of the press, of political discourses
> and of the administration . . . The intellectual who wants to do his

96. Merton, *Faith and Violence*, 62.

97. Ibid., 63.

98. Leclerq, *Love of Learning*, 202.

99. Vahanian, introduction to *Thought of Jacques Ellul*, xxix.

> work properly must today go back to the starting-point: the man
> who he knows, and first of all to himself... All other knowledge of
> the world, through statistics or news, is illusory.[100]

This concern for the common person pervades Ellul's work. He aims to illustrate the shortcomings of contemporary society—the technological society—not in order to add volumes to his copious body of work, but to allow the man on the street to reclaim the freedom that God gave the world through Jesus Christ and the Gospel message. He is thus in a sense a theologian, but not the typical pulpit preacher. His knowledge of classical theology and of Scripture allowed him to explain "the pressure on us moderns who must deal with a world changing so radically that it no longer has anything in common with the one which gave birth to Christianity."[101] Ellul's accusation that the institutional Church had abandoned contemporary Christians and firmly aligned itself with the demands placed upon it by society is detailed in chapter 3.

While it might appear in Merton's writing that he had entered the monastery to escape the concerns of his "neighbor Mario," as Ellul described his fellow man, Merton would in fact turn back towards the world in a revelation that has been recounted by numerous authors and by Merton himself. In doing so, he aligned himself with Ellul's concrete view of acquiring "knowledge of the world" that is immediately useful to the ones who need it the most—the individual caught in the collectivity that is trying to transcend the bonds of *technique* and return to the community. Merton's revelation took place in Louisville, Kentucky, on March 18, 1958. A sign marks this spot for any travelers to Louisville that might happen to find themselves at the same corner. Merton recalled, "in Louisville, at the corner of 4th and Walnut, suddenly realized that I loved all the people and that none of them were, or could be, totally alien to me. As if waking from a dream—the dream of my separateness, of the 'special' vocation to be different... I am still a member of the human race—and what more glorious destiny is there for man, since the Word was made flesh and became, too, a member of the Human Race!"[102] Merton also said that it was concern for the common man, for the individuals that make up contemporary society, that warrant his attention. He proclaimed as well in this passage an essential idea that will be expanded upon in chapter 6—the idea that

100. Ellul, *Presence of the Kingdom*, 99–100.

101. Vahanian, introduction to *Thought of Jacques Ellul*, xvi.

102. Elie, *Life You Save*, 254.

the Word was made flesh and entered into human history. Following this experience, Merton was prepared to judge the world—a world full of sinful people among which he included himself—and level the accusations of not only genocide and deicide, but of "cosmicide," or the attempted obliteration of the entire human race which the Cold War had brought to the forefront of possibility.[103] And also like Ellul, Merton's "academic analysis and un derstanding of contemporary society feed on his analysis and understand ing of faith, and vice-versa."[104] For both men, the concern for the common person drove their worldviews forward, and in some cases, as they both perceived the common person's situation becoming more perilous, their positions were presented with increasing radicalism. In Ellul's case, "his books are commonly approached with caution and accepted with even greater caution," and his writing can "force extremes on those who confront it."[105] Merton did not generally elicit a similar response, although some of his later poetry borders on the radical, and will be discussed in chapter

Having developed the foundations of their particular worldviews in the mid-twentieth century, Merton and Ellul were not alone in their cri tique of contemporary society. A prominent contemporary that took a similar stance regarding the deleterious effects of modern technology was the French philosopher Herbert Marcuse (1898–1979). An examination of Marcuse's thinking demonstrates that both Merton and Ellul, writing at the same time as Marcuse, have contributed to an existing philosophical debate that was ongoing throughout the height of the Cold War. Marcuse offered a scathing critique of the machine and its place in society. Both Marcuse and Ellul "paid particular attention to the negative aspects of technology's relationship to civilization and its predominantly deleterious effect on the human condition, and have expressed their criticism in uncompromising terms."[106] Merton would also find common ground with Marcuse, as they both saw the capitalist system of the West and the communist system of the East as inherently similar in many respects. Much like Ellul considered both of these economic systems to be equally captive to the demands of *technique*, Merton viewed these systems as equally totalitarian.

Marcuse wrote in the early 1960s that society was becoming richer, bigger and better by perpetrating the danger of atomic catastrophe.[107]

103. Pennington, *Toward an Integrated Humanity*, 22.

104. Menninger, "Ellul," 235.

105. Ibid., 236.

106. Matheson, "Marcuse, Ellul," 327.

107. Marcuse, *One Dimensional Man*, ix.

there are some similarities here to Ellul's belief in the advance of *technique* and efficiency, Marcuse would help Merton realize that some of his own thoughts that he had formulated and expressed in his social commentaries were shared by other noted intellectuals of his day. In his final speech entitled "Marxism and Monastic Perspectives," delivered in Bangkok hours before his death by accidental electrocution, Merton paid tribute to some of the ideas that Marcuse had supported concerning technology's deleterious effect on contemporary society. Unlike Ellul, Merton had not completely turned his back on Marx (as will be discussed in chapter 5). But including Marcuse in his final speech illustrates some of the salient features of not only Merton's own philosophy, but of some of the contradictions in his thought and the difficulties of situating him properly in the panoply of twentieth-century philosophers and theologians. Some of the inconsistencies are worth noting:

> Merton . . . ignored the fact that Marcuse, in agreement with his guru Marx, totally disregarded man's spiritual dimension—an indication of the incompatibility of Marxism and Christianity. Nor did he mention that the United States provided for spiritual freedom, including the right to embrace or not embrace monasticism, in contrast to the anti-monastic regulations in the Soviet Union. Most importantly, Merton overlooked that Marcuse's solution to the problems of the "One Dimensional Man" called for a revolution of "outcastes and outsiders" against the existing structure. Marcuse did not come to grips with man's inherent imperfection, his sinfulness, an article of faith in Christianity.[108]

How can we classify Merton, and how can we give credence to his ideas under the weight of these accusations? Like Ellul, he presented an uncompromising and often times excoriating attack on technology and contemporary society. After noting some of the inconsistencies in Merton's final speech, a fitting summary encapsulates an overview of his thought: "Certain reservations notwithstanding, one cannot but be impressed by his steadfast search for God through contemplation and action inside and outside the monastery, within and beyond the western tradition."[109]

It is Merton's—and Ellul's—search for God as a quest for freedom that provides the focus of this study. Their acceptance of the Gospel message and the pattern that this provided for their lives offers a living example of

108. Lipski, *Thomas Merton and Asia*, 69.
109. Ibid., 72.

their Christocentric view of freedom. Both men were influenced by parents that were artists, both were raised in rural environments in the post World War One years that had not yet been touched by the many technological advances that would characterize development in the twentieth century, and they both underwent intense religious conversion experiences in their early adulthood. These conversions are all the more remarkable in their similarity in light of the fact that both Merton and Ellul were raised in households in which religious belief and practice was largely absent. They both attempted throughout their lives to articulate a conception of freedom which relied heavily on their religious faith. The next chapter will examine how their theology informed their particular views, specifically addressing Karl Barth as an antecedent to their thought, as well as their critique of the visible, institutional church, which they both believed to have aligned itself firmly with *technique*.

3 Theological Perspective

Both Merton and Ellul relied heavily on their religious beliefs and on their particular theological views in formulating their understanding of freedom. This chapter examines their Christocentric view of freedom, focusing primarily on identifying some of the common antecedents to their thinking on the theological implications to human freedom, and identifying some additional aspects of their thought that are informed by their theology relating to technology's impact on freedom. They approach the topic from two different denominational perspectives, but the conclusions that they reached are remarkably similar.

Many philosophers have examined the impact technology has had on the human condition, including the effects that our increasingly technologically oriented mindset has had on the idea of freedom. In addition to the particular philosophers discussed in chapter 2, Ian Barbour, Langdon Winner, Wendell Berry, and Aldo Leopold are just a few of the more prominent contemporary thinkers to have engaged in this debate, although they all focused more on the sociological aspects of freedom than on the theological aspect. Merton also engaged some of the sociological implications stemming from contemporary technology in his later writing; however, his fundamental conception of freedom derived primarily from his theology and his faith. The same theological foundation was true for Ellul as well, as much of his work addressed the theological implications stemming from *technique's* rapid advance. Nevertheless, as with Merton, Ellul grounded the nature of freedom itself in theology. Merton and Ellul thus both bring a theological focus to the idea of freedom. In Ellul's case, his theology informed his entire notion of freedom, which provided the dialectical opposition to necessity in his work.

Leading thinkers in the study of the history and philosophy of technology have acknowledged that religious and theological ideas are often foundational aspects of technological thought. For example, Langdon Winner presents a number of ideas concerning the relationship between theology and technology in *Autonomous Technology* (1977). Winner was essentially trying to determine what characteristics inherent in Christian doctrine might account for man's domination of nature. Citing Max Weber's *Protestant Ethic and the Spirit of Capitalism* (1905) as one of the prominent explanations for the West's propensity to subjugate the natural world to the technical order, Winner asked whether Ellul's theory of *technique* might be more relevant to the discussion. He noted, "Ellul's theory of world history draws attention to two major examples in which *technique* was deliber ately and successfully limited" and that "a religious or moral conviction in the culture prevented an unrestrained development of technical means." The examples to which Winner refers are the ancient Greek culture and the culture of medieval Christian Europe. According to Ellul, the Greeks had mastered a certain "conception of life," the "apex of civilization and intelligence."[2] A certain hesitance to allow *technique* to dominate human ity has since been removed, according to Ellul, and contemporary society is overcome by *technique's* demands. A primary concern for both Merton and Ellul was the institutional church's surrender to *technique*—one of the salient ideas examined in this chapter.

Of particular emphasis in examining this theological focus will be the relationship that Merton and Ellul shared with the work of Swiss Protestant theologian Karl Barth (1886–1968). This chapter will identify the common alities between Ellul's and Merton's engagement with Barth and the impact that this engagement had on their respective views of human freedom, but will not attempt to provide a complete overview of Barth's extensive theol ogy. Ellul turned to Karl Barth's work in order to formulate, clarify, and re fine his own thinking. Thomas Merton appreciated many aspects of Barth's theology, but as a Roman Catholic, Merton held some of Barth's thinking at a greater distance. However, Barth clearly shaped both Merton's and Ellul's conceptions of the nature of freedom. Following a discussion of their en gagement with Barth, the study examines two other facets of their thinking and of their worldviews that fall within the purview of their theology. Both Merton and Ellul considered the institutional church, conformed as it is in contemporary society to *technique*, to be a hindrance to the dissemina tion and promulgation of the Gospel message, the acceptance of which is a

1. Winner, *Autonomous Technology*, 119.

2. Ellul, *Technological Society*, 29.

necessary first step on the road to true freedom. They believed that technology and the idea of progress had captivated the church, and they both level a harsh critique aimed at this phenomenon. Chapter 3 studies, refines, and clarifies Merton's and Ellul's thinking regarding what it means to be "free," setting the stage for an examination of their views on technology's impact on freedom through the sociological and the political lens in the following chapters.

The chapter concludes with a look at prayer and contemplation. For both men, prayer was a necessary ingredient in an individual's quest to understand the Gospel message and to accept the invitation to live life according to its precepts. In some sense, Merton and Ellul generally adhered to the "apophatic" tradition—a line of thought that emphasizes darkness, which is also known as "negative theology." This tradition relies heavily on images of darkness and negation, and it is an intellectual device employed at times by both men. Since God is the source of human freedom, this comparison of the methods used by Merton and Ellul to describe God and to comprehend the divine is of interest in the general comparison between the two.

KARL BARTH'S INFLUENCE

In order to understand Karl Barth's impact on Merton's and Ellul's theological methodology, it is necessary to put Barth's own theological work in perspective. Widely acknowledged as one of the greatest theologians of the twentieth century, he was a man "marked by an unusual intellect, a great capacity for work, seriousness of purpose, a democratic spirit, an appreciation for the arts—especially music—and finally, by a wry and engaging sense of humor."[3] In addition, like both Merton and Ellul, Barth found that social engagement was a topic in which all Christians should engage. After joining the Social-Democratic Party in 1915, Barth stated, "It was no longer possible for me personally to remain suspended in the clouds above the present evil world but rather it had to be demonstrated here and now that faith in the Greatest does not exclude but rather includes within it work and suffering in the realm of the imperfect."[4] Much like Merton and Ellul, Barth's concern was to proclaim Christianity's redemptive message in

---

3. Mueller, *Karl Barth*, 14. Studies of Barth's life and thought are vast and beyond the scope of this dissertation. However, for an introduction, see the helpful work of O'Grady, *Survey of the Theology of Karl Barth*.

4. *Revolutionary Theology*, 100.

such a way that it would directly influence the believer rather than simply provide a starting point for Biblical study and reflection. Writing in the first decades of the twentieth century, his work predates that of both Merton and Ellul, although there are two main avenues of thought through which one can trace Barth's influence on them both. These are the primacy of the Word of God as the source of human freedom, and a focus on dialectics. Explaining his view of freedom, Barth stated, "Finally, the Word of God is sovereign in that it is spoken and reaches us in divine freedom; not the blind freedom of fate, ruling by some unknown law over gods and men, but in the freedom of the divine mercy and patience. This is the freedom which gives freedom to others, which gives us and allows us our freedom, which asks of us that we place ourselves at its disposal in freedom—not forced, not pushed, not overpowered, but in adoration."[5]

Barth's *Church Dogmatics*, a thirteen-volume work, represents one of the premier theological works of the twentieth century. During the latter part of the nineteenth century and the early twentieth century, European Protestantism was divided into two camps—one liberal and one conserva tive. Barth parted ways with Protestant liberalism and its alliance with the anthropocentrism evident in theologians that adhered to the philosophy of Immanuel Kant (1724–1804) and Ludwig Feuerbach (1804–1872). These two German philosophers had presented a significant challenge to tradi tional theological orthodoxy. The Prussian philosopher Kant proclaimed that "we create a God for ourselves," and once created, he is given such attri butes that "we shall be able most easily to win Him over to our advantage." According to American philosopher William James, Kant allowed us to act "*as if* there were a God; feel *as if* we were free . . . and we find then that these words do make a genuine difference in our moral life."[7] James illustrated in this expression the idea that we can no longer assume an ontological awareness of God after Kant.

Following the Kantian attack, Bavarian philosopher Ludwig Feuer bach published *The Essence of Christianity* (1841). Many consider this work to have "led to the establishment of a new modern era."[8] It was incumbent upon theologians following Feuerbach to "demonstrate the possibility of Christian revelation—in some way—in the modern world"[9] One of Barth's

5. Barth, *God Here and Now*, 22–23.

6. Kant, *Religion within the Limits of Reason Alone*, 157.

7. James, *Varieties of Religious Experience*, 59.

8. Weber, "Feuerbach, Barth," 25.

9. Ibid., 28.

primary objectives in presenting his work was to refute the idea that theology and the existence of God was nothing more than an anthropomorphic projection of man's own being. Barth rejected "natural theology," believing that this intellectual construct left theology open to the anthropomorphic interpretation. It is this argument that has shaped much of twentieth-century theological thought, and this argument is specifically that which Barth sought to refute. The argument basically proposes that "In speaking about God, man is not dealing with a transcendent, objective reality, but with a postulate which he makes to serve a specific, moral function."[10] Ellul's assertion that "all morality, Christian or not, is destructive of freedom" demonstrates that he shares Barth's opinion on this matter.[11] He clearly sides with Barth in favor of revelation as an ontological truth over the Kantian idea that revelation is only useful to individuals if it serves to buttress the Categorical Imperative. Although in regards to Feuerbach's analysis, Barth does not solely disagree, and does actually attribute some merit to his case with statements such as:

> When we have grasped the significance of the direction in which human passion moves, we are confronted with the possibility of religion. Though religion, it is true, opposes the passion of men, yet it too stands within the bracket which is defined by the all-embracing word *sin*. With acute analysis Feuerbach has penetrated the truth when he points out that sinful passions are clearly seen, awakened, and set in motion, with the intrusion of the possibility of religion, and because of it.[12]

While Barth wrote extensively in order to refute both Kant, Feuerbach, and the idea that religion was a mere anthropomorphic projection, in evaluating Barth's impact on Merton and Ellul it is only necessary to examine Barth's thoughts on the Word of God and the freedom that can be derived from this Word. Engagement with Barth took place for both thinkers primarily in these two areas. It is Barth's declaration that "theology is a free science because it is based on and determined by the kingly freedom of the Word of God"[13] that provides much of the material for this comparison.

    In Barth's view, humankind's gift of freedom derives directly from God's Word. For him, all human freedom has its foundation in revelation.

---

10. Ibid., 24.
11. Ellul, *Ethics of Freedom*, 239.
12. Barth, *Epistle to the Romans*, 236.
13. Barth, *Dogmatics in Outline*, 5.

This idea is central to Barth's theology, and it is the one idea that most di rectly influenced Ellul. It will be important in Merton's thinking as well, although to a lesser degree. Ellul takes this Barthian line of reasoning and added that "everything comes from this first interchange: God speaks. Thus he manifests his freedom, just as a human speaker does. He invites his lis tener to the freedom involved in answering."[14] Ellul's intellectual debt to Barth has been covered extensively in various other scholarly works, as well as in works by Ellul himself.[15]

Andrew Goddard places Ellul "fully within the Reformed tradition and the thought of Kierkegaard and Barth."[16] The theological roots of free dom in Ellul's thinking are in part due to his appropriation of Kierkegaard's concept of *Inconditione*, or the idea that God has no conditions. There is a line of influence following from Kierkegaard that leads Ellul to Barth. Goddard noted, "Subsequently, after discovering Kierkegaard, Ellul was introduced . . . to Karl Barth, himself much influenced by Kierkegaard." Ellul scholar Patrick Chastenet adds, "Barth, in the direct line of Kierke gaard, who considered obedience to God the sole source of bliss, enabled [Ellul] to think dialectically about the obedience of the free man to the free God."[18] While Barth would indicate in later writings that his affinity for Kierkegaard wavered over time, the path from Kierkegaard to Barth through to Ellul is evident.[19] Barth's contribution to Ellul's thought includes the emphasis on dialectics, the association of the idea of freedom with the willful obedience to God's will, and the intellectual assent to Kierkegaard's thinking as well. While Ellul clearly benefitted from his reading of Barth's work, Barth himself showed an "interest in Ellul's early writings, holding a discussion on [Ellul's] book of law and apparently a query from Barth about what Ellul meant by '*la technique*' in *Presence*, encouraged [Ellul]

14. Ellul, *Humiliation of the Word*, 59.

15. Geoffrey W. Bromiley's chapter entitled "Barth's Influence of Jacques Ellul" in *Jacques Ellul: Interpretive Essays* provides a short yet concise overview. Madeleine Garrigou-Lagrange's interviews with Ellul, published in *Jacques Ellul: In Season Out of Season*, also addresses Barth's influence in Ellul's own words; see 17, 26, 60, 78 93, 175, 178.

16. Goddard, *Living the Word*, 65–66.

17. Ibid., 14.

18. Ellul and Troude-Chastenet, *Ellul on Politics*, 5.

19. Kierkegaard's influence on both Ellul and Merton will be covered in the next chapter.

to write [*The Technological Society.*]"[20] There is no similar relationship between Merton and Barth as the two never met and there is no indication that Barth ever read any of Merton's work.

Barth identified Feuerbach's theological musings as mere projections of man's own self-centeredness, nothing that "theology, declared Feuerbach, is anthropology. All talk about God is really indirect, projected talk about human beings."[21] It was not Barth's intent to prove Feuerbach wrong, but to provide a more robust alternative viewpoint regarding Christianity's historical role. If "Feuerbach was the catalyst who led Marx to turn Hegel on his head, to turn dialectical idealism into dialectical materialism," then this "anti-theologian provoked Barth not so much to turn anthropology on its head—as if theology and anthropology were opposites—as to seek in Christology a better theology *and* anthropology."[22] Ellul would carry on in this tradition, taking the idea of freedom and making it central to his own work.

Ellul praised Barth repeatedly, acknowledging his debt to Barth's ideas and methods:

> Whether we like it or not, Barth endures, not as a historical block of work that we can admire like Saint Thomas or Abelard, but as a current *resource* for continual theological research. Calling oneself "Barthian" would be unfaithful to the spirit of his thinking, which is provocative and evocative, always in motion, renewing itself, never following a merely logical development of principles, but rather expressing a wealth of life as well as of understanding. He did establish a "body of doctrine," but not so that disciples could apply it; so that subsequent generations could do *their* work proceeding from his.[23]

This idea applies as well to Ellul today, as few would refer to themselves as "Ellulians;" rather most of those who study his work seek to identify a point of engagement much like Ellul sought in Barth's work. It is precisely within this spirit of proceeding from Barth's work that Ellul developed much of his own thinking. He directly incorporated Barth's rejection of Feuerbach into his own theological worldview. Discussing what he believed, Ellul states succinctly "the affirmation of Feuerbach, that God is an absolutized value,

20. Goddard, *Living the Word*, 14.

21. Green, *Karl Barth*, 90.

22. Ibid.

23. Ellul, "Karl Barth and Us," 22.

was simplistic and puerile."[24] Ellul clarified his position with this further thought regarding his beliefs: "Faith in God—in a God who does not incarnate some natural force or who is not the abstract and hypostatized projection of one of our own desires or aspirations or values (Feuerbach), faith in a God who is different from all that we can conceive or imagine—cannot be assimilated to belief."[25] Presenting these thoughts on his beliefs concerning religion, Ellul demonstrated that Barth's rejection of Feuerbachian philosophy fundamentally shaped his theological worldview.

In addition, Ellul noted, "Barth also brought me freedom with regard to the biblical text—the only and unique pillar of the revelation of God, of course, but thanks to which God speaks in a multiple and diverse manner, allowing us to mine multiple riches from this unique treasure."[26] Revelation's centrality and the "contemporizing" role played by the church are elements of Barth's thought that are also found in Ellul's thinking, and to an extent in Merton's as well. In addition to stressing revelation's centrality, the idea that the Bible is a collection of questions rather than a book of answers is one that Barth and Ellul shared. Barth declared, "I sought to find my way between the problem of human life on the one hand and the content of the Bible on the other. As a minister I wanted to speak to the *people* infinite contradiction of their life, but to speak the no less infinite message of the *Bible*, which was as much of a riddle as life."[27] He went on to elaborate on his thinking about our relationship to God via the Bible, noting, "It is not the right human thoughts about God which form the content of the Bible, but the right divine thoughts about men. The Bible tells us not how we should talk with God but what he says to us; not how we find the way to him, but how he has sought and found the way to us."[28] This passage resembles Ellul's comments on biblical exegesis. He stated that the Bible does not provide answers, but instead contains God's questions to us.

How much does Ellul's dialectical method derive from Barth? Ellul stated, "We entered into a renewal of thought in the existential sense (well before the existential fashion spread by Sartre)" in which "the Bible ceased to be a collection of laws, commandments, or meditative texts, and became

---

24. Ellul, *What I Believe*, 4.

25. Ibid.

26. Ellul, "Karl Barth and Us," 24.

27. Barth, *Word of God and Word of Man*, 100.

28. Ibid., 43.

29. Fasching, *Thought of Jacques Ellul*, 9.

the place of a dialectical discussion shown to us 'of the sorrow and the promise' of life itself, *our* life itself."[30] He continued:

> We saw slowly and with difficulty, that this change originated from a new way of thinking as well as a new way of reading the Bible. At that period we scarcely spoke of dialectic. We knew little of Hegel . . . and little more of Marx. I had the greatest difficulty in understanding Barth's steps in thinking, always posing opposites and then going beyond them and synthesizing them in a new development—all of this not as an intellectual game, but because one was situated precisely at the existential level, where life itself unfolded.[31]

As these passages demonstrate, Jacques Ellul's intellectual debt to Karl Barth is significant. He patterned much of his theological methodology and his views on the idea of human freedom after Barth's thinking. He incorporated elements of Barth's thought regarding his dialectical approach and his notion of freedom. It would be difficult to imagine Ellul's corpus taking shape as it did without his having read and incorporated much of Barth's thinking and methodology. Incorporating portions of Barth's thinking "enabled Jacques Ellul to avoid the *"either-or"* dilemma of the non-believers, and helped him handle the *"already"* and the "not yet," in other words the promise and its fulfillment. But above all the Swiss theologian enabled Ellul to understand the central idea of the Biblical message essentially formulated in direct terms: the free determination of man in the free decision of God."[32] It is freedom and the nature of freedom that provides the most convincing link between Barth and Ellul. The situation will be much the same between Barth and Merton. The role that the church is expected to play in contemporary society is only one avenue through which Ellul and Merton find agreement with Barth.

As a Protestant thinker, Barth was not inclined to the cenobitic. Merton noted this, but much like Ellul's appropriation of Barth's dialectical method, "Merton continually uses Barth as one pole of his own search for truth," weighing Barth's thinking against other ideas "in an attempt to work out his own synthesis, and he often finds Barth salutary for his attempt."[33] Merton also added, "though Karl Barth has always defended the classic

---

30. Ellul, "Karl Barth and Us," 23.

31. Ibid.

32. Ellul and Troude-Chastenet, *Ellul on Politics*, 5.

33. Scruggs, *Faith Seeking Understanding*, 19–20. This excellent work represents the best comparison of these two thinkers available.

doctrines of the Reformation and is therefore not inclined to overestimate the value of asceticism as a way of Christian perfection, he still recognizes a vocation to celibacy, and esteems monasticism insofar as it seems to him to have been, historically, a protest against the secularization of the Church. Barth approves the call to special renunciation and to *liberty in Christ* which monasticism issues to Christians in the world"[34] This idea of "liberty in Christ" is central to both Merton's and Ellul's view that accepting the Gospel message is the first step on the road to freedom. While Merton and Ellul have appropriated some of the same ideas from Barth, and for mulated their thinking in ways that lead to a number of similarities in their assertion on the nature of freedom, it is perhaps the coincidental date of Merton's and Barth's death (December 10, 1968) that draws the most atten tion to these two individuals:

> One was a Protestant theologian who labored quietly in university towns of Switzerland and Germany for half a century. The other was a Roman Catholic monk who worked hermitlike on his writ- ings in the hills of central Kentucky. But while Karl Barth gave his life to scholarship and Thomas Merton to contemplation, both men were Christian activists who found in the Word a command to do. Barth stood courageously against Nazi totalitarianism. Mer- ton drove himself endlessly in championing the cause of the poor and oppressed. On their journey toward their deaths last week, each brought to his age, and to his fellow man, a message of love that was ardently Christian.[35]

Like Ellul, "Merton placed the Christian doctrine of the Incarnation at the very center of his thought and life in an attempt to hold all things together in Jesus Christ."[36] Moreover, like Ellul, and as the next section in this chapter on the visible and the invisible church will illustrate, Merton considered that the technological mindset presented a challenge to the ful fillment of the gift of freedom that was inherent in the acceptance of the grace offered by God through Jesus Christ.[37] Merton believed this was not a result of an emotional response from God directed at man in his fallen nature, but rather "that wholly destructive order of being which we set up

34. Merton, *Mystics and Zen Masters*, 191.

35. "Religion: The Death of Two Extraordinary Christians," *Time*, December 1968, http://content.time.com/time/magazine/article/0,9171,844711,00.html.

36. Scruggs, *Faith Seeking Understanding*, 10.

37. This idea is further examined in the section on The City as Manifestation of *nique* in ch. 5.

when we attempt to fill the space that should be filled by the freedom of the love of God."[38] Merton and Ellul both also envisioned the nature of the relationship between God and humankind in a manner similar to that held by Barth:

> Against the liberals who assumed the partnership of God and man, Barth proclaimed a radically transcendent Creator whose message had been hurled like a stone at humanity. In contrast to an ethical, teaching Jesus, Barth preached a divine Christ who was, in his person, God's message to man. Rejecting the higher criticism that reduced the Bible to human wish fulfillment, Barth proclaimed the objective authority of Scripture. The Bible, he wrote, was not man's word about God, but God's word about man. Barth's thinking, which came to be known as "crisis theology" or "neo-orthodoxy," stressed a God who stood in constant judgment about idolatrous counterfeits of faith who sought to create him in their own image.[39]

While this passage contains a number of ides which contrast with traditional Catholic orthodoxy, it reinforces the fact that Merton remained open to considering other faith traditions in formulating his critique. This is something which Ellul would occasionally do as well when he encountered Catholics who shared various aspects of his worldview, for example, devoting an issue of the journal *Foi et Vie* to French Catholic writer Charles Peguy.[40]

Both Merton and Ellul specifically acknowledge in their writing that reading Barth led them to change or reevaluate previously held beliefs. For example, Ellul wrote: "Barth made us undergo, a veritable conversion. It is in this sense that I would like to speak of a period 'after Barth'—not as something which is finished, but as an event which renders it impossible for us to return to former positions now radically suppressed."[41] Merton pays a similar degree of homage to his debt to Barth. He proclaimed straightforwardly that he never attempted to engage in any ecumenical debate while considering Barth's theology; rather he sought to "record ways in which theologians like Barth have entered quite naturally and easily into my own

---

38. Williams, "Not Being Serious."
39. "Religion," *Time*, Dec 20, 1968.
40. Thompson, "Jacques Ellul's Influence," 11.
41. Ellul, "Karl Barth and Us," 23.

personal reflections, indeed, into my own personal worldview."[42] Writing in his journal on June 10th 1967, he recorded, "Are the neologisms of Teilhard much better? Good intentions, heart in the right place, wanting the right thing, but did he really have the necessary gifts? If it comes to science I would gladly read later and better scientists. If it comes to poets . . . he does not even begin to be one. As for theology, I must admit that I become more and more suspicious of it in its contemporary form. After Barth . . ."

ton had appropriated elements of Barth's thinking, helping him to refine his worldview as he began to consider the impact that technology was having in contemporary society. Emphasizing the Protestant Barth's thinking over fellow Roman Catholic Teilhard de Chardin, Merton stated, "The Incarna tion is not something that can be fitted into a system, and although I know Barth draws from this many conclusions with which I would not agree . . . I would lean towards Barth much more readily than towards Teilhard de Chardin, for example."[44] It was not uncommon for Merton to turn to thinkers outside of his own faith tradition, and his appropriation of parts of Barth's thought represent this.

Merton's relationship to Barth is not as foundational to his future thinking as was that between Ellul and Barth. Perhaps the best summary of this relationship appears in the following quotation from a blog on the *America* magazine website:

> Barth and [Merton] shared deep Christian concern, a dissatisfac-
> tion with bourgeois Christianity, and a sense that we must be radi-
> cal, given over to faith, if we are to be alive spiritually at all. And
> of course they are different in so many ways: Barth was Protestant,
> a professor who died at the end of a long and fruitful life, a stub-
> born witness to the uniqueness of Christianity; Merton, become
> Catholic, died tragically in an accident in Bangkok Thailand when
> he was only 53, a stubborn witness to our need to let go, to go
> forth from our comfortable Christian security, to find God in real
> spiritual abandonment, freedom, even beyond what the Church
> has imagined possible. Barth, though thoughtful and complex in
> his reflections on religion and the religions of the world, seemed
> to hold back at the prospect that God could really work in and
> through people of deep faith in other religions; Merton kept push-
> ing us to be deep enough spiritually that we might be spiritually

42. Merton, *Conjectures of a Guilty Bystander*, 6.

43. Merton, *Learning to Love*, 247–48.

44. Merton, *Conjectures of a Guilty Bystander*, 9

alive, meeting one another across religious boundaries, unafraid . . . Looking back . . . I think it is true to say that we need both these versions of Christian witness[45]

This passage points out Merton's ecumenism, noting that while Barth did not share in that approach, his thinking helped propel Merton further along that path. Elaborating upon the Barth-Merton relationship, Merton scholar Ryan Scruggs suggests a number of commonalities within their thought as well as some of the salient differences. For the purposes of this study, it is only the points of commonality between Merton's and Ellul's interest in Barth that will be explored. A selection from Merton's journals in which he quotes Barth demonstrates that there are some similarities between their thinking that are worth exploring:

> From Karl Barth—*Christmas* 1931 . . . "Suppose a person living in Germany today had faith, then the comfort and direction he received (from the Christmas light) in all humility, *would consist in the permission and command to continue without those fixed ideas which at present he cannot avoid* . . . [Merton's emphasis]. Not only should man be able to live with principles, he should be able to live without them . . . The fact that God became man cannot be kept in a system . . . It cannot be proved . . . but it is as true as the eternal light which differs from all other lights inasmuch as it requires neither fuel nor candlestick."[46]

This passage sets the stage for the exploration of both Merton's and Ellul's critique of the visible church which will be presented in the next section of this chapter.

Merton first began to read Barth's *Church Dogmatics in Outline* in 1960. This was a time in Merton's life of great intellectual energy—evident in the enormous body of literature that he approached during the first few years of the 1960s. His inclusion of Barth, along with Hannah Arendt, Lewis Mumford, Gandhi, Jean-Paul Sartre, Carl Jung, and many other philosophers, thinkers, political and religious figures evinces the notion that Merton was no longer concerned that his reading come from "Good Catholics," but rather from individuals who would help him gain a greater understanding of contemporary society.[47]

---

45. Clooney, "Karl Barth, Thomas Merton," *America*, Dec 5, 2008.

46. Merton, *Turning toward the World*, 48.

47. Furlong, *Merton*, 239.

Merton incorporated some of Barth's thinking on the nature of free dom into his own thought. However, Merton found in Barth a point of agreement for positions that he had already reached as opposed to Ellul, to whom Barth was responsible for providing the foundation of his theo logical worldview. That is not to say that for both Merton and Ellul, Barth did not decisively influence critical facets of their theology. It is through Barth's "incarnational theology beginning with faith in Christ and then seeking understanding in reason and wisdom" which compelled Merton to not only read selected pieces of Barth's work, but to adopt some of his thought as a "point of contact for engagement with the world."[48] It would be Barth's notion of freedom that most attracted Merton. The Archbishop of Canterbury Rowan Williams observed, "The point is that . . . what Merton is picking up on is Barth's sense of God's freedom. God freely causes us to be involved in the life of the Spirit by freely choosing the means of salva tion, not being coerced, he says, by some eternal and impersonal force. God freely chooses to bring about salvation through poverty and death: through a renunciation which makes room for the freedom of God."[49] While Merton certainly benefited from reading Barth and considering the implications for freedom that he discussed in his work, Merton's steady aversion to a technical approach to theology increased during his last fifteen years of life.[50] He would find that while Barth did not believe revelation could be systematized, Barth's approach was itself systematic. He also believed that Barth was somewhat sympathetic to the mystical, contemplative tradition. Whether this is true or not, he recorded in his journal, "'Divine revelation cannot be discovered in the same way as the beauty of a work of art or the genius of a man is discovered . . . It is the opening of a door [that] can be unlocked only from the inside . . .' etc. I like Barth."[51] This is Merton's inter pretation of Barth's thinking on the matter, and does not necessarily reflect the opinion of the majority of Barth scholars.

For Ellul, Barth changed the significance of scripture in helping inter pret the meaning of everyday life. In addition, the dialectical method was first introduced, a method which Ellul would adopt in both his sociological and theological writing. For Merton, the idea that God's word equated to freedom would become part of his thinking on the topic of freedom. In

---

48. Scruggs, *Faith Seeking Understanding*, 11.

49. Williams, "Not Being Serious."

50. Teaghan, "Dark and Empty Way," 266.

51. Merton, *Turning toward the World*, 49.

addition, Merton added Barth to the list of thinkers who were decisively influencing his maturing critique of contemporary society. This is one of many indications that Merton, although a committed Roman Catholic, remained open to the ideas of religious thinkers from outside of his own tradition.

Thomas Merton and Jacques Ellul adopted parts of Karl Barth's theology as they pursued their own intellectual and spiritual development. Barth introduced the dialectical methodology, an appreciation for scripture as source of freedom, and emphasizing the Word of God as the means through which freedom is made known to humankind. While Barth's impact is more evident in Ellul's worldview, Merton appropriated portions of Barth's thinking to a lesser degree. For both, Barth provided an understanding of what it meant to be free in a Christian sense, as well as an appreciation of the dialectical methodology.

THE INVISIBLE AND THE VISIBLE CHURCH

In this section, the term "visible church" refers to the institutionalized structures that buttress both Ellul's French Reformed Church and Merton's Roman Catholic Church. These structures include not only the hierarchical structure of clergy and bishops, but also the intellectual constructs that are associated with the expressions of the faith, including ethical beliefs, acceptable standards of behavior, and moral precepts. They are entities that, while necessary, stand apart from what both Merton and Ellul consider essential for the needs and the requirements of the faithful.

According to both Merton and Ellul, the visible church has aligned itself firmly with the forces of efficiency that Ellul called *technique*. Although both men of intense faith and members of established religious denominations, it is difficult to label Thomas Merton and Jacques Ellul as stereotypical Christians. While both men maintained a Christocentric view of the nature of freedom, their opinions regarding the nature of the institutions through which the faithful practiced their beliefs were somewhat unorthodox. This section will examine their thinking on the relationship between the church as an institution and the Christian message as they each understood it by investigating the critique that both men leveled against the church, evaluating their claim that the church had compromised its mission through aligning itself with the idea of progress and the forces of *technique*.

Karl Barth dealt with the difference between the visible and the invisible church in his writing. Regarding the practice of religion as a human construct designed to allow individuals to achieve salvation, he wrote:

> Religious Righteousness! There seems to be no surer means of rescuing us from the alarm cry of conscience than religion and Christianity. Religion gives us the chance, beside and above the vexations of business, politics, and private and social life, to celebrate solemn hours of devotion—to take flight to Christianity as to an eternally green island in the gray sea of safety and security from the unrighteousness whose might we everywhere felt. It is a wonderful illusion, if we can comfort ourselves with it, that in our Europe—in the midst of capitalism, prostitution, the housing problem, alcoholism, tax evasion, and militarism—the church's morality, and the "religious life" go their uninterrupted way. And we are Christians![52]

He clearly differentiated in this passage between the idea of adhering to a system of beliefs and maintaining a faithful adherence to the Christian message. He added, "what is the use of all the preaching, baptizing, confirming, bell-ringing, and organ-playing, of all the religious moods and modes, the counsels of 'applied religion' . . . the community houses with or without motion-picture equipment, the efforts to enliven church singing . . . and whatever else may belong to the equipment of modern ecclesiasticism?" Barth's thinking on this topic mirrors that of both Ellul and Merton. Ellul's message can be seen in part as an attempt to illustrate that contemporary society has suffered because the visible church had aligned itself with the forces of *technique*. The Western world (within which he would include the communist bloc countries of the Cold War era) is, as one Ellul scholar noted, "nothing other than the fruit, bitter but no less desired, of the theology of a correlation of world and faith, of human audacity and God's transcendent presence and humility."[54] In Ellul's thinking, this correlation of world and faith has resulted in *technique*'s continued and largely unchecked advance.

Ellul, like Merton, believed that the visible church was prone to align itself with *technique*. An unrestrained materialism characterized the visible, institutional church, to include any church in which a hierarchical

---

52. Barth, *Word of God and Word of Man*, 19–20.

53. Ibid., 20.

54. Vahanian, introduction to Fasching, *Thought of Jacques Ellul*, xvi.

structure appeared. Ellul hoped to establish differing conceptions of the idea of religion on the one hand and the Christian revelation itself on the other, as he noted, "I would therefore like to establish a difference and even an opposition between religion . . . and the Christian Revelation or Christian faith rather than Christianity, because the suffix *ty* already implies a shift to the sociological. Following Karl Barth, I would like to show the difference between the two."[55] In this passage, "religion" refers to the visible church, while "Christian Revelation" refers to the invisible church.

Ellul was not a theologian in the ecclesiastical sense; his concern was to situate religion in the pantheon of ideas that pertain to the human condition in the here and now. What can scripture tell us about our human condition, and is there anything that we can learn to help us change the situation in which we find ourselves? Ellul is not attempting to argue the finer points of dogma with ecclesiastical authorities. He is simply trying to take the revealed word of God and incorporate it into the realm of human freedom, using it as a foundation for defending the necessity of living freely and outside of the bonds imposed on people by *technique*. This further precluded transforming the Gospel message into any kind of system subject to the demands of *technique* and efficiency. It was due to the incompatibility of God's design with human design that the Gospel message, according to Ellul, must not be too closely associated with temporal society through institutions such as the visible church, which are susceptible to being co-opted by the forces of *technique*. The three intellectual constructs through which Merton and Ellul critiqued the contemporary church are, first, their claim that the church had been dominated by *technique*; second, that the visible church, manifest through institutionalized religion rather than focusing solely on revelation had been elevated to the sacred; and third, that the church had failed in its mission to lead a social revolution. This third aspect—revolution—is not an area in which Barth had any impact, but that Merton and Ellul proclaimed apart from his influence.

In order to further the Gospel message, the source of human freedom in Ellul's worldview, individual believers must internalize the message and decide whether to accept or reject it. Christianity—in Ellul's view—had emphasized the periphery over the core, and as such, he wrote:

> Christianity has had a social role and this has not corresponded to what one might have hoped for, to what the premises of the faith might have led us to hope for. Over against this is the reality of the

55. Ellul, *Perspectives on Our Age*, 93.

Christian message, the biblical revelation, which must be regarded as such. The difficulty is that we cannot clearly set the two aspects in antithesis to one another. Christianity is represented not only by the church's authorities but also by hidden currents and secret actions. Again, authentic believers are not alone but by the very fact of their faith they are inserted into a certain community of believers and thus come under the judgment that may be passed on its historical-social behavior.[56]

This "historical continuity" is not necessarily the vehicle through which one achieves the freedom offered to individuals. Nor is the institutional church to be seen as that vehicle. One must make the decision to follow the Gospel message without being compelled or forced—there can be no as pect of threat or fear in one's decision. The decision not to respond to God's love—to reject the Gospel message—is inherent in the offer. "Since there cannot be any restricting or restraining of love, humanity could decide not to respond," Ellul wrote, and continued this idea, stating, "It follows the theme of . . . freedom and non-freedom, which finds expression in the at titude of Adam, from whom Elohim awaits a response."[57]

Merton scholar Robert Inchausti summarizes Merton's view on this topic: "God must be free *not* to respond to man—just as man must be free not to respond to God—if true communion is to take place."[58] There is a dialectical tension inherent in this view of freedom—humans and God are both free to respond or not to respond, and the institutional church has little to do with coercing a person's response. This notion that one decides to accept God's Word and the corresponding gift of freedom was also part of Barth's thought. He stated, "What is man under the sovereignty of the Word of God? No abstractions now, please! No absolute claims for any self-made, independent, human understanding of the self! No anthropol ogy isolated from Christianity! What is man, who has such a share in this, that Jesus Christ wished man to share in Himself . . . Here there is only one answer: This man is man in the *decision of faith*."[59] God's Word is the vehicle through which humankind is granted the gift of freedom, and it is up to individuals to decide to accept or reject that gift. In those instances in which the visible church has aligned itself with *technique*, the church

---

56. Ellul, *Subversion of Christianity*, 139.

57. Ellul, *Jacques Ellul on Freedom*, 35.

58. Inchausti, *Merton's American Prophecy*, 133.

59. Barth, *God Here and Now*, 24–25.

actually stands as a barrier to the Word's promulgation to the faithful. It is important to note that both Merton and Ellul do not entirely condemn the visible church, but they believe that the tendency has been towards alignment with *technique*, as this section demonstrates.

Ellul explained what it is that he thought the visible church should be doing. It should not be attempting to coerce individuals into accepting the Gospel message, but rather should be leading a social revolution; however, this revolution is not the type that seeks to replace one temporal power with another.

> The Church should be revolutionizing the world towards freedom. The mistake has been of equating revolution with Stalinism or Maoism and thinking that revolution can be brought about at the end of a gun. Power can be won in this way, but never freedom. We are going to have to find a completely new way to go about achieving freedom, one far removed from the traditional context.[60]

However, Ellul did not believe that the church was leading this revolution. Rather, the visible, institutional church was caught up in *technique's* steady advance, pushing its own morality and its own agenda at the expense of interpreting the Gospel message—which is the wellspring of freedom. Ellul believed that

> we have to admit that there is an immeasurable distance between all that we have read in the Bible and the practice of the church and of Christians. This is why I can speak validly of perversion or subversion, for, as I shall show, practice has been the *total* opposite of what has been required of us. As I see it, this is the unanswerable question that Kierkegaard faced in his day. Today we must attempt something different. We must follow a different path and take up again this searching for conscience.[61]

Ellul refers to Kierkegaard in this passage, which touches upon a branch of study known as political theology. Although neither Ellul nor Merton are considered to have contributed to the emerging field of political theology *per se*, Karl Barth is often referenced in political theology studies, a field of inquiry which proposes "a unique theological-political crisis within Christianity has opened up the path the West has taken."[62]

60. Ellul and Troude-Chastenet, *Ellul on Politics*, 31.

61. Ellul, *Subversion of Christianity*, 7.

62. Lilla, "Persistence of Political Theology," 41. Political theology is a subject that lies beyond the scope of this paper, but for a more detailed examination of this topic, see

Chapter 4 will explore some of the commonalties between Ellul and Merton and their appropriation of Kierkegaard's thinking. Again referring to the passage cited above, Ellul proclaimed that the visible church had proposed a set of practices that had not placed it in the vanguard of "social revolution." The fact that it had proposed its own moral code was part of the process that led to its adherence to *technique*. Along these lines, Ellul added, "Contemporary morality, such as it exists in our society, and which is currently called bourgeois morality, is made up of two quite different elements."[63] He went on to say that

> one of these is what is left of the Christian morality developed in the Middle Ages and transformed in the sixteenth and seventeenth centuries . . . The other is a technological morality, emphasizing collective virtues and oriented toward work. We must remember, moreover, that these two elements are not contradictory. It is Christian morality, in the form which it took from the sixteenth century on, which has been preparing the way for the development of technological morality.[64]

Not only had the church juxtaposed a set of moral standards over the Gospel message, but according to Ellul it had also furthered *technique's* advance under the guise of Christian morality.

Ellul accused the church of not only failing to lead the revolution against the state, but of actually entrenching that very state which placed itself at the service of the visible church. He claimed: "The church alone can limit the state . . . because she represents the Wholly Other."[65] institution tied to the state apparatus, the Wholly Other becomes part of the technologically justified contemporary state, sacrificing its redemptive power. However, it is not solely the visible church's fault that it has failed to carry out its mission, as Ellul went on to say, "it is not technology itself which enslaves us, but the transfer of the sacred into technology . . . It is not the state which enslaves us, not even a centralized police state. It is the sacral transfiguration . . . which makes us direct our worship to this conglomerate of offices . . . The religious, which man in our situation is bound to produce, is the surest agent of his alienation, of his acceptance of

---

Scott and Cavanaugh, *Blackwell Companion to Political Theology.*

63. Ellul, *To Will and to Do*, 185.

64. Ibid.

65. Goddard, *Living the Word*, 291.

the powers which enslave him."[66] This sacralization of technology leads to religion—which is a purely human construct and is part of the idea of the visible church—being held in the regard due to the Gospel message (the invisible church), hindering our realization that this very message provides humankind with the first step on the path to freedom.

Merton added his thoughts on this topic with the statement:

> Technology is not in itself opposed to spirituality and to religion. But it presents a great temptation. For instance, where many machines are used in monastic work (and it is right that they should be used), there can be a deadening of spirit and sensibility, a blunting of perception, a loss of awareness, a lowering of tone, a general fatigue and lassitude, a proneness to unrest and guilt which we might be less likely to suffer if we simply went out and worked with our hands in the woods or in the fields.[67]

It is clear from both of these statements regarding the perception of technology as sacred that both Ellul and Merton saw this situation in a similar light. However, there may have been other no less compelling reasons why they believed that the visible church had both been co-opted by contemporary technological morality and had failed to deliver on its mission. Ellul believed that another reason that the church was failing in its mission was God's refusal to "send more people" or to continue to inspire. He stated, "It is possible that God is allowing us to follow our own path of madness, but it is also possible that he is awakening people and no one is listening to them or joining with them. In the domain of theology, it seemed likely that Barth was the awaited prophet. But now, several years after his death, we see the eclipse of Barthian thought. In the same vein, the extraordinary opening made by Vatican II has strangely closed back up or been turned aside."[68] Merton would add to the idea that the church was failing in its mission by implying that perhaps one of the contributing factors to the church's failure to remain faithful to promulgating the Gospel message was that science and technology were themselves becoming religions. According to Christopher Kelly, "secularization was also a concern for Merton, but the problem of alienation is not only to be found in the secular world. One gets the sense from reading the works of Thomas Merton that while he was no religious anarchist, he did find fault in those religious organizations that were over-

66. Ellul, *New Demons*, 206–7.

67. Merton, *Conjectures of a Guilty Bystander*, 25.

68. Ellul, *In Season, Out of Season*, 93.

bearingly authoritarian and so caught up in tradition and rigid doctrine so as to be part of the problem rather than the solution."[69] Concerned about the ongoing Second Vatican Council, Merton recorded in his diary that "I think as long as they don't take account of the real problems posed by technology, anything they say or do will be beside the point."[70] It was also at this time in Merton's life that he was reading Ellul's *The Technological Society*, and his agreement with Ellul on the insidious nature of *technique* was at its height.

Addressing themes that will be covered in chapter 4 in the section on media and advertising, Merton shared his thoughts on the church's adoption of new technologies. He was generally opposed to this, but did grudgingly admit that perhaps there was some role that these new ideas and instruments could play:

> It is quite true that the Church must make use of the great new inventions of our age in order to preach the Gospel far and wide. But the Christian apostle must learn how to use these things in a different spirit and with different techniques from the man of the world. The radio and newspaper publicity that surrounds for example the death of a Pope, his burial, and the election and coronation of his successor, can immensely debase the dignity and significance of the Church's symbolic rituals by presenting them in the senseless clichés of journalese.[71]

Somewhat problematically, Merton did not specify what it was that he thinks the church should adopt as far as these new technologies were concerned. However, he did display his concern for maintaining the dignity of the church. As harsh as his critiques could be, he never wavered in his commitment to the Roman Catholic Church as the one institution which represented the source of truth and the interlocutor of God's message, however imperfectly it went about this task.

Ellul, on the other hand, had few qualms about attacking the church head-on for its shortcomings, as evidenced by statements such as, "alas, time and again for almost 2,000 years the churches have obstinately done exactly the opposite of this 'ought'—concealing the gravity of the problems, evading the issues, opposing all revolutionary tendencies, holding to the forces of order, conservatism and traditional morality and adapting themselves to

69. Kelly, "Contemptus Mundi," 6.

70. Merton, *Dancing in the Waters of Life*, 193.

71. Merton, *Disputed Questions*, 143.

these."[72] This overarching denunciation of Christian churches in general is more severe than one finds from Merton. However, Barth echoed this sentiment. "Whenever, therefore, a theologian or denomination makes something other than the revelation of God attested in Scripture normative, they have departed from the foundation which provides the only secure basis for all theological formulations."[73] While not implying that this has been the norm throughout Christianity's long history, he certainly identified a common element of the visible church's shortcomings:

> It is important to note . . . Barth has been the foe of religion understood as the product of man's attempt to reach God on his own. Thus defined, religion is synonymous with the attempt of man to justify and save himself. In short, man's religion is always idolatry. On this account, Barth opposes the influential practice in modern Christian mission strategy of regarding other religions as a point of contact for the Gospel. He does so for the same reasons he will not allow man's natural knowledge of God (natural theology) to be regarded as a level preliminary to Christian faith and therefore something with which Christian faith can be coordinated.[74]

It is precisely the technological morality that leads one away from the realization that self-transcendence (see chapter 4) is the path to freedom. The path is one that, according to both Merton and Ellul, is for individuals to traverse alone.

Although the next chapter will address technology's role in the creation of the amorphous "mass" of people which collectively form the crowd, this phenomenon is also applicable in examining the relationship between the individual believer and the small band of the faithful to whom Merton and Ellul believed that the Gospel message resonated with most significantly. Merton himself would add to this debate with his thoughts concerning proselytism and the "herd mentality" that characterized the contemporary Church:

> The spirit of proselytism grows out of human cupidity and ambition, and it is this which endangers the purity of the Christian faith in our age, by making Christianity sometimes too like the mass movements that are springing up everywhere. For proselytism, not being "rooted and grounded in charity" (Ephesians 3:17) but

72. Ellul, "Between Chaos and Paralysis," 750.

73. Mueller, *Karl Barth*, 50.

74. Ibid., 92.

> springing rather from a hidden anxiety for domination and power, is over-anxious to imitate the techniques and the policies of politicians and business men.[75]

He would go on, admonishing not only the church itself but also the Christian (specifically, the Roman Catholic) and his collective penchant for conformity and his embrace of *technique* and efficiency:

> We are living in an age of universal alienation and mass movements. Christian circles are by no means immune from the contagion of totalitarianism. It is all too easy for us to seek a kind of massive, monolithic strength in discipline, publicity, and proselytism. It is all too easy for us to lose sight of Christ and his charity, and to exchange the basic truths of the Gospel for new slogans that promise to be "more effective" in rallying thousands to our cause. Let us beware. The blaring of loudspeakers, the roaring of slogans, the tramp of marching thousands, will never produce anything but alienated fanatics. Christianity can never be allowed to savor of a mass movement. Christians can never, with a good conscience, yield to the lure of totalitarianism. Even when a political system promises a strong arm with which to defend the Church, if that arm ends in a mailed fist, and if the "protection" offered is that of a secret police and concentration camps, we cannot accept its protection.[76]

Ellul echoed this idea, and concurred that the technological society—the mass, the crowd of people formed and shaped by the ideas promulgated by the media and the power brokers—is an obstacle to achieving self-transcendence, and thus an obstacle on the path to freedom. He stated, "Paradoxically in appearance, only a community of 'united and isolated' men would guarantee the existence of an authentic inner life denied by the technological civilization."[77] Ellul would ascribe to the rising faith in technology as a panacea to humankind's ills the mantra of "false-idol." Ellul believed that "the attachment to any part of the order of necessity in the will-to-power is (in biblical terms) part of the worship of a false idol," and that "since liberty comes only from the right relationship with God, this making of idols out of the order of necessity becomes eventually only enslaving and self-defeating."[78] The order of necessity referred to in this

75. Merton, *Disputed Questions*, 143.

76. Ibid., 147.

77. Ellul and Troude-Chastenet, *Ellul on Politics*, 11.

78. Temple, "Task of Jacques Ellul," 348.

passage is the worship of progress and an uncritical acceptance of technology. Ellul took his critique of the institutional church to more radical lengths than Merton would, and in doing so provides much to consider regarding the role of the church in the contemporary world. One can trace these sentiments back to Barth's affirmation that Christianity is not, nor should it ever be, considered a "religion" in the sense that it is a structure upon which morality, ethics, and society should be based. Ellul believed, "Christianity has everywhere introduced the negation of what it affirms."[79]

In another expression of this idea, he stated, "It is a terrible thought that the church has often used fear and constraint in all their different forms, that it has crushed man with anxiety, when the key to the whole law is the freedom which God himself gives us to live without fear or worry."[80] These critical attacks continued with the observation that, "similarly, Christianity destroyed the religions that enabled people to live with the moral and psychological courage that they give, and it put nothing in their place, for it is not a religion."[81] It is not only that the institutionalization of the Gospel message through the visible church has put a barrier in the path of the one seeking true freedom, but also that institutionalization has rationalized the continued advance of *technique* and the worship of progress.

Ellul went on to note:

> These various orientations that result from Christianity are not the fruit of revelation but historically are its products and have found historical incarnation. We need hardly insist on the well-known fact that desacralization has permitted the development of technology and the unlimited exploitation of the world. In our very nihilism we have believed that everything is legitimate, and Christians have tried to support this possibility from Genesis, arguing that God has appointed the human race to exploit the earth.[82]

According to Ellul, "Christianity is the very opposite of nihilism, but alas, things are not as simple as that, and Christianity is in fact at the root of all the historical evil of modern nihilism."[83] Having accepted that our invitation to subdue the earth is legitimate, the result is always the same. Moving forward without guilt and with the affirmation that our work is justified,

---

79. Ellul, *Subversion of Christianity*, 140.
80. Ellul, *Ethics of Freedom*, 138.
81. Ellul, *Subversion of Christianity*, 141.
82. Ibid., 143.
83. Ibid., 140.

Ellul proposed that "once we begin to attain to the conviction that we are not sinners, what do we see around us? What is brought to us by the thou sands of pictures transmitted by television? Epidemics, famines, massacres, genocides, revolutions everywhere leading to innumerable executions even when the intentions are the best, the installation of bloody and capricious dictatorships, socialism transformed into an instrument of oppression, of murder, and of hatred, the spoliation of the planet by technology." must be revelation and an acceptance of God's gift of freedom that frees humankind from this conviction that we are not sinners, and that our own technology and progress in the form of *technique's* continued advance of fers solutions to contemporary problems. This message must not be pre-packaged and presented as a consumer choice, as Ellul noted, "thus, if the church wants to be faithful to his revelation, it will be completely mobile, fluid, renascent, bubbling, creative, inventive, adventurous, and imagina tive. It will *never* be perennial, and can *never* be organized or institutional ized . . . Thus even onto the humble level of the church, revelation cannot be organized or experienced socially. How much less so when Christians find themselves in charge of society!"[85] It is these Christians that Ellul accuses of allowing *technique* to have overwhelmed and co-opted the Gospel message.

Ellul repeatedly claimed that individual members of the broader cul ture throughout history continuously reinterpreted the revelation. As such, successive generations might interpret scripture differently. To illustrate his point, he used the first two chapters of Genesis as an example. Ellul claimed that these chapters had nothing to do with creation or evolution, but in stead were solely concerned with "the intended relations between God, his people, and the land."[86] While not needing to go too deeply into the meth odology that Ellul employed to make his point in this study, it is important to note that this example reinforces the idea that our contemporary cultural attributes can influence our interpretation of scripture.

It has been noted that neither Merton nor Ellul were raised in Chris tian households. While they both had mothers who were Christian and who adhered to the tenets of Christian belief and practice, the young Mer ton and Ellul were shielded from exposure to religious belief. Both men ex perienced conversions to religious belief and practice, and as they matured, they formulated their viewpoints on the role and nature of faith and the

84. Ibid., 144.

85. Ibid., 157.

86. Vanderburg, "How the Science versus Religion Debate," 430.

implications of their faith for the ways in which they would live their lives. For Merton, the public declaration of faith, similar to the one he himself proclaimed upon becoming a Roman Catholic, differed substantially from the inner workings of faith and true belief. He stated that, "on the one hand, there is the idea that the church is primarily an official and authoritative public organization and the act of faith is the intellectual acceptance by the individual of what this organization publically and officially teaches. Thus the act of faith becomes a profession of orthodoxy and of regularity, a protestation of conformity (backed no doubt by sincere good will) in order to merit, so to speak, a religious security clearance."[87] This statement summarizes his thinking regarding the condition of the visible, institutional church, especially in the contemporary world. Subjected to the demands of *technique*, the church's ability to promulgate the redemptive Gospel message to the faithful has been compromised. Merton summarized his critique with the statement:

> A mere outward conformism, a formalistic ritual participation in the ceremonies of collective worship not only does little to stimulate our interior liberty but even tends to stifle our freedom and stunt our spiritual growth. Why? Because it evades that interior option, that moral and spiritual self-commitment which the liturgy really demands of us. "This people honours me with their lips," says the Lord, "but their heart is far from me."[88]

Ellul made a similar claim to the relationship between living faith and adherence to dogma. Ellul's belief was that "the Christian calling is to a way of life expressing a living personal relationship with God in Christ, not adherence to a set of injunctions."[89] He also introduced his idea of dialectics into the debate on the church and society. He stated, "Thus the whole deployment of the existence of the people of God (the church) and individual Christians is dialectic and in the constant renewal of promise and fulfillment (or, in other words, of the already and the not yet) . . . The Christian life is lived in this contradiction."[90] In this passage Ellul presented the dialectic as not merely an intellectual device used to bracket his worldview, but as an actual ontology. Additional thoughts concerning

87. Merton, *Mystics and Zen Masters*, 271.

88. Merton, *New Man*, 161.

89. Goddard, *Living the Word*, 108.

90. Ellul, *What I Believe*, 38.

the church and its relationship to the world will be covered in the section on non-violence in the next chapter.

Merton had much more to say about the condition of the church in the modern age. He observed that "the whole massive complex of tech nology, which reaches into every aspect of social life today, implies a huge organization of which no one is really in control, and which dictates its own solutions irrespective of human needs or even reason. Technology now has reasons entirely its own . . . and this huge inhuman mechanism, which the whole human race is now serving rather than commanding, seems quite probably geared for the systematic destruction of the natural world."

also noted *techniques* insipid effect on the spiritual landscape. He stated that the first duty of the Christian is "to be aware . . . at the present time, all so-called progress consists in developing this technical framework of our civilization," and that "all parties, whether revolutionary or conserva tive, liberal or socialist, of the right or of the left, agree to preserve these fundamental phenomena: the primacy of production, the continual growth of the state, the autonomous development of *technique*."[92] Ellul and Merton also proposed that the church is one of the parties that has been responsible for *technique's* growth.

In a comical illustration of Ellul's thinking on the church and technol ogy, James Douglas contributed a short passage explaining how technol ogy would come to the rescue when pollution overwhelmed the earth and humans were fated to wear helmets in order to breathe:

> For those who have confronted the threat of nuclear war, the vi-
> sion is a familiar one . . . men in glass masks roaming a landscape
> of death . . . The survivors will be, as after a nuclear war . . . dedi-
> cated to a crash program for lower-income breathing (awaiting the
> results of a Presidential commission). Ethical debates will recall
> earlier dilemmas: What to do if my "clean air room" is too small
> to include my neighbors? The churches will pray for air. The Pope
> . . . will appear without helmet on his balcony as a sign of hope
> for the world. The Third Vatican council will debate the role of
> the Church in pollution, with the American bishops arguing that
> technology is not intrinsically evil. (Wasn't technology responsible
> for the life-saving helmets visible everywhere in St. Peter's?)[93]

91. Merton, *Hidden Ground of Love*, 383.
92. Dietrich, "Jacques Ellul and the Catholic Worker," 5.
93. Douglas, "On Transcending *Technique*," 140.

This passage summarizes Ellul's assertion that the church is no different from any other secular institution and engages in the same rationalization that any organization would do if presented with such a crisis.

Ellul's thinking on the topic of institutionalized religion and personal faith shares some similarities with Karl Barth. In fact, "Barth made clear that religion and revelation in Jesus Christ do not belong to the same realm."[94] Referring again to the *Church Dogmatics* and Barth's thought regarding the nature of God's revealed Word, he stated, "It (God's Word) cannot therefore be systematized, or be made a *corpus* of revealed propositions."[95] He also believed that "the existence of such phenomena as Christian Zen, [and other ecumenical movements] signals a wholly new way of coming to grips with religious 'otherness'; however in order for this phenomenon to prosper, "the center of gravity had to shift from the objective institution to the subjective individual."[96] Merton exemplified this ecumenical movement as he spent a great deal of time investigating other systems of belief, attempting to find common ground rather than engage in any form of syncretism. In doing so, he added:

> Let no one hope to find in contemplation an escape from conflict, from anguish or from doubt. On the contrary, the deep, inexpressible certitude of the contemplative experience awakens a tragic anguish and opens many questions in the depths of the heart like wounds that cannot stop bleeding. For every gain in deep certitude there is a corresponding growth of superficial "doubt." This doubt is by no means opposed to genuine faith, but it mercilessly examines and questions the spurious "faith" of everyday life, the human faith which is nothing but the passive acceptance of conventional opinion. This false "faith" which is what we often live by and which we even come to confuse with our "religion" is subjected to inexorable questioning.[97]

One should not hold the church accountable for the average believer's mere adherence to dogma over genuine belief. The Catholic Church in particular had already addressed technology through a number of papal encyclicals that had dealt either implicitly or explicitly with technological advancement. These encyclicals addressed four general areas in which

94. Weber, "Feuerbach, Barth," 31.
95. O'Grady, *Survey of the Theology of Karl Barth*, 8.
96. Dupre, "Spiritual Life in a Secular Age," 24.
97. Merton, *New Seeds of Contemplation*, 12.

technology posed the most significant challenges to contemporary society: "the destruction of cultures among underdeveloped peoples, damage to the inner life (self-consciousness, awareness, contemplative life), and the triumph of the scientific technical positivist ideology."[98] It was within this general critique that Merton was able to continue to sound the alarm, and by doing so he was able to claim that he was continuing in the Catholic theological mainstream. However, Merton accused the church of furthering these trends. He directed his critique not only at the dogmatic nature of contemporary belief, but also asserted that the church itself had a role in this issue with the statement, "If in practice the function of organized religion turns out to be nothing more than to justify and to canonize the routines of mass society; if organized religion abdicates its mission to disturb man in the depths of his conscience, and seeks instead to 'make converts' that will smilingly adjust to the status quo, then it deserves the most serious and uncompromising criticism."[99] Many of Merton's sentiments in this passage could be taken for Ellul's comments on the church and revolution.

For Merton, an uncritical acceptance of technology and refusal to challenge the idea of progress characterized the contemporary, visible church. This idea reflects Ellul's assertion that the church had abandoned its responsibility to lead the faithful away from any idea or belief that would compromise the sacredness of the Wholly Other God. According to Merton scholar Robert Inchausti, it was an "abdication of moral responsibility" and was "symptomatic of our inability to think rationally about the tools that shape our lives and revealed the mythic role technological determinism plays as a surrogate 'religious' value."[100] This is an idea with which Ellul would have concurred.

Merton had found a sense of community in the monastery at Gethsemani, but he feared that the sense of community that all believers should share had withered. He stated, "My one real difficulty with faith is in really accepting the truth that the Church is a redeemed community, and to be convinced that to follow the mind of the Church is to be free from the mentality of the fallen society. Ideally, I *see* this, but in fact there is so much that is not 'redeemed' in the thinking of those who represent the Church." he proceeded to write more and more in the spirit of dialectical tension be

98. Silva, "Notes on the Catholic Church," 11.

99. Merton, *Mystics and Zen Masters*, 273.

100. Inchausti, *Subversive Orthodoxy*, 98.

101. Merton, *Vow of Conversation*, 199.

tween community and collectivity, this idea became more prominent. One of the most glaring errors on the part of the visible church was the ready acceptance of nuclear weapons on the part of most Americans proclaiming to be Christian.[102] Chapter 5 will cover Merton's comments on nuclear war and the Cold War in more detail.

American historian and journalist Henry Adams (1838–1918) presented the idea that Christianity served as an "organizing principle."[103] This principle portrayed Christianity as "project—reference point, narrative, and source of authority—imparted to history a semblance of cohesion and purposefulness."[104] The church's acquiescence in the continual advance of modern technology and the uncritical acceptance of the idea of progress undermines this sense of authority and purposefulness. Both Merton and Ellul suggested that in order to transcend the bonds of *technique*, one must embrace a revolutionary Christianity and radically break from the corrupted message offered by the visible church, inasmuch as it has been subdued by *technique*. Although neither commented directly on Adams' ideas, they can both be considered to have asserted that Christianity should be adopted as a "disorganizing principle" as opposed to Adams' "organizing principle."

Neither Thomas Merton nor Jacques Ellul spared the visible church from uncompromising criticism. Linking the church with the technological society, accusing the church of abandoning its mission to promulgate the Word of God, which is essential for those who wish to discover true freedom, both men leveled a radical and withering attack on the visible church. Merton included in this attack those Christians that went along with the visible church in its engagement with *technique*, many of whom benefited from the arrangement:

> That there are large numbers of Christians who live somewhat easily in this climate of opinion is clear from the popular religious press. This is not surprising if we reflect that most Christians belong to the rank and file of common humanity and that the Catholic press has a tendency to follow accepted and prevalent opinions in matters of world politics. It is also possible that a certain negativism and pessimism which had been widespread in both Catholic and Protestant spirituality since the Renaissance and the

102. Farrell, "Thomas Merton and the Religion of the Bomb," 78.
103. Bacevich, "Selling Our Souls," 11.
104. Ibid.

> Reformation may account for the willingness with which believ-
> ers accept the idea of a crusade against the nations that can quite
> easily be caricatured as essentially wicked and perverse: made up
> of beings hardly human, never deserving of trust, always worthy
> of being destroyed.[105]

Merton demonstrated his belief that the dominant "lived morality" of our
time is the technological morality. He stated, "We are entering into a new
form of morality which could be called technological morality, since it
tends to bring human behavior into harmony with the technological world,
to set up a new scale of values in terms of technology, and to create new
virtues."[106] The section on propaganda and the mass man in chapter
address the idea that the church has followed the popular press, presenting
arguments that tend to vilify the enemies of the state, and that the average
believer is part of the "rank and file."

It is not necessarily the church's fault that society has replaced its sense
of "religiosity" with the belief that technology instead had become sacred.
Ellul wrote, "The realm of the gods and non-natural powers is empty.
Those who live in a technological milieu know well that the spiritual is
nowhere to be found. And yet we are seeing a strange reversal. Unable to
live without the sacred, we attach our sense of the sacred to the very thing
that has destroyed the previous object of this sense, namely, technology."
This phenomenon continues into the twenty first century, although on a
scale and with intensity that for Ellul and Merton would have been diffi
cult to comprehend. It has been observed that "the Information Age does
something else as well, however: it displays in stark terms our propensity to
bow down before freedom's reputed source. Anyone who today works with
or near young people cannot fail to see this: for members of the present
generation, the smartphone has become an amulet. It is a sacred object."
As manifestations of *technique*, twenty-first-century gadgets represent for
some the victory of efficiency and progress. The sacred is evident in many
of these hand-held devices.

Both Thomas Merton and Jacques Ellul adhered to a Christocentric
view of the nature of human freedom. They derived their respective views
in part from the tradition of Western philosophy itself and in part from

105. Merton, *Seeds of Destruction*, 106–7.

106. Ellul, *To Will and to Do*, 185.

107. Vahanian, introduction to Fasching, *Thought of Jacques Ellul*, xix.

108. Bacevich, "Selling Our Souls," 13.

their reading of scripture. In formulating their views, they relied to a degree on Karl Barth's thinking on the nature of freedom. Ellul's contribution to contemporary theology is "monumental . . . his work is a *tour de force* carried out over several decades."[109] Ellul not only provides a thorough analysis of the technological society, he also reveals the theological issues that negatively influence human freedom, while demonstrating that Karl Barth still has something to add to the discussion.[110]

THOUGHTS ON PRAYER AND CONTEMPLATION

Within the debate over the role of institutionalized religion and faith is the subject of the nature of personal faith itself. Expressed through prayerful devotion or through a mystical, contemplative approach, prayer takes many forms. Merton and Ellul demonstrated some similarities in their thinking regarding personal faith, contemplation, and prayer. While Merton has been described as a mystic, Ellul did not believe that the mystical approach was a valid practice. Regarding prayer, Ellul wrote, "The true content of prayer is not expressed in what is said, whence, among other things, the great mistake of analyzing prayer on the basis of the apparent content of the discourse, and the distinction between the prayer of petition of praise, of intercession, etc. That sort of thing can be useful from the pedagogical point of view, but it falsifies the true nature of prayer."[111] In addition, he stated, "It is the entire prayer which is the prayer of the Holy Spirit. Only when the Holy Spirit intercedes, and in a way which cannot be expressed, that is, which transcends all verbalizing, all language, then is the prayer, and it is a relationship with God."[112] This sentiment seems to reflect a mystical approach to prayer and contemplation, but Ellul eschewed mysticism repeatedly in his writing.

If Ellul's ideas on prayer do not fall into the category of mysticism, they do maintain some similarity to Merton's thinking on the topic. Distinguishing between contemplation and prayer, Merton stated, "Contemplation is not prayerfulness, or a tendency to find peace and satisfaction in liturgical

---

109. Fasching, *Thought of Jacques Ellul*, 177.

110. Ibid.

111. Ellul, *Prayer and Modern Man*, xx.

112. Ibid.

rites."[113] Therefore, there is a distinction to be made between Ellul's prayer, which addresses God, and Merton's contemplation, which involves thought about God. However, upon further analysis, it appears that they might be referring to a similar phenomenon. Merton's description of contemplation runs markedly similar to Ellul's description of prayer. Merton stated that

> poetry, music, and art have something in common with the contemplative experience. But contemplation is beyond aesthetic intuition, beyond art, beyond poetry. Indeed, it is also beyond philosophy, beyond speculative theology. It resumes, transcends, and fulfills them all, and yet at the same time it seems, in a certain way, to supersede and deny them all. Contemplation is always beyond our own knowledge, beyond our own light, beyond systems, beyond explanations, beyond discourse, beyond dialogue, beyond our own self. To enter into the realm of contemplation one must in a certain sense die: but this death is in fact the entrance into a higher life. It is a death for the sake of life, which leaves behind all that we can know or treasure as life, as thought, as experience, as joy, as being.[114]

This passage illustrates a number of important concepts. It first demonstrates an affinity to Ellul's notion of prayer as transcending both language and verbalization of any kind. It also introduces the concept of self-transcendence. Merton discussed a similar phenomenon:

> There are many other escapes from the empirical, external self, which might seem to be, but are not, contemplation. For instance, the experience of being seized and taken out of oneself by collective enthusiasm . . . the false mysticism of the Mass Society captivates men who are so alienated from themselves and from God that they are no longer capable of genuine spiritual experience.[115]

This passage introduces some ideas that chapter 4 will discuss in greater detail, such as the mass society and the force of ideas which in manifest through propaganda.

The apophatic tradition, from the Greek term *apophasis*, meaning a negation of, or a denial, is commonly associated with Gregory of Nyssa (335–395), John Scotus (1265–1308), and Meister Eckhart (1260–1327

---

113. Merton, *New Seeds of Contemplation*, 9.

114. Ibid., 2.

115. Merton, *New Seeds of Contemplation*, 11–12.

116. Teaghan, "Dark and Empty Way," 263.

The tradition centers on the idea that reason is not the only path through which one can come to know God. In place of pure reason, one approaches God by transcending sensory perceptions, images, and ideas.[117] Merton's writing reflected this pattern, and in some sense we can attribute a similar style to Ellul, as demonstrated in the examination of Ellul's emphasis on the radical transcendence of God and the *via negativa*. The apophatic tradition "suggests radical transformation of the self into God more than it advances propositions about the nature of the God thus found."[118] The suggestion of self-transcendence is inherent in the tradition. While Ellul and Merton approached the idea of prayer and contemplation from different denominations, they both place great importance on the practice of contemplation as a means to face *technique* head-on. Surveying Ellul's writing on the topic of prayer and contemplation, "no one can mistake Ellul for a proponent of escapism," as he reminds modern day readers that a contemplative is "dialectic, dynamic, vital . . . at once impossible and essential" as a defense against "the self, against 'religion'" and against "death and nothingness."[119] While not specifically promoting a contemplative stance, Ellul implicitly presents his ideas on contemplation, while Merton remained far more explicit throughout his writing.

Presenting their views on freedom from a Christocentric standpoint, Merton and Ellul expressed their understanding of the God that imparts this freedom through the "apophatic tradition." Merton owed his reliance on this tradition to his reading of Saint John of the Cross (1542–1591), Meister Eckhart, and the Rhineland Mystics. He tended towards the mystical after having read Aldous Huxley's *Ends and Means* (see chapter 4), however, Ellul held mysticism in contempt. There is common ground between Merton the Catholic and Ellul the Protestant in the idea that "the apophatic mystics further claim that it is impossible to reach God through reason alone."[120] While Merton embraced this way of thinking, Ellul only hints at it obliquely as seen in the passages in which he describes true prayer as communication which goes beyond words and dialogue. However, Ellul's poetry is presented in a manner "reminiscent of the mysticism of St. Theresa of Avila and St. John of the Cross."[121] Saint Theresa and St. John of the

117. Ibid.

118. Ibid., 264.

119. Wentworth, "On the Lookout for the Unexpected."

120. Teaghan, "Dark and Empty Way," 264.

121. Lynch, "Poetry of Jacques Ellul," 11.

Cross are figures that feature in Merton's adoption of the apophatic tradi
tion, and so while Ellul does not present his formal work in this manner,
it is interesting to note that he is sympathetic to it in his personal writing.
Chapter 6 will present a comparison of some of both Merton's and Ellul's
poetry. The similarities are striking, and it is interesting to note that the
apophatic tradition established in the thirteenth and fourteenth century
served as a springboard for these men as they presented portions of their
technological and sociological critique in the twentieth century.

This chapter presented a summary of Karl Barth's contribution to
Merton's and Ellul's thinking, as well as the content of their critique against
the visible church and it's acquiescence to *technique*. This failure on the
part of the visible, institutional church results in its diminished capacity
to lead the faithful on the path to freedom, which for both Merton and
Ellul is found through an acceptance of the Redemptive message imparted
in the Gospels. This examination of the theological perspective provides a
framework for evaluating their view of technology's impact on freedom in
contemporary society. The next chapter will examine some aspects of both
Merton's and Ellul's sociological critique. Departing from the transcendent
viewpoint within which their theology is located, the next chapters will
work the discussion down to the immanent level of actual politics and a
way of life designed to allow the individual that has chosen to accept God's
gift of freedom to conduct his or herself in contemporary society.

4 Sociological Perspective

Theology informs a particular view of freedom that Thomas Merton and Jacques Ellul believe has been threatened by contemporary technology and the forces of *technique*. Moving from the transcendent perspective of their theology, this study next considers some of the sociological ramifications of technology's effect on freedom. Chapter 4 follows the same structure as the previous chapter by examining some antecedents to their thought and then tracing some of the commonalties in their thinking on a point-by-point basis. A look at Merton and Ellul on the idea of self-transcendence opens the chapter. Also considered will be their views on propaganda, the concept of the "mass man" and the crowd, and the idea of the city as an expression of *technique*.[1] Merton and Ellul both drew upon the thought of Danish philosopher Søren Kierkegaard (1813–1855) as well as English philosopher Aldous Huxley (1894–1963). A section will be devoted to the influence that both of these individuals had on Merton and Ellul, while a section on non-violence and war will conclude the chapter and will set the stage for an examination of technology and freedom through the political lens in chapter 5.

TRANSCENDING THE SELF

The idea that one must "transcend the self" is inherent in a number of religious doctrines, and is an idea to which both Merton and Ellul refer in much of their writing. Self-transcendence is a central concept for them, and the idea will appear again in this chapter in their discussions on the media, advertising, and propaganda. A solid understanding of their views on this

---

1. The term "mass man," while by no means gender-neutral, was the term used by Kierkegaard as well as others to denote humankind's condition when conformed to society.

topic is important in order to situate their thinking on technology's impact on freedom. In order to be free, one must slip the bonds of the false self. Forces such as propaganda and advertising, most evident in the city, serve to work against individuals in their quest for self-transcendence.

Throughout their writing, both men refer to the self in various guises. Ellul refers to the notion of self-justification and to the idea that *technique* engenders purely manufactured desires that appeal to the false self. The products of our work are objects of self-justification in Ellul's worldview. He stated, "To be freed from the self is true freedom."[2] Tying the notion of self-transcendence to his Christocentric view of freedom, he went on to say that "God grants us freedom by lifting the burden of self-centeredness from us."[3] With this statement, Jacques Ellul firmly aligned his notion of freedom with self-transcendence.

Merton refers to the "false self" as opposed to the "true self." He wrote, "The word of God calls man back out of this delusion to his true self." also referred to his own past and considered the false self as the entity that was born into the world upon his birth. As has already been noted in chap ter 2, Merton recalled that at his birth he was, "free by nature, in the image of God," but he "was nevertheless the prisoner of my own violence and my own selfishness, in the image of the world into which I was born."[5] Merton indicated in this passage that he was born free, in the image of the God that gave humankind the gift of freedom, yet a false self-imprisoned him even at this early age. Clearly, Merton believed that self-transcendence was a necessary ingredient in the pursuit of freedom, or in finding the freedom that is given at birth as he indicated in the first pages of his autobiography. For both Merton and Ellul, technology and the forces of *technique* this effort and tend to inhibit our ability to transcend the false self, thus curtailing the attainment of this gift. Merton's entrance into the monastery can be seen as "a kind of instinctual flinch at the culture of modernity, a life-preserving, involuntary recoil from civilization . . ."[6] The monastery was where Merton would seek to transcend the false self.

---

2. Ellul, *Ethics of Freedom*, 137.

3. Ibid.

4. Merton, *Mystics and Zen Masters*, 272.

5. Merton, *Seven Storey Mountain*, 3.

6. Inchausti, *Merton's American Prophecy*, 41.

Self-justification through worshipping the products of our work is one of the salient features of Ellul's thought regarding self-transcendence.[7] Putting the idea of worshipping our work in perspective, he stated:

> Work which is purely material and which has results that are purely material . . . is triumphantly transformed by man into a value, i.e., into a criterion of good and evil, into a significant aim in life, into an irreplaceable factor without which life would not be worth living. The work of our hands is what justifies life and gives it meaning. Instead of being a purely useful and utilitarian affair which is modestly kept in its own place, it takes on the significance of truth or justice or freedom. It is itself truth, justice, or freedom. We ascribe to it that which really belongs to God.[8]

This passage demonstrates that not only can self-justification through our work divert us from the task of self-transcendence, it can actually be confused for a *faux* freedom. Additional points on self-justification through work link the idea of work to the unquestioned acceptance of progress as a panacea, "the belief that man's salvation will come through technical progress, or the uncontested idealization of productivity and a higher standard of living" rather than through understanding that freedom is a divinely-offered gift.[9]

Merton also believed that there was a danger in identifying too closely with our work—or more precisely in the work of trying to achieve a type of "perfection." He preferred the term "holiness" to "Christian perfection" as this latter term contained the seeds of self-centeredness and could tend to inflate the ego. Merton believed that "though often draped with orthodoxy and piety, perfectionistic "spirituality may be completely self-centered," practiced by high-minded men who have "forgotten the terrible paradox that the only way we become perfect is by leaving ourselves, and, in a certain sense, forgetting our own perfection, to follow Christ."[10] Those who are trying to set out on the path to true freedom often end up, according to Merton, further entrenching the notion of the false self.

In another demonstration of his affinity for Karl Barth, Ellul went so far as to compare worshipping our work with Feuerbach's anthropomorphic view of God and religion. He stated, "[Work] is ourselves objectified and

---

7. Ellul, *Ethics of Freedom*, 142.

8. Ibid., 143.

9. Ibid.

10. Merton, *New Man*, 27.

detached from us. We may apply to it the analysis which Feuerbach applied to God."[11] In order to separate oneself from this objectification, Ellul stated that we must "stand at a distance from ourselves in a kind of duplication." This "duplication" resembles Merton's thinking on the true and false self.

Merton led a life of contemplative study from the time he entered the monastery in December, 1941. According to Robert Inchausti, "Merton's life as a contemplative placed him in a radically different relationship to his times. Not only did he see through the false claims of modernity (prog ress, scientific objectivity, the end of ideology) very early, but he spent over twenty years living an alternative, religious existence."[13] Merton would tar get his false self for destruction upon entering the monastery, as he shared in his own words:

> What I abandoned when I "left the world" and entered the monas-
> tery was the understanding of myself that I had developed in the
> context of civil society—my identification with what appeared to
> me to be its aims. Certainly, in the concrete, "the world" did not
> mean for me either riches (I was poor) or a life of luxury . . . But it
> did mean a set of servitudes that I could no longer accept . . . Many
> of these were trivial, some of them were erroneous, all are closely
> related . . . The image of a society that is happy because it drinks
> Coca-Cola, or Seagram's, or both and is protected by the bomb.
> The society that is imaged in the mass media and in advertising,
> in the movies, in TV . . . in all the pompous and trifling masks
> with which it hides callousness, sensuality, hypocrisy, cruelty, and
> fear.[14]

Echoing many of the concerns addressed in this book, such as advertising, media, TV, and the bomb, Merton boldly proclaimed that he specifically sought to refute the self that had been molded for him by society. His ob jective in entering the monastery was to escape this false self, and so his thought and his writing in the late 1940s and into the 1950s reflects this theme to a greater degree than one finds in Ellul's writing of the same time. There are, however, additional similarities between the ends and means of self-transcendence in their thought.

---

11. Ellul, *Ethics of Freedom*, 144.

12. Ibid.

13. Inchausti, *Merton's American Prophecy*, 84.

14. Inchausti, *Subversive Orthodoxy*, 95.

Demonstrating that one must make a distinction between the self that we present to others, Merton stated, "We must be saved from immersion in the sea of lies and passions which is called 'the world.' And we must be saved above all from that abyss of confusion and absurdity which is our own worldly self. The person must be rescued from the individual."[15] Linking self-transcendence to God's gift of freedom, he went on to say, "I must learn to 'leave myself' in order to find myself by yielding to the love of God."[16] This statement resembles Ellul's aforementioned claim that transcending the self is the first step to attaining freedom.

Merton's ideas are similar to Ellul's in that man's ability to rise above the socially constructed self is a crucial first step in embarking on the path to true freedom through accepting God's Word. Merton linked the tendency to fixate on the false self with *technique's* insidious effects when he stated, "When man is reduced to his empirical self as he is in a technological age, he cannot 'see' the symbols because he is incapable of interior response."[17] Merton urged his readers to weave together the symbols of "language . . . humanity, nature, and God together in a living and sacred synthesis, to express and encourage our acceptance of our own ontological roots in a mystery that transcends our individual egos."[18] This idea is found in Thomas Merton's literary work, and will be explained further in chapter 6.

Merton elaborated upon the idea of self-transcendence in much of his work. A contemplative, he was eager to share the notion that true communion with God was to be found only upon overcoming the false self. In *New Seeds of Contemplation*, his one work that can be considered a systematic treatment of theology, he stated that "the true inner self must be drawn up like a jewel from the bottom of the sea, rescued from confusion, from indistinction, from immersion in the common, the nondescript, the trivial, the evanescent."[19] Further elaborating on this idea, he stated, "The creative and mysterious inner self must be delivered from the wasteful, hedonistic and destructive ego that seeks only to cover itself with disguises."[20] However, the notion of self-transcendence runs much deeper than a mere

15. Merton, *New Seeds of Contemplation*, 38.

16. Ibid., 16.

17. Merton, *Love and Living*, 57.

18. Inchausti, *Merton's American Prophecy*, 136.

19. Merton, *New Seeds of Contemplation*, 38.

20. Ibid.

encouragement to escape the trappings of contemporary society. There was a theological basis for self-transcendence in Merton's worldview that went far beyond Ellul's assertion that transcending the false self is a necessary first step towards reasserting the individual in the technological society. For Merton, the very understanding of who we are as human beings created in God's image rests on discovering the true self. He wrote, "To say I was born in sin is to say I came into the world with a false self. I was born in a mask . . . thus I came into existence and non-existence at the same time because from the very start I was something that I am not."[21] There is an existential element to Merton's thinking on the topic of self-transcendence that sets him apart from Ellul. Merton added to the discussion by stating, "To be 'lost' is to be left to the arbitrariness and pretenses of the contingent ego, the smoke-self that must inevitably vanish. To be 'saved' is to return to one's inviolate and eternal reality and to live in God."[22]

The idea of the true self is an aspect of Merton's thought that reflects the Catholic imagination at work. The Protestant Ellul was more concerned with the false self that one must overcome on the path to attaining freedom and transcending technique, but he did not go as far as Merton in elaborating upon the idea of the true self. While Merton and Ellul agreed that self-transcendence is a necessary prerequisite to attaining freedom, neither thinker relied on the other when formulating their ideas. They presented similar findings, but arrived at these conclusions separately.

In a letter to his friend Abdul Aziz, Merton provided further thoughts regarding his notion of the false self and the barrier that this self presents to realizing that the Word of God is the path to true freedom. Merton explained that pride and desire centers around the false self, and that "God Himself works to purify us of this inner 'self' that tends to resist Him and to assert itself against Him."[23] Merton identified many of the great intellectual traditions as means that one can employ in order to rise above the false self, "the great question, not only for Marxism, but for liberal democracy, for Christianity, and for Zen, is how, in practice, such freedom can be the possession of any but the rare few who have undergone the trouble, discipline, and sacrifice necessary to attain it."[24] These "rare few" are those who have turned away from the false self. One should not conclude that either

21. Merton, *New Seeds of Contemplation*, 33–34.

22. Ibid., 38.

23. Merton, *Hidden Ground of Love*, 53.

24. Merton, *Mystics and Zen Masters*, 283.

Merton or Ellul ever completely succeeded in transcending their own "false selves," even insofar as they emphasized the importance of doing so. While the rare few have achieved some degree of self-transcendence, even those who realize the necessity to grapple with the difficult task can be considered part of the rare few as well.

Søren Kierkegaard's Influence

Danish philosopher Søren Kierkegaard's writing is an antecedent to that of both Merton and Ellul. In *The Present Age* (1846), Kierkegaard presented the concept of "leveling" as well as of the "mass man." Examining this idea will lead us to conclude that both Ellul and Merton incorporated some of its basic tenets into their own thinking on the condition of man and society in the twentieth century.

Ellul first read Kierkegaard at age seventeen, and remembered that it was "thanks to him I understood that I knew nothing of real despair."[25] A line of influence extends from Kierkegaard through to Barth and eventually to Ellul, as indicated by Barth biographer David Mueller, "It is generally held that Barth is indebted to this [Kierkegaard] for the dialectical method so characteristic of [Barth's work]."[26] Ellul's work is presented in a manner consistent with Kierkegaard's worldview—situated "at the interface between concrete existence and life's possibilities."[27] In addition, Kierkegaard led Ellul to an understanding of the Gospels that was "radical and disruptive."[28] Finally, Kierkegaard asserted that his age was lacking in passion, an idea that both Ellul and Merton also echo in their work.

Merton stated that Western society was in the grip of pseudo-passion, "fabricated in the imagination and centered on fantasies."[29] Merton explained that "modern man has surrendered himself to be used more and more as an instrument, as a means, and in consequence his spiritual creativity has dried up at its source. No longer alive with passionate convictions, but centered on his own empty and alienated self, man becomes destructive, negative, violent."[30] This passage contains elements of many of the

25. Ellul and Troude-Chastenet, *Ellul on Politics*, 4.

26. Mueller, *Karl Barth*, 24.

27. Ellul and Troude-Chastenet, *Ellul on Politics*, 5.

28. Ellul, *In Season, Out of Season*, 59.

29. Merton, *Conjectures of a Guilty Bystander*, 32.

30. Merton, *Faith and Violence*, 54.

ideas reviewed thus far; self-transcendence, a focus on means rather than ends, and as will be seen in this chapter, violence. Merton added, "Man has gradually had the life of the spirit and the capacity for God crushed out of him by an inhuman way of life of which he is both the 'product and slave.'" Presenting ideas which connect back to his thoughts on the church's en slavement to technology, Merton accuses church and society with complic ity in the following charge:

> Instead of striving to change these conditions, and to build an or der in which man can gradually return to himself, regain his natu ral and supernatural health, and find room to grow and respond to God, we are rather busying ourselves with relatively insignifi cant details of ritual, organization, ecclesiastical bureaucracy, the niceties of law and ascetical psychology. Those who teach religion and preach the truths of faith to an unbelieving world are perhaps more concerned with proving themselves right than with really discovering and satisfying the spiritual hunger of those to whom they speak.[32]

These concerns with mundane ritual and organizational details have re placed the passions and the "spiritual hunger" that Merton believed should be the hallmark of those who have accepted the Gospel message and real ized that it is the wellspring of true freedom.

Ellul scholar Darrell Fasching associates Kierkegaard with an even more fundamental element of Ellul's thought. Fasching noted, "Kierkeg aard . . . insist[s] that a human being is not a 'fixed animal' defined by an 'essential' human 'nature,' but rather that 'existence precedes essence,' and hence history is the realm of freedom and cannot be defined in advance like the unfolding of the oak tree from an acorn. To be human is to choose one's self, to transvalue all values, to shape one's self and world in terms of yet unrealized possibilities."[33] This passage attributes to Kierkegaard a very important role in Ellul's intellectual development. Ellul himself rarely refer enced any of Kierkegaard's philosophy, but he did refer to him briefly in *Technological Society*, in which he stated, "In the middle of the nineteenth century, when *technique* had hardly begun to develop, another voice was raised in prophetic warning against it. The voice was Kierkegaard's. But his

---

31 Merton, *Faith and Violence*, 56.

32. Ibid.

33. Fasching, *Thought of Jacques Ellul*, 183.

warnings . . . were not heeded. They were too close to the truth."[34] Comparing many of the core tenets of his belief to ideas held by Kierkegaard, Ellul wrote:

> Kierkegaard then shows with prophetic vigor the kind of noise we experience today, whose importance he has discerned: the racket of the city, of speed, of politics and revolution, the racket of the press and of advertising, "urban chattering and gossip, like a snowy whirlwind"—all this (and what would he say in our day!) utterly suffocates the word. "The problem with the daily newspaper is that it is expressly designed to glorify the present moment"; "nonsense, gossip, foolishness . . . these things are caricatures of the word; they transform it into impious chattering, yack-yack, so that the content of the message is scattered by senseless noises."[35]

The city, advertising, the shallowness of the media—these thoughts are present in much of Ellul's own writing. They appear in Merton's work as well.

Kierkegaard referred to leveling as an "abstract power."[36] He also referred to his times not only as an age lacking in passion, but also as an "age of advertisement and publicity."[37] The notion of advertising is important to the process of leveling, forcing man into a herd-like existence, devoid of passion and individuality. Describing the forces responsible for the process of leveling and its results, Kierkegaard stated that "the Press is an abstraction . . . which in conjunction with the passionless and reflective character of the age produces that abstract phantom: a public which in turn is really the leveling power."[38] Merton picked up on this theme in his own writing when he stated that "the inner life of the mass man, alienated and leveled in the existential sense, is a dull, collective routine of popular fantasies maintained in existence by the collective dream that goes on, without interruption, in the mass media."[39] This mass man is alleged to be unable to transcend the false self, jeopardizing his or her ability to attain true freedom.

34. Ellul, *Technological Society*, 55.

35. Ellul, *Humiliation of the Word*, 196.

36. Kierkegaard, *Present Age*, 52.

37. Ibid., 35.

38. Ibid., 64.

39. Merton, *Mystics and Zen Masters*, 268.

Ellul claims that *technique* "attacks man, impairs the source of his vital ity, and takes away his mystery."[40] In presenting an idea that corresponded to both Kierkegaard's leveling process and to the idea of *technique* as a force which will act on all men, Merton stated that "the abstract leveling process, that self-combustion of the human race produced by the friction which arises when an individual ceases to exist as singled out by religion, is bound to continue like a trade wind until it consumes everything."[41] Merton and Ellul both appropriated elements of Kierkegaard's worldview, incorporat ing central tenets into their own thinking.

ALDOUS HUXLEY'S INFLUENCE

Merton read Aldous Huxley's *Ends and Means* (1940) as a college student at Columbia University. Huxley's relationship to Merton is in a sense simi lar to Karl Barth's relationship to Ellul. Barth was a formative influence on Ellul, but he essentially reinforced some of Merton's already-established beliefs. Huxley set Merton on the path towards contemplation and mysti cism, playing a formative role in his thinking. As Merton himself noted in his journal on November 27, 1941, just a few weeks before he entered the monastery, "I spent most of the afternoon writing a letter to Aldous Huxley and when I was finished I thought: 'Who am I to be telling this guy about mysticism?' I reflect that until I read his book, *Ends and Means* four years ago, I had never even heard of the word mysticism. The part he played in my conversion, by that book, was very great."[42] After enter ing the monastery, Merton maintained some passing interest in Huxley's thought. While he had not yet clearly formulated his technological critique, Merton may have relied on Huxley as a springboard for the development of his thoughts on technology and freedom. For example Phillip Thompson observes, "A few random comments [in his journals] suggest some aware ness of the corruptive possibilities in technology. There was admiration for Aldous Huxley's *Ends and Means*, in which the Englishman asserted that evil means such as violence and war, even in a just cause, corrupts the user by asserting the primacy of material and animal urges."[43] However, in

40. Ellul, *Technological Society*, 415.
41. Merton, *Mystics and Zen Masters*, 264.
42. Merton, *Secular Journal*, 266.
43. Thompson, "Jacques Ellul's Influence," 11.

Ellul's case, Huxley reinforced beliefs that Ellul already held. He read Huxley's *Brave New World* (1932) "with enthusiasm," and although it was not "the inspiration of his ideas, certainly confirmed his intuitions."[44] In addition, in 1960, Huxley recommended Ellul's *Technological Society* (although at that time it was still only available in French under the title *La Technique*) to the Center for the Study of Democratic Institutions as one of the most "important contemporary works on technology."[45]

Huxley noted in *Ends and Means* that "the more there is of self, the less there is of God"[46] Merton mirrored this idea with much of his writing on the subject of the true and false self, with phrases such as: "The obstacle is in our 'self,' that is to say in the egotistic will. It is when we refer all things to this outward and false 'self' that we alienate ourselves from reality and from God."[47] Summarizing Merton's view that the false self is reinforced by mass society, Merton declared, "From the moment one elects to exist truly and freely, all this comes to an end. Decision begins with the acceptance of one's own finiteness, one's own limitations, in fact, one's own nothingness: but when one's own nothingness is seen as part of the vast, formless void of the anonymous mass, it acquires a name, a presence, a voice, an opinion in the actions of the real world—not the abstract world of the public but the concrete world of living men."[48]

Huxley commented on the insidious nature of propaganda in his writing. He stated, "At no period of the world's history has organized lying been practiced so shamelessly or, thanks to modern technology, so efficiently or on so vast a scale as by the political and economic dictators of the twentieth century. Most of this organized lying takes the form of propaganda."[49] These observations echo a major theme of Ellul's work, as Huxley explained that technology and progress are not the panacea that they are commonly believed to be. Implying an idea similar to Ellul's statement from *The Technological Society* that our modern technology propels us along the path of carefully considered means to carelessly considered ends, Huxley had this to say about technology: "Such is the world in which we find ourselves—a world which, judged by the only acceptable criterion of progress, is mani-

---

44. Ellul and Troude-Chastenet, *Ellul on Politics*, 4.

45. Lovekin, *Technique, Discourse and Consciousness*, 29.

46. Huxley, *Perennial Philosophy*, 96.

47. Merton, *New Seeds of Contemplation*, 21.

48. Merton, *Mystics and Zen Masters*, 266.

49. Huxley, *Ends and Means*, 7.

festly in regression. Technological advance is rapid. But without progress in charity, technological advance is useless. Indeed, it is worse than useless. Technological progress had merely provided us with more efficient means for going backwards."[50] Ellul stated in a chapter entitled "Ends and Means" from his monumental work *The Presence of the Kingdom*: "The first great fact which emerges from our civilization is that to-day everything has be come 'means.' There is no longer and 'end'; we do not know whither we are going. We have forgotten our collective ends, and we possess great means: we set huge machines in motion in order to arrive nowhere."[51]

As a complement to Huxley, Ellul commented on those who studied technology's influence in contemporary society by noting that "if they are intellectuals, they study the question both at its heart, and in its repercus sions, like Huxley."[52] While Merton died before he was able to fully assimi late what he had learned from his visit to Asia in 1968 and his meetings with the Dalai Lama and other Buddhists into his worldview, it is safe to say that "they must have deepened his devotion to the traditions of what Huxley called 'The Perennial Philosophy': his Christian and above all his Trappist values would have been undiminished."[53] Huxley's *Perennial Philosophy* an anthology that presents a number of similarities in the worldviews of the great religious traditions—precisely the type of inquiry with which Merton was most concerned.

Merton biographers Cornelia and Irving Süssman provide one of the best explanations for the important relationship that existed between Mer ton and Huxley. They noted that

> Aldous Huxley had sent money to Friendship House [in New York City] after reading about it in a review that Thomas Merton had written of one of Huxley's books. So they affected each other . . . Both were men of rich literary and cultural backgrounds— Merton the younger, sought in Catholicism what Huxley sought in Buddhism: a springboard for a high dive into the Infinite Sea. The shape of Western spirituality would be changed by them more than anyone can assess—Christian and Buddhist spirituality com ing together in a way no one had thought possible.[54]

50. Ibid., 8.

51. Ellul, *Presence of the Kingdom*, 63.

52. Ibid., 61.

53. Woodcock, introduction to Merton, *Thoughts on the East*, 7.

54. Süssman, *Thomas Merton*, 95.

The definitive work on Merton and Huxley remains to be written.[55] However, some of the commonalities between Merton and Ellul regarding their relationship with Huxley's work bear mentioning in order to situate Merton and Ellul within the panoply of twentieth-century thinkers. Like Huxley, Merton and Ellul are not opposed to technology *per se*. Both Merton and Ellul recognized that our fascination with the products of technology and our uncritical acceptance of the idea of progress directly placed technology under the guise of the false self.[56] They both also recognized that technology can be a barrier to one's ability to transcend the false self, creating the paradox that "it is precisely when one is most successful and in control of one's life that one is most likely in the grip of an illusion."[57] Overcoming this illusion is the task of the contemplative and is an essential first step on the road to freedom.

Not only did Merton and Huxley influence each other, but Huxley himself was greatly influenced by Ellul. Having already recounted that Huxley introduced Ellul to American readers, it should also be noted that after reading Ellul's *The Technological Society* in its original French edition, Huxley commented that it made the case that he had tried to make himself in *Brave New World* (1931).[58] There is thus a link between Huxley and both Merton and Ellul. Huxley was a formative influence on Thomas Merton, while he reinforced ideas that Ellul had already formulated on the insidious nature of *technique*.

LEVELING AND THE "MASS MAN"

While Ellul presents his idea of *technique* as the primary obstacle to human fulfillment, Merton presents the idea of the "mass man" in many of his works. The mass man is essentially one that has surrendered the autonomy of a thinking individual for the comforts and conveniences of the contemporary world. Merton was leery of mass movements that "carry you away with the tide of activism and mask individual responsibility."[59] In other words, mass man can be seen as the man or woman unknowingly cast

55. Woodcock's introduction to Merton's *Thoughts on the East* states on p. 4 that "a good study relating Huxley and Merton remains to be written."

56. Inchausti, *Subversive Orthodoxy*, 98.

57. Ibid., 189.

58. Ellul, *In Season, Out of Season*, v.

59. Thompson, *Between Science and Religion*, 113.

into an allotted position in society based on the unseen and all-powerful demands of *technique*. Merton says of this person, "The inner life of the mass man, alienated and leveled in the existential sense, is a dull, collective routine of popular fantasies maintained in existence by the collective dream that goes on, without interruption, in the mass media."[60] *Technique* helps to create the mass man through propaganda, which manufactures not only the products that the mass man sees through advertising, but also manufactures the desire to purchase and to own the product. According to Ellul:

> Mass production requires mass consumption, but there cannot be mass consumption without widespread identical views as to what the necessities of life are. One must be sure that the market will react rapidly and massively to a given proposal or suggestion. One therefore needs fundamental psychological unity on which advertising can play with certainty when manipulating public opinion. And in order for public opinion to respond, it must be convinced of the excellence of all that is "American." The conformity of life and conformity of thought are indissolubly linked.[61]

Merton saw this phenomenon first hand and recounted:

> Last time I was in town—we had to drop something at the G.E. plant—Appliance Park . . . Surrounded by open fields with nothing whatever in them, not even thistles, marked "Property of General Electric. No Trespassing" . . . What struck me most was the immense seriousness of the place—as if at last I had found what America takes seriously. Not churches, not libraries. Not even movies, but THIS! This is it. The manufacture of refrigerators, of washing machines, of tape recorders, of light fixtures. This is the real thing. This is America.[62]

Merton and Ellul both proposed the idea that contemporary society creates both the desire for consumption as well as for the products that are consumed. Merton went on to postulate that this phenomenon is responsible for creating the "real thing" in America, and in a sense meeting those manufactured desires provides meaning to American life, and to America itself. What is really being manufactured is an identity that society bestows upon us, based upon consuming an ever-increasing diversity of products,

60. Merton, *Mystics and Zen Masters*, 268.

61. Ellul, *Propaganda*, 68.

62. Merton, *A Search for Solitude*, 218–19.

few of which anyone really needs, but ultimately which members of mass society "want" by virtue of acquiescing to the false self.

The notion that the "mass man" has become a phenomenon that threatens to overwhelm the individual in society is not an idea found only in Merton and Ellul. In 1941, *The Report of the Archbishop of York's Conference* stated that "the 'impoverishment of the agricultural community' must be halted and that the 'unnatural imbalance' in favor of industry corrected; that the trend towards the collection of people in enormous urban centers must be reversed, for the huge metropolis is more conducive to the creation of the mass man rather than the man of the community."[63] Industry and the growth of the city were identified as threats in this passage. Merton echoed similar concerns with comments such as, "the thought patterns which began to assert themselves in the Renaissance, and which assumed control at the French Revolution, have now so deeply affected modern man that even where he perceives certain traditional beliefs, they tend to be emptied of their vital inner reality, and to mask instead the common pseudo-spirituality of the outright nihilism of mass-man."[64]

Largely separated from the false self, mass man stumbles on, ignorant and deprived. Addressing whether or not mass man is actually free, Merton stated, "In any case, membership in a mass-movement is too often merely an 'escape from freedom,' a renunciation of personal responsibility, in order to live not by one's own mind and one's own freedom but by the thought and decisions of the group."[65] Relating the phenomenon of inclusion in the mass to self-transcendence, Ellul added:

> To be alienated means to belong to someone other (*alienus*) than oneself; it also can mean to belong to someone else. In a more profound sense, it means to be deprived of one's self, to be subjected to, or even identified with, someone else. That is definitely the effect of propaganda. Propaganda strips the individual, robs him of part of himself, and makes him live an alien and artificial life, to such an extent that he becomes another person and obeys impulses foreign to him. He obeys someone else.[66]

Propaganda propels individuals further into the mass. Ellul noted that "these systems seem to me dangerous, because they demand of man a sort

63. Germino, "Two Types of Recent Christian Political Thought," 464.
64. Merton, *Faith and Violence*, 48.
65. Ibid., 135.
66. Ellul, *Propaganda*, 169.

of renunciation of autonomous action. But this adaptation of man to the system is precisely the greatest danger inherent in a technological, bureau cratic society."[67] The mass man must be adjusted to the mass society, and *technique*, acting through propaganda, adjusts him. Using the automobile again as a metaphor for this process, *technique*'s insidious march can be more readily explained:

> The limited example of our use of that supposedly neutral means, the automobile, may serve to illustrate [*technique*]. If we are to use automobiles, we need techniques to find oil and other raw materials required to make an automobile and to use it; highways must be built, requiring the manufacture and development of materials needed for the task; service stations must be developed; governments must set up licensing procedures, must take steps to insure safety, legislative and judicial determinations must be made . . . In short, the automobile as a means had its own weight, sending us out in search of a vast array of other means.[68]

Writing in his journal in 1939, Merton recorded similar thoughts on this very topic. While he seemed to be somewhat facetious in this particular journal entry, he describes the very forces that *technique* has unleashed in order to facilitate the automobile's continued utility. He wrote, "Some bea vers, in Connecticut, have built a dam and are flooding a lot of roads. The highway department of the county where this disaster is taking place has brought the matter to court, asking for the power to remove these auda cious beavers."[69] The automobile is again symbolic of a determinism that forces actions upon society and upon those who pretend to be the ones in control.

The leveling process molds the mass man to the crowd. Adding propa ganda and advertising to the mix strengthens the grasp that the technologi cal society maintains over its citizens.

PROPAGANDA AND ADVERTISING

Propaganda is a phenomenon that is also subject to the demands of *nique*, but there is a symbiotic relationship between *technique* and propa ganda. Ellul stated:

67. Ellul, "Between Chaos and Paralysis," 748.

68. Punzo, "Jacques Ellul on the Technical System," 24.

69. Merton, *Secular Journal*, 11.

> I want to emphasize that the study of propaganda must be con-
> ducted within the context of the technological society. Propaganda,
> which is defined as information presented to compel individuals
> to act in a certain, preconceived manner, is called upon to solve
> problems created by technology, to play on maladjustments, and
> to integrate the individual into a technological world. In the midst
> of increasing mechanization and technological organization, pro-
> paganda is simply the means used to persuade man to submit with
> good grace.[70]

It is along this line of thinking that we see the first comparisons between
Ellul's thoughts on propaganda, and Merton's. It is within the framework of
studying propaganda that Merton was introduced to Ellul. Wilbur Ferry,
the Vice President of the Center for the Study of Democratic Institutions at
Santa Barbara introduced Merton to Ellul's writing:

> Ferry introduced Merton to . . . the French social philosopher,
> Jacques Ellul. Actually, it was Ferry . . . who introduced Ellul, not
> only to Merton, but to American scholars in general. In 1961, the
> center had already been much occupied with the subject of tech-
> nology. This interest prompted them to ask Aldous Huxley about
> European works on the subject. Huxley recommended, above all,
> Jacques Ellul's work, *La Technique*, which had been published in
> 1954 . . . Merton read it as soon as he was able to get a copy.[71]

Merton's review of *La Technique* (translated into English as *The Technological Society)* for *Commonweal* was covered in chapter 2, the chapter which
also introduced some ideas regarding "being" and "doing." The study of
propaganda expands on this line of thought, adding the contrast between
"having" and "being." Ellul noted that "having does not enhance being
(notwithstanding the stupid ideology of our technicians), but there is no
expanded being without some having: the golden mean."[72] The golden
mean (or the point at which one determines that they have enough to support themselves and their family) is clearly neglected as advertisements
tout the benefits of a mindless consumption, producing both the products
that are meant to be consumed as well as the desire to consume. The result,

70. Ellul, *Propaganda*, xvii–xviii. While Ellul's treatment of propaganda is extensive, this dissertation seeks to identify commonalities between Merton and Ellul, not
to provide a detailed review of Ellul's thought on the subject. For a summary of Ellul on
propaganda, see Real, "Mass Communication and Propaganda," 108–25.

71. Shannon, *Thomas Merton's Paradise Journey*, 261.

72. Ellul, *What I Believe*, 54.

according to Ellul, is that "our gadgets are as necessary to us as food." lul made this statement many years before the advent of the iphone and ipod—gadgets which many people today cannot imagine living without.

What role did Merton ascribe to propaganda? Much like Ellul, he saw propaganda as conditioning man to accept the reality of his condition as mass man. Merton believed that "action is not governed by moral reason but by political expediency and the demands of technology—translated into simple abstract forms of propaganda."[74] He went on to say that propaganda conditions the mass of men and women to react in a certain way to various stimuli. He mentioned Ellul specifically in *Conjectures of a Guilty Bystander* Referring to propaganda, Merton stated, "Jacques Ellul shows that a mass of factual and correct information can, even if not illogically presented, have the same effect as completely false and irrational propaganda."[75] Merton equated the mass media with technology and propaganda, often using the term "mass media" interchangeably with "propaganda." He noted, "We are in the same world as everybody else, the world of the bomb, the world of race hatred, the world of technology, the world of mass media."[76]

Propaganda is not only subject to the forces of *technique*, but is it self also a *technique*. It is a *technique* that Canadian philosophy professor Randal Marlin believes results "partly from the application of the social sciences, including psychology, to technology."[77] Marlin concurs with many of Ellul's conclusions regarding propaganda's pervasiveness. He notes that "viewing the technological system as a whole, we see that maximum effi ciency—defined, for example, as maximum return on investment over a given period of time—may no longer involve adapting products to human wants, practices, and capacities" but may instead "require adaptations of human beings to the requirements of the system."[78] Although Marlin pres ents a different definition of efficiency than Ellul, his thoughts on adapting human needs to efficiency's demands are similar.

---

73. Ellul, *What I Believe*, 133.

74. Merton, *Conjectures of a Guilty Bystander*, 65. Merton uses the term "propa ganda" frequently, yet he does not provide any sociological or historical study of the phenomenon comparable to Ellul's *Propaganda*.

75. Merton, *Conjectures of a Guilty Bystander*, 236.

76. Ibid., 157.

77. Marlin, *Propaganda & the Ethics of Persuasion*, 32.

78. Ibid.

Marlin provides a link between Ellul's thoughts on the subject and the continued study of this important topic in contemporary academia. He illustrates many of the social and ethical issues surrounding contemporary propaganda, noting that

> for instance, in the healthcare profession, more and more reliance is being placed on gadgetry and monitoring than on human contact between patient and caregiver. But if the frenetic pace of modern life is too upsetting to some individuals, the system itself does not have to slow down. What we see is the development and marketing of mood enhancing drugs to enable people to cope. As Ellul points out, one branch of technology makes up for deficiencies in another, but the technological system as a whole keeps growing.[79]

Marlin indicates that Ellul believed propaganda conditions people to accept their role in the technological society.

While Ellul and Merton both spent some time in their respective writing dealing with particular forms of propaganda, such as Communist and Capitalist propaganda, not to mention Nazi propaganda, it is in a general, all-encompassing propaganda that is found in the mass media, such as the press, television, and through advertising that the similarities between Ellul and Merton on the topic of propaganda are most pronounced. They looked at propaganda as an indispensable condition for the continued development of technical progress and the establishment of a technological civilization. Ellul stated that propaganda was not only responsible for *technique*'s continued advance, but is itself a *technique*. He wrote, "Not only is propaganda itself a *technique*, it is also an indispensable condition for the development of technical progress and the establishment of a technological civilization. And, as with all *techniques*, propaganda is subject to the laws of efficiency."[80] Ellul would elaborate on propaganda, citing it as a force that must be overcome as it stifles democracy, thereby inhibiting freedom at the societal level, not just at the level of the individual, adding, "For what is under attack in our present political society is the autonomy of the citizen, his ability to judge for himself. He is up against networks of information, public relations, propaganda in diverse forms. Hence we can attain democracy if we start out from the possibility of critical renewal, but not if we start out from new institutional systems, or by joining a party or by propagandizing

79. Ibid., 33.
80. Ellul, *Propaganda*, x.

for some group that may seem to be better than another."[81] It is, however, the insidious effect on the individual that most concerns both Ellul and Merton. Ellul stated this clearly with the comment that "propaganda is called upon to solve problems created by technology, to play on maladjust ments, and to integrate the individual into a technological world."[82] of the overall technical system, propaganda both propels the system for ward and acts a palliative for the individual caught in the tide. Ellul added, "in the midst of increasing mechanization and technological organization, propaganda is simply the means used to prevent these things from being felt as too oppressive and to persuade man to submit with good grace."

Clearly, both Merton and Ellul believed that propaganda inhibited in dividual freedom and is a manifestation of the technical system. They also shared the idea that individuals cannot choose to disregard the message that is continually broadcast through propaganda. According to Merton, one of the primary reasons for this is that in the West, it is customary to assume that technological progress is seen only as something inherently good, as well as *inevitable*.[84] The idea that technological progress is inevitable is con gruent with Ellul's explanation of automatism as a defining characteristic of *technique*. Ellul explained that *technique* is self-augmenting; as he wrote in *The Technological Society*, "Let no one say that man is the agent of technical progress . . . and that it is he who chooses among possible *techniques*. He can decide *only* in favor of the *technique* that gives maximum efficiency. But this is not choice."[85] Merton shared a similar observation concerning freedom and choice, stating, "Because we live in a womb of collective illusion, our freedom remains abortive. They can never be used. We are prisoners of a process, a dialectic of false promises and real deceptions ending in futility."

Merton's view of the inevitability of technical progress is similar to Ellul's view that *technique* determines its own path, irrespective of man's choices. Regarding choice, "Merton saw the effect of the secular myth of progress as a surrendering of human freedom and spontaneity to an unseen yet pervasive principle of efficiency that promises to fulfill our desires if we accept our roles as cogs in the machine."[87] Here we see similarities to not

81. Ellul, "Between Chaos and Paralysis," 749.

82. Ellul, *Propaganda*, xvii.

83. Ibid.

84. Merton, *Turning toward the World*, 4.

85. Ellul, *Technological Society*, 80.

86. Merton, *Raids on the Unspeakable*, 14.

87. Kelly, "Thomas Merton's Critique," 5.

only Ellul's idea of *technique*, but also the notion that our desires are created for us by the system, and that it is through propaganda that these desires are both manufactured and made known to us.

Propaganda not only blurs the distinction between the true and the false self, but also blurs the distinction between the self and society. Resembling Merton's concern with the collectivity eclipsing the community, Ellul asserted that propaganda's most insidious effect is to eclipse *any* notion of the person as a self; whether that "self" is the true or the false self is of no consequence. He stated:

> When the propagandee tries to assert himself as a living reality, he demonstrates his total alienation most clearly; for he shows that he can no longer even distinguish between himself and society. He is then perfectly integrated, *he* is the social group, there is nothing in him not of the group, there is no opinion in him that is not the group's opinion. He is nothing except what propaganda has taught him. He is merely a channel that ingests the truths of propaganda and dispenses them with the conviction that is the result of his absence as a person. He cannot take a single step back to look at events under such conditions; there can be no distance of any kind between him and propaganda.[88]

Merton returned to the idea of the true and the false self in his assessment of the lure posed by propaganda:

> There are many other escapes from the empirical, external self, which might seem to be, but are not, contemplation. For instance, the experience of being seized and taken out of oneself by collective enthusiasm, in a totalitarian parade: the self-righteous upsurge of party loyalty that blots out conscience and absolves every criminal tendency in the name of Class, Nation, Party, Race or Sect. The danger and the attraction of these false mystiques of Nation and of Class is precisely that they seduce and satisfy those who are no longer aware of any deep or genuine spiritual need. The false mysticism of the Mass Society captivates men who are so alienated from themselves and from God that they are no longer capable of genuine spiritual experience. Yet it is precisely these forms of ersatz experience that are "opium" for the people, deadening their awareness of their deepest and most personal needs, alienating them from their true selves, putting conscience and personality to

---

88. Ellul, *Propaganda*, 171.

sleep and turning free, reasonable men into passive instruments of the power politician.[89]

Merton saw little hope for humankind ever gaining some degree of control over technology, as evidenced in this passage. He recorded in his diary that "those who foresee and work for a social order—a transformation of the world—[must work] according to these principles: primacy of the person . . . control of technology . . . etc."[90] Control of technology can be seen in this light as either the freedom from the demands of *technique*, or a refusal to continue to participate in the mindless consumption so prevalent in American society; as Merton went on to say in the same diary entry, "Primacy of wisdom and love, against materialism, hedonism, etc."[91] Propaganda's deleterious effect on human freedom is manifest in many ways.

Technique is intimately connected to propaganda, and to advertising as well. Ellul noted a circular relationship:

> Finally, there is the creation of a need to compensate in the form of *technique*s of well-being (jogging, dieting, yoga, camping, etc.). In this case needs lead to well-being. This is not done only for consumption; one is searching for a "better life" (according to the banal slogan), or for being "in shape" (pushed by advertising). But there is a close connection between the better life or being in shape and *technique*, for we have to be in shape to be able to work. An ethic of production finds inner expression in the concern for a better life.[92]

This passage demonstrates Ellul's belief that propaganda is one of the most significant obstacles to human freedom. It is insidious, and often is unrecognized by the consumer, since "propaganda hinders humankind's ability to not only achieve freedom, but to even recognize it. Ellul's message is to free oneself of illusions, which are often packaged in the form of propaganda and promulgated by the state, commercial entities, or some other movement.[93] Langdon Winner has added:

> But while ends have become passive in the face of technical means, the reverse is not true. Indeed, the nature of the means requires

89. Merton, *New Seeds of Contemplation*, 11–12.
90. Merton, *Turning toward the World*, 10.
91. Ibid.
92. Ellul, *Technological Bluff*, 260.
93. Marlin, *Propaganda & the Ethics of Persuasion*, 31.

that the ends be precisely redefined in a way that suits the available *technique*. Abstract general ends—health, safety, comfort, nutrition, shelter, mobility, happiness, and so forth—become highly instrument-specific. The desire to move about becomes the desire to possess an automobile; the need to communicate becomes the necessity of having telephone service; the need to eat becomes a need for a refrigerator, stove, and convenient supermarket.[94]

Technique drives propaganda forward. Providing the illusion of choice, propaganda actually limits choice, constricting our freedom in the process:

> *Technique* itself, *ipso facto* and without indulgence or possible discussions, selects among the means to be employed. The human being is no longer in any sense the agent of choice. Let no one say that man is the agent of technical progress . . . and that it is he who chooses among possible *technique*s. In reality, he neither is nor does anything of the sort. He is a device for recording effects and results obtained by various *technique*s. He does not make a choice of complex and, in some way, human motives . . . A machine could effect the same operation. Man still appears to be choosing when he abandons a given method that has proved excellent from some point of view. But his action comes solely from that fact that he has thoroughly analyzed the results and determined that from another point of view the method in question is less efficient.[95]

Examining Jacques Ellul's and Thomas Merton's writing on propaganda, it would appear that we have little hope of recapturing anything resembling an authentic human life outside of the bonds of the mass. Jacques Ellul and Thomas Merton share many similarities when it comes to their views on the nature of propaganda. They both saw it as a force that compels man to accept his position in a technological society, and as mass man.

Non-Violence and Peace

Propaganda and the mass media are focal points for Ellul and Merton when considering the issue of non-violence. Echoing Ellul's concern that propaganda represented a manifestation of *technique*, and that *technique* propelled humankind along at its own pace and towards its own ends, Merton identified propaganda and the media as culprits in the Cold War.

94. Winner, *Autonomous Technology*, 234.
95. Ellul, *Technological Society*, 80.

In a series of letters known as "The Cold War Letters" Merton identified a number of forces that he believed were responsible for the coming nuclear holocaust.[96] Merton wrote, "This country has become frankly a warfare state built on affluence, a power structure in which . . . the interests of the military . . . dominate and dictate our national policy" and that "the people of the country are by and large reduced to passivity . . . so that they blindly follow any line that is unraveled for them by the mass media."[97] In order to transcend this passivity furthered by the mass media, Merton believed it was imperative to formulate an ontology of non-violence and peace. Merton and Ellul both adhered to a very strict ethic of non-violence.[98] For these two men, violence was not simply manifested in war and conflict between states or between individuals. According to Ellul, propaganda is a form of violence. He stated that "the force of propaganda is a direct attack against man."[99] However, it is their concern with the violence wielded by states that deserves the most attention in their writing, and that will be the focal point for comparing their views on this subject. The single point of convergence between Merton and Ellul on non-violence is found in the idea that man can no longer contain violence, as evidenced by Ellul's question whether or not "violence can be kept in the service of order and justice and even peace" but rather follows *technique's* demands.[100]

Both Merton and Ellul took different approaches to conceptualizing non-violence. They have different opinions as well regarding the just war tradition and pacifism in particular. Thomas Merton "never fully embraced pacifism. Like Thomas More and Erasmus, he believed in the theoretical applicability of the just war. Yet, like the Renaissance Humanists, he looked at the horrors of contemporary warfare and concluded that the just war theory was irrelevant in practice. He was, in fact, one of the first 'nuclear pacifists.'"[101] Merton specifically identified a non-violence "metaphysic." Referring to French philosopher and Christian mystic Simone Weil, Merton noted that Weil "has had things to say of her experience of sufferings

96. Douglas, *JFK and the Unspeakable*, 11.

97. Merton, *Cold War Letters*, 4.

98. For a full discussion on the nuclear disarmament debates occurring in the the same time that Merton and Ellul presented their thinking on non-violence, see Gaddis, *Cold War*.

99. Ellul, *Propaganda*, xvi.

100. Ellul, *Violence*, 5–6.

101. Musto, *Catholic Peace Tradition*, 250.

of Christ which are not only deeply Christian but also speak directly to the anguish and perplexity of modern man. This intuition of the nature and meaning of suffering provides, in Simone Weil, the core of a metaphysic, not to say a theology, of non-violence. And a metaphysic of non-violence is something that the peace movement needs."[102] Clearly Merton was not interested in simply examining or justifying any legal or ethical framework within which warfare and violence between states can be justified. As with all of his writing, his thinking on non-violence "reflect[s] his search for a spiritual orientation that seeks reality and meaning amidst a disorienting century."[103]

Jacques Ellul critiqued the just war tradition, presenting himself as "a trenchant critic of [the just war tradition] and yet, as often in his writing, his comments are lacking in detailed engagement with the specific arguments of his opponents."[104] Without delving into the just war tradition itself, it is sufficient to assert that Ellul's issue is with the practicality of the tradition's application in contemporary, or technological, society. In providing his own rationale for his stance in opposition to the just war, he critiqued Karl Barth's *ultima ratio*—a view that proposed that the state has the right to employ violence in order to maintain its own survival, but only after every other conceivable means has been exhausted. Ellul commented that "Barth's view . . . seems unsatisfactory."[105] Karl Barth himself attempted to intervene in a non-violent manner against Hitler in 1934, as evidenced through his participation in the Confessing Church and the signing of the Barmen Declaration.[106] However, citing Barth's *ultima ratio*, Ellul believed this approach justified the Munich decisions and the decision not to contest the Italian advance into Ethiopia, ultimately allowing Germany and Italy to continue to prepare for a larger European war. Ellul stated, "All the world knows that if other nations had intervened against Hitler and Mussolini in 1934–1935, those two regimes would have foundered, and millions of lives would have been saved."[107] How those millions of lives would have been

102. Merton, *Faith and Violence*, 78.

103. Thompson, "Jacques Ellul's Influence," 11.

104. Goddard, "Ellul on Violence and Just War," 3. Ellul's stance on the just war and on non-violence in general has been critiqued, most notably by Kenneth J. Konyndyk's article "Violence."

105. Ellul, *Violence*, 7.

106. For a full description of the Barmen Declaration and Karl Barth's resistance to the German Christian Church under Nazi rule, see Busch, *Karl Barth*, 235–48.

107. Ellul, *Violence*, 7.

saved through applying Ellul's principles of absolute non-violence is un
clear, yet as in Merton's case, he does not project a simplistic pacifism, and
accepts that in some cases, violent means of resistance may be required.

Technique inevitably pushed violence further in accord with its own
ends of efficiency, limiting and ultimately removing humankind's control
over violence. The concept of violence appears in their writing in many
different manifestations. Of obvious concern to Merton, writing in the
1960s, was America's involvement in Vietnam, about which he asked, "Is it
perhaps this insatiable hunger for visible and quick returns that has driven
the majority of Americans to accept the war in Vietnam as reasonable? Are
we so psychologically constituted and determined that we find real com
fort in a daily score of bombed bridges and burned villages, forgetting that
the price of our psychological security is the burned flesh of women and
children who have no guilt and no escape from the fury of our weapons?"
In this passage Merton associated American involvement in Vietnam with
deterministic forces beyond human control. There is no analysis of national
security objectives or strategic calculation, merely a suggestion that our
subconscious has been molded in such a way that resorting to violence is
not necessarily a choice freely made. He continued:

> Or perhaps our scientific and technological mentality makes us
> war-minded. We believe that any end can be achieved from the
> moment one possesses the right instruments, the right machines,
> the right technique. The problem of war turns into a problem of
> engineering. We forget that we are dealing with human beings
> instead of rocks, oil, steel, water, or coal. Hence the signal failure
> of the bulldozer mentality in Vietnam. Yet apparently the only
> answer of the Pentagon is to get a bigger bulldozer. The answer is
> neither scientific nor humane.[109]

Linking his notion of non-violence to the myths that buttress society, cre
ated and dispersed through propaganda, Merton stated, "The supposed
objectives of war are actually myths and fictions which are all the more ca
pable of enlisting the full force of devotion to duty and hatred of the enemy
when they are completely empty of content."[110] This passage presents the

---

108. Merton, *Faith and Violence*, 45. For a full account of the protest movements
against the Vietnam War, see Karnow, *Vietnam: A History*.

109. Ibid.

110. Ibid., 79.

idea that states inculcate hatred of the enemy through propaganda, a theme that will be addressed in chapter 5.

Speaking of the political leaders of the twentieth century, Merton stated that

> the best that could be said of them may be that they sometimes combined genuine capability and subjective honesty. But apart from that they seemed to be the powerless victims of a social dynamic that they were able neither to control nor to understand. They never seemed to dominate events, only to rush breathlessly after the parade of cataclysms, explaining why these had happened, and not aware of how they themselves had helped precipitate the worst of disasters. Thus with all their good intentions, they were able at best to rescue themselves after plunging blindly in directions quite other than those in which they claimed to be going. In the name of peace, they wrought enormous violence and destruction. In the name of liberty they exploited and enslaved. In the name of man they engaged in genocide and tolerated it. In the name of truth they systematically falsified and perverted truth.[111]

Many interesting ideas appear in this passage, to include Ellul's notion that contemporary man is determined by *technique*, and that *technique* propels us on the path of carefully considered means to carelessly considered ends. Propaganda's role also appears in the passage, and Ellul explains how one must respond to this situation. He believed that we "must struggle against violence precisely *because* . . . violence is the form that human relations normally and necessarily take."[112] Struggling against violence is necessary to Ellul because the struggle against necessity is a manifestation of freedom. By struggling against necessity, of which violence is a part, we proclaim our desire to be free. This is representative of the dialectical nature of his thought illustrated through the lens of non-violence.

Merton noted a difference between "what Gandhi called the non-violence of the weak . . . it submits to evil without resistance. Effective non-violence ('the non-violence of the strong') is that which opposes evil with serious and positive resistance, in order to overcome it with good."[113] Part of this task requires the Christian to work for the abolition of war:

111. Merton, *Seeds of Destruction*, 224.

112. Ellul, *Violence*, 127.

113. Merton, *Faith and Violence*, 83.

The task is to work for the total abolition of war. Unless we set ourselves immediately to this task, both as individuals and in our political and religious groups, we tend by our very passivity and fatalism to cooperate with the destructive forces that are leading inexorably to war. First of all, there is much to be learned. Peace is to be preached, non-violence is to be explained as a practical method, and not left to be mocked as an outlet for crackpots who want to make a show of themselves. Prayer and sacrifice must be used as the most effective spiritual weapons in the war against war, and like all weapons, they must be used with deliberation: not just with a vague aspiration for peace and security, but against violence and war.[114]

Wendell Berry, once a friend of Thomas Merton's, and a noted poet and public intellectual living in Kentucky, provides a contemporary view on non-violence and peace. He believes that peace "calls for discipline and intelligence and strength of character, though it calls also for higher prin ciples and aims. If we are serious about peace, then we must work for it as ardently, seriously, continuously, and bravely as we now prepare for war." This observation could have been written be either Merton or Ellul, and il lustrates that there is a connection to both men's thinking and those writing on the topic in the twenty-first century.

The more technology advances, the more powerful humankind's war-making capacity becomes. As this loop gathers momentum, we are inexorably left with the idea that "war is therefore made in order to keep or to increase the means of making war."[116] An important consideration when examining Ellul's view of non-violence is his conflation of the state with the city—the two entities that are most important when considering *technique*'s manifestation in the world. He considers the state to be on par with the city; and "although he admits that the state is ordained of God, we must regard it as Babylon, the *civitas mundi*."[117] The city is a focal point for the continuation of violence, "a center from which war is waged. Urban civilization is warring civilization. Conqueror and builder are no longer distinct. Both are included in one man, and both are an expression of that desire for might which is revolt against the Lord."[118] It is the city that acts

114. Forest, "Thomas Merton and the Catholic Worker," 321.

115. Berry, "Citizen's Response," 237.

116. Merton, *Faith and Violence*, 83.

117. Konyndyk, "Violence," 254.

118. Ellul, *Meaning of the City*, 13.

as the engine, driving not only technique but violence constantly forward. The final section of this chapter considers Merton's and Ellul's thoughts on the implications of the city in the technological society.

THE CITY AS MANIFESTATION OF TECHNIQUE

The city plays a role in Ellul's thinking, and to lesser degree, in Merton's thinking as well. Ellul's *Meaning of the City* (1970) is the "theological counterpoint" to *The Technological Society* (1964).[119] For Ellul, the city represented humankind's attempt to distance himself from God, but in doing so, mankind puts his own freedom further in the distance. [120]

For Merton, the city held a metaphoric value. There are some differences in nuance between Ellul's stark portrayal of the city as man's attempt to alienate himself from God, and Merton's idyllic view of the country (or the monastery) juxtaposed against the hectic image of the city. Referring to the city, or the *polis*, Merton wrote, "Barth's terrific chapter on Pilate . . . I think I will have to become a Christian. ('In this meeting of Jesus and Pilate everything is together that should be thought and said from the side of the Gospel regarding the realm of the "*polis*" ["city"]:')"[121] Ellul did not use the rural setting of the monastery or anything else to make his point; the city *per se* is the subject of his critique. There is no indication that either Ellul or Merton were influenced by each other's thinking on the city. However, for both thinkers, there are connections between the idea of the city and other elements of their thought, to include propaganda and advertising, self-transcendence, and the city's role in hindering this process.

Thomas Merton spent a great deal of his young life in some of the largest cities of his day, to include New York City. Much of his autobiography describes his reactions to the city—to the noise and the crowds—but these observations do not reveal any hint of the later development of his thought on the city as metaphor for man's fallen state. As with Ellul, "the City in Merton's thought was the social order established by men without the aid and counsel of God, and he identified it with several symbolic names from the Bible, church history, and his own experiences, calling it variously Babylon, The Tower of Babel, and his old hometown New York

119. Ibid., viii.

120. Although some similarities exist, comparisons between the City in Ellul and Merton with St. Augustine's *City of God* are beyond the scope of this study.

121. Merton, *Dancing in the Waters of Life*, 27.

City."[122] Describing the city, Merton noted that "one must move through noise, stink and general anger, through blocks of general dilapidation, in order to get somewhere where anger and bewilderment are concentrated in a neon-lit, air-conditioned enclave, glittering with products, humming with piped-in music and reeking of the sterile and sweet smell of the technologically functioning world."[123] This passage illustrates two frameworks for conceptualizing technology—the products of technology themselves that cause the disruption in the city and the process of technological progress which accounts for the appearance of these products in the first place. Ellul brought both of these intellectual methodologies to bear in his own critique of the city. He noted that "throughout the Bible, the human city . . . represents all the aspects that go into the attempt to enhance human greatness—including economics, materialism, war, self-realization, the conquest of time and space and nature, all political machinations and, especially for our time, *technique*."[124]

The city intensifies propaganda and the tension between the true and the false self, as evidenced by the passage below from Ellul:

> The man who disappears into the city becomes merchandise. All the inhabitants of the city are destined sooner or later to become prostitutes and members of the proletariat. And thus man's triumph, this place where he alone is king, where he sets the mark of his absolute power, where there are no traces of God's work because man has set his hand to wiping it out bit by bit, where man thinks he has found all he needs, where his situation separated from Eden becomes tolerable—this place becomes in truth the very place where he is made slave. And a remarkable slavery it is since already we see him subject to the power of money and luxury. By his own work he dispossessed himself of what was left to himself; he became an alien—for the benefit of money and government, themselves diverted from their original usefulness. And the place where all these metamorphoses take place—a place worthy of magic enchantments—is the great city. Professional historians tell us this: "Cities have always been centers for man's progress, and for the concept of liberty." But clearly, in God's sight, cities belong to an entirely different realm.[125]

122. Baker, *Thomas Merton: Social Critic*, 54.

123. Merton, "Conjectures of a Guilty Bystander," 259.

124. Temple, "Task of Jacques Ellul," 347.

125. Ellul, *Meaning of the City*, 55.

Merton also juxtaposed the twin ideas of the false self and of the city. His most searing criticism of the city was "that it confuses man about who he is, opposing the effect of contemplation which reveals man's true identity. The city's society always mistakes the outer shell of the person for the real person, and he is taught to believe that this 'personality,' which is no more real than the artificial buildings, is really his true self."[126] Similarly, Ellul observed, "Standing before a city, man finds himself faced with such a perfect seduction that he literally no longer knows himself, he accepts himself as emasculated, stripped of both flesh and spirit. And acting so, he considers himself to be perfectly reasonable, because the city's seduction is in fact rational, and one really must obey the orders of reason."[127] The two previous passages demonstrate that for both Thomas Merton and Jacques Ellul, the city was both lure and trap. Merton took the argument even further, describing the city not only seductive, but bent on its own destruction.

Not only had the city blinded those who live in the technological society, it had also captivated the church. Considering Ellul's views on *technique's* impact on the visible church, the city plays a major role in this phenomenon. He stated, "The city is truly the place of the genuine captivity of the church."[128] Ellul proposed that introducing God into the city equates to a "revolutionary act."[129] Anticipating the discussion on "revolution" that the next chapter will examine, the introduction of God into the city—this revolutionary act—portends the establishment of the city of God on earth, but cannot in and of itself actually bring about the kingdom. "Christ," says Ellul, "has not come to reconcile the world to itself in self-sufficiency and self-satisfaction, but to reconcile the world to God in holiness, shattering the world's self-sufficiency so that all things might be possible."[130] This self-sufficiency is reinforced by *technique*. Ellul concluded that the city "is the exact counterpart of what man had wanted to do—not in the sense of obverse and reverse, or type and antitype, but rather in the sense of the back of a woven rug and its right side. While the side man works on is a formless mess, the side God works on is the right side, the side of the New Jerusalem."[131]

126. Baker, *Thomas Merton: Social Critic*, 54.

127. Ellul, *Meaning of the City*, 30.

128. Ibid., 20.

129. Fasching, *Thought of Jacques Ellul*, 136.

130. Ibid.

131. Ellul, *Meaning of the City*, 190.

Ellul and Merton both emphasized the idea of the city as counterpoint to God's realm and to His creation. For Merton, the city, built by man, occupies a position that is set apart from places where man can engage in contemplation and find God, although it is not simply a matter of urban against rural. The same for Ellul; the city, built to liberate us from nature and from want, is in reality a hindrance to our God-given gift of freedom, and represents a manifestation of necessity and *technique*.

Both Merton and Ellul believed that freedom was found through self-transcendence. Technology, manifest as the force of *technique*, hinders this effort through the dissemination of propaganda, and is most evident in the city. Having progressed from the transcendent perch of the theological perspective into the sociological perspective, this study will next move to the immanent realm of politics and worldly affairs. Karl Marx, as has been noted, was an intellectual antecedent to both Merton and Ellul, although to varying degrees. His impact on their thinking will be followed by a point-by-point analysis of their political ideologies, culminating with an explanation of their "third way" approach to contemporary society's shortcomings. They both formulated a distinct ontology, one which situates freedom at its center and locates freedom firmly within the Gospel. In order to discern whether or not they are able to articulate this vision into a practical formula for everyday life, chapter 5 will examine their views on a variety of political issues and will present their thinking on "the third way" which they believe offers a means for individuals in contemporary society to transcend the bonds of *technique* and take the first step on the road to freedom.

5   Political Perspective

Both Thomas Merton and Jacques Ellul wrote extensively on political matters. Having moved from the transcendent position of their theological perspective, this chapter will examine the influence that Karl Marx had on both men's worldview. A look at how Marx influenced both men will be followed by an overview of the similar approach that Merton and Ellul demonstrate in comparing the capitalist system of the West with the communist East, and the idea that humankind's freedom is impeded in both systems equally is the topic of the second section in this chapter. The Catholic Worker movement in New York, an organization to which Merton maintained close ties, was also ironically influenced by the Protestant Jacques Ellul. Founded in 1933 by Dorothy Day and Peter Maurin, this movement strived to exemplify freedom as an acceptance of life lived in accordance with the Gospel. Merton's direct engagement with the movement and the similarities between the Catholic Worker philosophy and Ellul's worldview is the subject of the third section. The fourth section deals with the role of anarchy and revolution in their thought. Finally, both men propose a "third way": a methodology for patterning one's life outside of the reigning ideologies that dominated the mid-twentieth century. A look at how they developed their thinking on this third way concludes the chapter.

According to Ellul, "The universal catastrophes of the present time are not due to accident, or to 'bad luck,' nor are they mere breakdowns in the happy mechanism of 'progress,'" but are instead "the inevitable product of the essential structure of our civilization."[1] These essential structures result from the political process and political decisions, as well as on the politics that takes place between nations. Ellul's French Protestant Church was in a difficult position following the liberation of France in 1944, and much of his political thought stems from this era. He noted, "We found

1. Ellul, *Presence of the Kingdom*, 33.

ourselves confronted with communism in 1944. What attitude should we adopt? Many French pastors and theologians . . . assented to communist doctrine."[2] Ellul explained that this situation led to a split within the French Reformed Church, a situation that brings to light some of the ideas inher ent in this study, for example, the visible church's failure to promulgate the Gospel message, studied in chapter 3, and the denigration of the revealed Word, explained in chapter 6. Concerning this split, Ellul wrote, "On the one hand we find those who considered the only calling to evangelism: making the Gospel known and enabling people to share in the salvation of Jesus Christ. On the other, those who considered a Christian could witness to his faith only through political action . . . Remarkably, [the latter] group managed to prevail, through utterly insidious means."[3]

With these proclamations, Ellul explained that he saw a disconnect between political action and the promulgation of the Gospel message. In other words, his Christocentric view of freedom dictated that the contem porary political process was of little or no use in helping those who have chosen to accept the Word of God find their way on the path to freedom. Along this line of thinking, Karl Barth said to Ellul, "I don't understand your interest in politics. How can that possibly change the essential human situation?"[4] Politics in Ellul's worldview was thus viewed from the perspec tive that *technique* had fatally compromised the traditional practice of poli tics in contemporary society.[5]

Congruent with themes that have been discussed in previous chap ters, Ellul's discussions concerning the state of contemporary society and the political structure of that society are subject to the pervasive impact of *technique*. Ellul thought that *technique* was "attaining proportions un precedented and even unimagined in the past, and that contemporary technological development has established a near autonomous system of social and cultural imperatives, to be called here the technical universe." It is within this technical universe that the contemporary nation-state

2. Ellul, "Be Reconciled," 2. For an account of Protestantism in France in during the war years, see Adams, *Political Ecumenism.*

3. Ellul, "Be Reconciled," 2–3.

4. Goddard, *Living the Word*, 15.

5. Ellul's *Political Illusion* is dedicated to this idea. However, the scope of Ellul's politi cal thought is beyond the scope of this study, and only those areas of political inquiry that demonstrate a marked similarity to Merton's thought will be explored. For a concise overview of Ellul's politics, see Menninger, "Politics or Technique?"

6. Menninger, "Political Dislocation," 74.

lives and functions. But there is a difference between the contemporary international order and that which came before, and that difference can be summarized by Ellul's phrase that the contemporary system "continues to grow around us" and within this system "politics has been dislocated."[7] Harking back again to his discussion of ends and means, a discussion to with which Merton has also contributed, "The nature of [the state's] responsibility to provide answers to social problems has been distorted through certain confusion between means and ends generated by technological development."[8] The contemporary nation-state had been overcome by the forces of *technique* in the same manner as the visible, institutional church, a phenomenon discussed in chapter 3.

Through their reading of Marx, their comparisons of the similarities between the realities existing in both American and Soviet societies, and their commitment to social justice, both Merton and Ellul exhibit some similarities in their political views. Before engaging with some of the specifics regarding their views on the facets of contemporary society that are most impacted by technology, it will first be necessary to look at the impact that Karl Marx's thinking had on both men.

THE INFLUENCE OF KARL MARX

The Depression heralded a time of want for Ellul's family, much more so than for Merton's. Seeking an explanation for the great economic injustice that plagued the land, both young men would find some degree of solace and intellectual comfort in Karl Marx's writing. While Merton even became a communist for a short time while at Columbia University, Ellul never joined the party. In fact Ellul would turn away from Marx after integrating a Marxist dialectical approach into his own worldview, while Merton never completely disowned Marx or separated himself from Marxist ideas.

Politically, both Merton and Ellul showed an early affinity for Karl Marx. Ellul described his initial fascination with Marx, noting that in his first encounter with *Das Kapital*, he "had the sudden impression of a connection . . . I discovered a global interpretation of the world, the explanation for this drama of misery and decadence that we had experienced. The excellence of

---

7. Ibid. Similarities to the thinking of American theologian and commentator Reinhold Niebuhr, comparing Ellul and Merton with his thought is outside the scope of this study. For a detailed summary of Niebuhr's philosophy, see Fox, *Reinhold Niebuhr*.

8. Menninger, "Political Dislocation," 74.

Marx's thinking, in the domain of economic theory, convinced me." impact that Marx had on Ellul's sociological thought cannot be underesti mated, and Ellul biographer Andrew Goddard considers Marx's influence to be of paramount importance, and he stated that "in order to understand Ellul's political commitments in this period it is necessary to return to the context in which he began his university studies and to his relationship with . . . Barth and Kierkegaard [and] Karl Marx."[10] Having found some intellectual "solid ground" to help explain the state of affairs in which his family found themselves during the Depression, Ellul would go on to adopt much of the style that Marx used in his writing. Although he later would turn to other sources for further guidance and to refine his thinking, Marx's thought affected him in profound ways. He recounted:

> All at once I felt as if I had discovered something totally unex-
> pected and totally stupefying, precisely because it related directly
> to my practical experience . . . I felt I understood everything. I felt
> that at last I knew why my father was out of work, at last I knew
> why we were destitute . . . Marx was an astonishing discovery of
> the reality of this world . . . I plunged into Marx's thinking with
> incredible joy: I had finally found *the* explanation . . . I discovered
> in Marx the possibility of understating what was going on. I felt
> I had a deeper insight into the things I was being taught at the
> Faculty of Law.[11]

It is no coincidence that Ellul describes his first encounter with *Das Kapi tal* with the same emotional overtones used to describe his conversion experience.

It is important to keep in mind that although Marx provided an in tellectual foundation for his worldviews, Ellul never became a committed Marxist. He was never convinced that those who had adopted Marxism were adhering to the core tenets of the ideology. To Ellul, Marx represented "a model of the social theorist's personal resistance to impersonal social forces."[12] He remained convinced that had Marx written *Das Kapital* the twentieth century, he would have concluded that *technique* was the greatest threat to civilization rather than economic modes of production. However, Ellul was not as concerned with modes of production as he was

---

9. Ellul, *In Season, Out of Season*, 11.

10. Goddard, *Living the Word*, 15.

11. Ellul, *Perspectives on Our Age*, 4–6.

12. Menninger, "Marx in the Social Thought of Jacques Ellul," 18.

with identifying technique as the ultimate determining factor in contemporary civilization. Ellul scholar David Menninger asserts that Ellul at times presented the concept of *technique* as metaphor for sin, since Ellul's attitude toward *technique*, "as he presents it in *The Technological Society*, is a moral one. This fact becomes clear if one reads Ellul's more explicitly moral works—*The Presence of the Kingdom*, for example—where the idea of *technique* as 'sin' is quite apparent."[13] This passage displays the similarity between Ellul's *technique* and Marx's vision of the forces of production. In order to illustrate some of the influence that Marx had on Ellul's thinking regarding the growth of *technique* and the overwhelming change in society that this growth had wrought in the nineteenth and twentieth century, Menninger juxtaposes a citation from Marx with one from Ellul. First, the citation from Marx:

> There is one great fact, characteristic of this our nineteenth century, a fact which no party dares deny. One the one hand, there have started into life industrial and scientific forces that no epoch of the former human history had ever suspected . . . Machinery, gifted with the wonderful power of shortening and fructifying human labor, we behold starving and overworking it . . . The victories of art seem brought by the loss of character . . . Even the pure light of science seems unable to shine but on the dark background of ignorance. All our inventions and progress seem to result in endowing martial forces with intellectual life, and in stultifying human life into material force.[14]

This citation is contrasted with the following from Ellul's *Presence of the Kingdom*, revealing the extent to which Ellul appropriates parts of Marx's thought:

> The first great fact which emerges from our civilization is that today everything has become means. There is no longer an end; we do not know wither we are going. We have forgotten our collective ends, and we possess great means: we set huge machines in motion in order to arrive nowhere . . . Thus *man*, who used to be the end of the whole humanist system of means, *man*, who is still proclaimed as an end in political speeches, has in reality himself become the means of the very means which ought to serve him, as, for instance, in economics or the state . . . He becomes an obedient

---

13. Ibid., 20.

14. Tucker, *Marx-Engels Reader*, 19; cited in Menninger, "Marx in the Social Thought of Jacques Ellul," 20.

consumer . . . he swallows everything that economics puts in his mouth . . . we are turning him into an instrument of those modern gods, which are our means.[15]

Ellul appropriated from Marx not only the dialectical methodology, which he had also encountered in Barth's writing, but the idea that humankind was being propelled along by forces outside of their control. In Marx's view, these were the forces of production, while for Ellul, it was *technique*

Thomas Merton would move away from Marxist teaching as he began to develop his own worldview, but he would continue to write and to act in accordance with principles which he believed were consistent with the social justice that Marx espoused. He agreed with Marx's analysis of contemporary society's ills, but he "completely rejected Marx's solutions to these problems," particularly rejecting his conclusions on the role of religion and faith.[16] Like Ellul, Merton concluded that Marx the thinker and the Marxist movement which grew out of his thinking were two different entities. Merton believed Marx to be a "true humanist," but held Marxists in contempt for becoming the "demons which Marx condemned."[17] Merton stated, "Marx is, in some strange way, an heir of Ezechiel and Jeremias. Not that he is a conscious and willing instrument of God—but an instrument. We have to listen to his tune and understand it. Because it does not mean exactly what Marx himself thought it would mean or what the communists made it mean, (for Marxism, in a sense, is dead. But the unintentional consequence lives on and their work is terrible)."[18]

Merton was attracted to Karl Marx's writing while a student at Columbia University in the 1930s. He was perhaps not so much drawn to Marx out of an attraction to his economic theories as much as out of an aesthetic fascination.[19] Like Ellul, Merton would formulate much of his worldview through the dual lens of Marxism and Christianity. While Marx provided both men with an early model for further inquiry and further development of their intellectual foundations, in Merton's case, his interest in Marxism may have been an early attempt at self-justification, since "the ideas of Marx had appealed to Merton precisely because they served his youthful need for self-justification. Marxism may have offered a way to repudiate an ob

15. Ellul, *Presence of the Kingdom*, 63.

16. Baker, *Thomas Merton: Social Critic*, 67–68.

17. Ibid., 68.

18. Merton, *Search for Solitude*, 90.

19. O'Connell, "Communism," 71.

viously flawed social order without having to acknowledge any particular moral flaws in himself, and so it played into his own rootless egotism by exempting him from any rigorous examination of conscience."[20] As Merton recalled in his journals, his university years were ones in which he largely went about life aimlessly and without direction, so it is no surprise to see that he might have had difficulty grounding his reading of Marx at that time into any established worldview. However, his interest in Marx contributed to his mature worldviews even though he began to distance himself from the communists while still a student at Columbia. While grappling with Marxism,

> Merton quickly became disillusioned with what he called "the radical mystique," but he never lost his conviction that extreme measures were needed to meet the crises of the age. He had just become convinced that those measures had to be personal and symbolic ones. The so-called activists were actually making things worse by accentuating the very features of modernity most in need of reform: its penchant for shrill, reductive explanations of complex social phenomena and its fascination with change for change's sake.[21]

Whatever Merton's early motives for turning towards Marx, having been exposed to such powerful ideas in his university days would further his desire to engage with issues relating to economic justice and social equality in the future.

For both Merton and Ellul, exposure to Marx's thinking provided an impetus to their critiques of contemporary society and the role of technology in the twentieth century. The idea that they did not adhere to Marxism does not, however, imply that they were committed Capitalists. They both viewed the essential structures of the communist East and the capitalist West as fundamentally the same in many ways.

SIMILARITIES BETWEEN THE USA AND THE USSR

Both men believed that the USA and the USSR were fundamentally the same in that they were two political entities subject to the same demands placed upon them by technology and continued technological progress.

20. Inchausti, *Merton's American Prophecy*, 11.
21. Ibid., 12.

Writing in the mid-twentieth century, Merton and Ellul found themselves facing the harsh reality of the Cold War. While chapter 4 introduced their thinking on non-violence *per se*, this section deals with the political realities in which they lived. Both men lived in the capitalist societies of the West, and both addressed the issues surrounding the confrontation between East and West in somewhat different formats. For Merton, living in a monastery in the United States, there were periodic reminders of this confrontation as a US Air Force B-52 bomber on training missions often times made low passes close to his hermitage. For Ellul, his home in France was much closer to the "front" in Western Europe, and so his perspective is somewhat different. However, both men consistently identified the many similarities between the nature of society in both the West and the communist East, specifically the Soviet Union.

While many philosophers, politicians, and literary figures of the time identified the West as the land of freedom, and the Soviet Union as its an tithesis, Merton and Ellul did not join in this line of reasoning. They are thus members of a small coterie of thinkers who consistently refused to be influenced by what they saw as the propaganda put forth by their govern ment and their society as a whole. For example, French philosopher Her bert Marcuse's *One Dimensional Man* (1964) portrayed both capitalist and socialist societies as components of a vast, repressive technological civiliza tion that was bringing every aspect of humanity under its control. similar vein, Ellul's appropriation of certain elements of Marxist thought is evident in the statement that "essentially, for instance, Communist soci ety is based on the same facts as Capitalist society: and at the bottom, the U.S.S.R. obey [sic] the same rules as the U.S.A. Man is no more free on the one side than on the other; he is simply used for production in different ways."[23] One would be tempted upon reading this to proclaim Ellul a Marx ist, and one might also question whether or not his true allegiance is actu ally to Marxism as a system, although this would be a mischaracterization. For Ellul, production was an integral part of the technological system, and so his emphasis here is not to throw his support to Marx, but to illustrate that the technological system did not exist any differently on either side of the Iron Curtain. Referring to the communist nations as a whole, he stated, "It was clear to me that except for some spectacular but futile gestures such as nationalization the socialists should be forced to enter the same path

22. Winner, *Whale and the Reactor*, 66.
23. Ellul, *Presence of the Kingdom*, 36.

of technological progress as any other government."[24] To Ellul, *technique* made no distinction between different ideological and political systems.

Ellul "saw capitalism as a system that results in the 'subservience of being to having' and socialism as a system that results in the 'subservience of being to doing and to collective having.'"[25] He also noted that propaganda was identical in either system, that "the phenomenon [of propaganda] is essentially the same in China or the Soviet Union or the United States or Algeria."[26] This is because "communism, socialism, and capitalism are all driven by the same mechanical techniques."[27] These techniques included propaganda, which was wielded within both the United States and Soviet Union for the same ends—leveling the masses. Echoing this statement is Canadian philosophy professor Randal Marlin, introduced earlier in chapter 4 in the section on propaganda. He stated that, "for example, in the US, the 'American way of life' is the backdrop for much propaganda. Once one accepts the American way of life as superior, it becomes a criterion of good and evil; things that are un-American become evil."[28] Ellul is not alone in his assertion that propaganda exists in all societies—not just those in the grip of totalitarianism.

Both Merton and Ellul had similar opinions concerning the outcome of the Second World War, and this thinking affected their opinions on the political realities of the post-war world. Both men have asserted that although the Third Reich was destroyed as a political entity, the *mindset* that created the Third Reich and sustained the German war effort had essentially been adopted by the victorious Allies. Merton held to a belief that while Germany's defeat saved civilization from entering a new dark age, there was a significant risk that the means that Germany employed in its rise to power might be adopted by those nations responsible for her defeat.[29] Writing about America's war in Vietnam in his journals, lamenting over the fact that so many Americans believed in a "divine mission to destroy communism," Merton observed that this belief was "too much like the

---

24. Ellul, *What I Believe*, 8.

25. Ellul, *Money and Power*, 20.

26. Ellul, *Propaganda*, xiv. Ellul's thoughts on the Algerian War (1954–1962) are beyond the scope of this paper. However for a full account of the opinions of other members of the French intelligentsia during this crisis, see Horne, *Savage War of Peace*.

27. Nielsen, "Technology and Ideology," 132.

28. Marlin, *Propaganda & the Ethics of Persuasion*, 37.

29. Inchausti, *Merton's American Prophecy*, 42.

basic principle behind Hitler's thinking, which led to World War II."
he began to focus his thinking more on technology's impact on freedom, he
would engage in topics that many people considered "off limits" for a monk
living in a monastery. For example, he would oppose American philoso
pher John Dewey's (1859–1952) belief that the post-World War II rise in
monasticism's popularity was evidence of a "loss of intellectual nerve." Mer
ton responded that "such criticism . . . was itself symptomatic of another
kind of loss of nerve: a refusal to face up to the lessons of the holocaust,
Hiroshima, and the two world wars, to own up to the radical truth that we
have become moral and intellectual dwarfs overwhelmed by the power of
our machines, actively participating in the worldwide triumph of a techno
logically enhanced militarism." [31] He continued, stating: "To embrace new
methods, arrangements, or political strategies as *the solution* to this star
tling new state of affairs was itself a retreat into *technique* and method and
away from responsibility." [32] Illustrating the theme that the motives behind
Hitler's rise to power might be evident in the post-war West, Ellul stated
somewhat caustically that contemporary society

> believed so completely in the takeover by the machine, and in
> plenty . . . nevertheless, hope persists whenever tomorrow's beck-
> on; say Hitler's Thousand years, or the bourgeois' s stupid notion
> of progress. The hope is still the same but the human being (model
> 1950) tells himself that he can only attain Paradise through the
> destruction of his enemies . . . When man finds the foe who stands
> in his way and who alone has barred paradise to him (be it Jew,
> Fascist, capitalist, or Communist), he must strike him down, that
> from the cadaver may grow the exquisite flower the machine has
> promised. [33]

This passage suggests that those who believed in Hitler's vision are little dif
ferent from the mass of post-war citizens who continue to, as a group, cling
to the idea that their enemies must be destroyed. This is an idea furthered
by propaganda, fed to the masses that have been leveled in the existential
sense and duped into blindly supporting either the capitalist system in the
West or the communist system in the East. For Ellul, and for Merton, there

---

30. Merton, *Dancing in the Waters of Life*, 231.

31. Inchausti, *Merton's American Prophecy*, 50.

32. Ibid.

33. Ellul, *Technological Society*, 191.

is little difference between the two. Merton expressed this idea quite clearly in a letter to Nicaraguan poet Pablo Antonio Cuadro, in which he stated:

> It is certainly true that the storm has arisen out of our own hearts. It has sprung unbidden out of the emptiness of technological man ... I know it is not accepted as a sign of enlightenment to question the enlightenment and sincerity of the twentieth century barbarian. But I no longer have any desire to be considered enlightened by the standards of the stool pigeons and torturers whose most signal claim to success is that they have built so many extermination camps and operated them to the limit of their capacity ... I had not clearly understood that Gog and Magog were to fight one another ... The truth is that there is a little of Gog and Magog even in the best of us.[34]

Merton did, however, acknowledge that there is a qualitative difference between West (Gog) and East (Magog). He recorded in his journal that "our system makes for 'better living' (i.e. comfort), but theirs is more efficient in war and foreign policy—though we can fight wars when we set our mind to it."[35] He also acknowledged in his letter to Pablo Antonio Cuadra that perhaps Magog would not have allowed him to live, while Gog did allow him to live and to write, but Merton would not internalize the propaganda that drove the Cold War forward.

Ellul echoed these sentiments with the statement that

> once the postulates of our civilization are admitted, appearances alone can change. Individual or State capitalism, Western or Eastern democracy, all these are different costumes worn by the same man—but "it isn't the habit that makes the monk." Yet it is on account of this habit that the men of our own day are summoned to kill each other, in order to achieve this revolution for which they long; yet the very conditions of their conflict prevent them from achieving it.[36]

What Ellul has done with this passage is summarize a number of the themes that this study has presented thus far. He noted that people in all societies worship *technique*, power, and money. He also illustrated the role that propaganda and leveling plays in making this condition a reality, and the church, which also worships these facts and encourages their acceptance

---

34. Merton, *Emblems of a Season of Fury*, 70–71.

35. Merton, *Turning toward the World*, 20.

36. Ellul, *Presence of the Kingdom*, 36.

in place of belief in the Revelation, is implicated as well. He went on to explain that neither a capitalist nor a communist system of government exhibits any difference whatsoever in the basic reality that "technological mechanisms, the demand for economic growth, the primacy of science, bureaucratization, manipulation of man to adapt him at whatever cost to the life others make for him, the development of the 'society of spectacle,' urbanization, the collectivization of life (whether in the shape of American conformism or communist integration)—these are the real forces at work in our world."[37] Ellul was not alone in expressing this sentiment. It is also an example of Merton's thinking, as well as the thought expressed by Dorothy Day, the founder of the Catholic Worker movement:

> For Dorothy Day, social injustice demanded dissent, and—given the challenges and the political fault lines of her time—political protest simply came with the Christian territory . . . But [contemporary protest movements do not] take seriously her admonishments to build alternative communities and to go back to the land to fight the social alienation brought about by both communism and industrial capitalism.[38]

Some observers would accuse Day's Catholic Worker movement of having pro-communist sympathies, but as the next section will demonstrate, the organization was dedicated to addressing poverty and injustice outside of any ideological constraint.

THE CATHOLIC WORKER MOVEMENT[39]

A common belief shared by many of the Christian charity movements in the early twentieth century was that "the primary threat to human autonomy no longer comes from 'nature' or from 'tyrants' but from economic, political, and social systems of our own making that have become increasingly powerful, increasingly self-perpetuating, and increasingly out of control." Among these groups was the Catholic Worker movement, founded by Dorothy Day and Peter Maurin in 1933. Largely recognized as operating

37. Ellul, "Between Chaos and Paralysis," 747.

38. Inchausti, *Subversive Orthodoxy*, 93.

39. For the best summary of the Catholic Worker Movement, see Zwick and Zwick, *Catholic Worker Movement*.

40. Inchausti, *Subversive Orthodoxy*, 84.

outside of traditional Catholic dogma and often times considered to have been acting on the fringes of the Catholic hierarchy, Merton would come to see the movement as a genuine opportunity to follow Christ. Ellul is also associated with this movement, as the editor of *The Ellul Forum* noted, "When I first read Ellul, the affinity of his thought with that of both Dorothy Day and Thomas Merton immediately struck me."[41] It is important to keep in mind that Ellul never visited New York and never participated in any Catholic Worker activities. Often accused of communist leanings, the economic philosophy of distributism underpinned much of the Catholic Worker movement. Distributism was a system advocated by some conservatives as well, to include Russell Kirk (1918–1994), author of *The Conservative Mind* (1953). Other Catholics such as G. K. Chesterton (1874–1936), Hilaire Belloc (1870–1953), E. F. Schumacher (1911–1977), and Pope John Paul II (1920–2005) also advocated distributism.[42]

Describing Ellul's influence on her decision to become involved in the Catholic Worker movement Katherine Temple stated, "Ellul also quite indirectly helped me become open to the Catholic Worker movement, founded in 1933 by the peasant-worker-scholar Peter Maurin. It may sound odd to claim that an arch-Protestant pushed me towards a group with arch-Roman Catholic origins, and it is true that the links are not strictly linear."[43] Temple found in Ellul a powerful voice geared towards questioning the structure of contemporary society. While she was a common worker in the movement and not a founder or leader, she would compare Ellul and Catholic Worker movement cofounder Peter Maurin further, and although she noted that their respective religious beliefs were not something to be easily overlooked, she was certain that "what [bound] the two men together is stronger than whatever separates them. Each has turned against the tide to develop critical analyses that move us beyond ideologies and state power; each is rooted in Christianity that pre-dates confidence in 'life, liberty and the pursuit of happiness'; each has understood the Christian response as one of personalism, self-sacrifice, poverty, the daily works of mercy; each is a Christian intellectual in the true sense."[44] Temple illustrated the similarities between Ellul's worldview and the view espoused by those who were

41. Fasching, "In This Issue," 1.

42. Pearce, *Literary Converts*, 371; quoted in Scheske, "Conservative Convert." For a full description of the tenets of distributism, see Cooney, *Distributism*.

43. Temple, "Jacques Ellul," 7.

44. Ibid.

involved with the movement, of which Thomas Merton was at times closely affiliated. She sat for an interview for the *Ellul Forum* in which she explained that it was actually through Ellul's writing that she came to live the Catholic social worker life. She stated, "In some ways, I came to the Catholic Worker movement through the writings of Jacques Ellul."[45] This example of Ellul's thought influencing the movement is a powerful statement of the link be tween his vision and Merton's vision of some of the options available to those who wish to transcend *technique's* crushing impact on contemporary society.

Portraying themselves as a remedy to the carnage caused by industrial capitalism, the Catholic Worker movement sought to alleviate these condi tions; conditions which bore a remarkable similarity to those described by Ellul throughout much of his writing:

> Man was placed here with his talents, to play his part, and on every side he saw the children of this world wiser in their generation than the children of light. They built enormous skyscrapers, with imagination and vision they made their blue prints, and with reckless and daredevil financing made them actual in steel and concrete. Wheels turned and engines throbbed and the great pulse of the mechanical world beat strong and steady while men's pulses sickened and grew weaker and died.[46]

These sentiments are similar to Merton's own observations of twentieth-century America, and also offer a striking parallel to both Merton's and Ellul's observations on the city, described in chapter 4.

The idea that work could be misinterpreted as self-justification in El lul's thinking is also evident in the work that the Catholic Worker move ment accomplished on the part of the poor. Reflecting a unique viewpoint of the nature of work, the movement held to the belief that

> the problem was not work *per se*. Moderate amounts of labor could "purify and pacify the mind and dispose [a person] for contempla-tion." The problem was that excessive amounts of work agitated the soul. The interior life must not be subjugated to "unnatural, frantic, anxious work, work done under pressure of greed or fear or any other inordinate fashion." Even if such work were freely

45. Temple, interview by Jeff Dietrich, 8.

46. Elie, *Life You Save*, 69.

chosen, it signaled that a form of proportionate labor had been lost in the modern world.[47]

Dorothy Day mirrored Ellul's belief that we justify ourselves through our work, thus impeding the ability to transcend the false self. She referred to the 'heresy of good works' those 'accursed occupations' that keep us from thinking."[48] Another comparison between Day and Ellul can be seen in the statement, "Dorothy Day would have loved Ellul's remark that what constantly marked the life of Jesus was not nonviolence but in every situation the choice not to use power. This is infinitely different."[49] The many similarities between Day's thinking and Ellul's reinforces the idea that Merton, a Roman Catholic, and Ellul, a Protestant, were able to find common ground on many of the issues facing society in the post-war years.

In "Thomas Merton and the Bomb," author James J. Farrell asserts that Merton drew heavily on the personalist beliefs exemplified by the movement in formulating his views on non-violence:

> In Merton's life and writing after 1957, he combined personalism and the civil voice of nuclear discourse in a synthesis that would be increasingly influential in American culture. Merton's personalism drew on the Catholic Worker movement, [founded by] Peter Maurin and Dorothy Day. Catholic Worker personalism asserted the absolute primacy of the human person and decried violence to persons in modern institutions, including war, the nation-state, and both Marxist and capitalist economies.[50]

There is thus a link between Ellul's fundamental beliefs concerning the deleterious impact that the technological society has had on contemporary society, manifest through those such as Katherine Temple who were motivated to join the Catholic Worker movement after having read Ellul, and Thomas Merton's views on non-violence. Regarding Merton's opinion that the Catholic Worker movement's "personalist" nature translated into his thinking on non-violence, it is interesting to note that Ellul was also a member of the French personalist movement in the 1930s, and this movement is considered to have influenced Day and Maurin as they built the Catholic Worker movement in New York.[51]

47. Thompson, *Between Science and Religion*, 124.

48. Inchausti, *Subversive Orthodoxy*, 93.

49. Ibid., 89.

50. Farrell, "Merton and the Bomb," 81.

51. Ellul, *In Season, Out of Season*, 24–25n1.

Noting another connection between the movement and ideas that have been presented thus far, those associated with the Catholic Worker movement, to include Merton, "often found the practice of religion incon sistent with the values of religion, and they decried the hypocrisy of much modern religion."[52] There is thus a commonality between the movement and Merton's (and Ellul's as well as discussed in chapter 3) views on the ten sion between the visible and the invisible church. Ellul and Merton merge on the most pressing issues of their day, and their thoughts regarding the church and its relationship to contemporary society are identical in many ways. Ellul elaborated further on this idea with the statement that "one can normalize atomic disintegration, but not the disintegration produced by the gospel."[53] This assertion ties together many themes relating to the chap ters presented to this point. Non-violence, the Cold War, and the visible church's acquiescence to *technique* come together in this statement.

There is a metaphysical rationale behind Merton's thinking regarding social work and charitable work involving the very relationship of man to society. It can be seen in some ways as the culmination of much of Merton's worldview. As noted in *Man Before God: Thomas Merton on Social Respon sibility* (1974):

> The question of the relationship of the person to the social orga-
> nization in which he lives is one of the most important problems
> of modern times. Every ethical problem of modern times can be
> traced back to this root question. The problem is met everywhere,
> but since men are tending more and more to be "organization
> men" (in the West) or "new mass-men" (in the East) modern man
> is becoming so conditioned that he fails to recognize his own per-
> sonal relationship to his immediate society as a personal problem.
> Modern man has moved very close to losing his personality and
> freedom in a general wave of conformism and passivity.[54]

Merton would go on to address this topic of the relationship of man to society in much of his writing in the 1960s. He would propose, "The work of collaborating with others to establish the reign of God in the hearts of men is not the work of individuals or mass-men, but of persons who have reached not only maturity but their full stature as free Christians."

52. Farrell, "Merton and the Bomb," 81.

53. Ellul, *Subversion of Christianity*, 158.

54. Kelly, *Man Before God*, 176.

55. Ibid., 177.

It is the use of the word "free" in this passage that demonstrates Merton's commitment to a Christocentric view of freedom similar to that proposed by Ellul.

Freedom is thus a requisite for the Christian who hopes to contribute to bringing about the realization of God's kingdom, and the social realm is the milieu in which this realization will occur.

> Christian social action is first of all action which discovers religion in politics, religion in work, religion in social programs for better wages, etc., not at all to "win the worker for Christ" but because God became man, because every man is potentially Christ, because Christ is our brother, and because we have no right to let our brother live in want, or in degradation or in any form of squalor whether physical or spiritual. In a word, if we really understood the meaning of Christianity in social life, we would see it as a part of the redemptive work of Christ, liberating man from misery, squalor, subhuman living conditions, economic of political slavery, ignorance and alienation.[56]

Thomas Merton saw the Catholic Worker movement as more than simply an organization dedicated to feeding the hungry. He saw in the movement that "the Christian commitment had radical social consequences."[57] After Merton's experience on Fourth and Walnut in Louisville that was recounted in chapter 2, he began to see the lines that separated the monastery from the outside world as less distinct. Merton "realized that people in the Catholic Worker movement were trying to live a vocation that had much in common with the monastic life and gave even more striking witness to the presence of God in each person" and "he valued Dorothy and the Catholic Worker movement for daring to connect love and justice and for taking an active stand against war—something practically no other Catholic institution, certainly no monastery, was willing to do."[58] Living the Christian life and accepting this life as an embodiment of freedom rather than its antithesis is a central tenet in all of Ellul's thought, and it occupies a central place in Merton's thought as well.

Merton shared the following sentiment with Dorothy Day, the founder of the Catholic Worker movement, "If there were no *Catholic Worker* and

---

56. Merton, *Conjectures of a Guilty Bystander*, 81–82.

57. Forest, "Merton and the Catholic Worker," 321.

58. Ibid.

such forms of witness, I would never have joined the Catholic Church."
This link provided by the Catholic Worker movement between Merton's
conversion to Catholicism and Ellul's intellectual foundations of the move
ment itself and for motivating some of its members to join the movement is
a powerful illustration of the similarity in worldview that both men leveled
against contemporary society, and the role of technology and *technique*
is through this unique response to technology's crushing impact on human
freedom that Ellul and Merton find much common ground. The Catholic
Worker movement provided the opportunity to live out the Gospel mes
sage and truly embrace the Christocentric view of freedom that Merton
and Ellul espoused. Their relationship with the Catholic Worker movement
demonstrates a commitment to living out this radical commitment to the
freedom that they both believed was offered in the Gospel message.

MERTON AND ELLUL ON REVOLUTION

Jacques Ellul was not a committed "revolutionary," and neither was Thomas
Merton. Merton sought solace and an escape from the world when he
joined the monastery in December 1941. He thought at the time that he
was done with the world, and that he would spend the rest of his life dedi
cated to seeking out God. Ellul, on the other hand, spent his young adult
life in search of revolution, and was especially active in this effort immedi
ately after the German surrender in 1945. He had hoped that France would
experience a complete social and political upheaval, and when this failed
to occur, he turned his back on social activism and dedicated his time to
writing. Merton moved from contemplation to action in 1958 after his Lou
isville experience (recounted in chapter 2)—and Ellul moved from action
to contemplation after the immediate post-war years. However, both men
formulated significant portions of their worldview in both the active and
contemplative phases of their lives.

Ellul's early involvement in the personalist movement, which hoped
for radical societal and governmental change in France after the liberation
in 1944, led to a crushing sense of failure. He turned away from direct ac
tion but his writing continued to be presented as a means for others to
act and to engage head-on with the pressing issues of the times. Ellul has
been described as a "Marxist turned Christian political activist who later

59. Merton, *Hidden Ground of Love*, 151.

renounces his activism by stressing the importance of contemplation."[60] Outlining his thinking on revolution, he stated:

> More and more frequently we hear talk of "revolution," of "overthrows," as characterizing our times. It is true that we are witnessing the development of so-called "revolutionary" movements (communist movements, revolts of the poor or of former colonial peoples, and so on). But to describe them as "revolutionary" is to judge superficially, for these movements regularly end by reproducing and indeed reinforcing the trends present in the old society (nationalism, the power of the state and the bureaucracy, economic and technological expansion). The only change is in the controlling personnel and in a modification of the old *formal* structures . . .[61]

This statement summarizes his view of revolution and is in stark contrast to the proclamations of practically all historical revolutionary figures. The passage demonstrates that in Ellul's view, revolution is useless when considering the idea of transcending the grip of *technique*. He continued with, "I insist, our society remains as it was—permanent, stable, even rigid. What disturbs me is not any 'overthrow,' but on the contrary the absence of overthrow of the basic, actual structures of the modern world."[62]

Regarding the revolutionary mindset and the idea that revolution offered an option for "overthrowing" *technique*, he stated, "The attitudes usually taken in face of this movement of mechanization, of crystallization of the social body—especially under the influence of technology—seem to me mistaken."[63] Ellul had no faith in revolution as a cure for the ills plaguing the technological society.

Thomas Merton's thoughts on "revolution" differ in some respects when compared to Ellul. He did not attempt to provide an overarching framework through which one can view revolution, but his hope for social change through non-violent revolution occasionally finds its way into his journals, as he wrote, "Today I said Mass for Latin America—not that the revolution should not happen, but that there may be a truly just social order, established not through chaos and violence, but solidly and in true

---

60. Burke, "Jacques Ellul," 13.
61. Ellul, "Between Chaos and Paralysis," 747.
62. Ibid.
63. Ibid.

equity."[64] Merton often used the term revolution in the context of social reform—never suggesting that violence should be in any way involved. He stated, "We are now in possession of atomic power, we have the moral obli gation to make good use of it, rather than turning it to our own destruction. But we will not be able to do this without an interior revolution that aban dons the quest for brute power and submits to the wisdom of love and the Cross."[65] Revolution in Merton's worldview mirrored Ellul's thought on the topic in that he did not seek to employ violence—nor does he enjoin others to do so. Revolution was not meant to be a course of action through which violence could be applied in order to further the conditions in which hu mankind seeks the path to true freedom. For Merton, Buddhist and Chris tian monasticism considered human beings themselves to be the starting point for radical change, and so it would first be necessary to address the problems of individuals rather focusing on changing social structures. The methodology for this type of change involved self-transcendence as addressed in chapter 4.

Ellul outlined a political stance that he believed Christians should take, stating, "The only Christian political position consistent with rev elation is the negation of power: the radical total refusal of its existence, a fundamental questioning of it, no matter what form it may take." addition to his ideas on revolution, Ellul also discusses anarchy in some of his writing. The common understanding of anarchy implies disorder and chaos, and a lack of any authority. Ellul presented an idea of anarchy that is different from this understanding, and that stems from his theology and his belief that the institutional church has abandoned its mission to preach the gospel message as discussed in chapter 3. Ellul stated, "Without a doubt the official Church, transformed into a power, taught the opposite of biblical teaching . . . both the Old and New Testaments take exception to all political power. No power can claim to be legitimate in itself. Politi cal power and organizations are necessities in society but only necessities. They attempt repeatedly to take God's place, since magistrates and kings

---

64. Merton, *Dancing in the Waters of Life*, 81. While Liberation Theology in Latin America is outside the scope of this study, for an account of Merton's relationship with this movement, see Cunningham, *Thomas Merton and the Monastic Vision*.

65. Merton, *Seeds of Destruction*, 124.

66. Labrie, "Merton on Marx and Marxism," 11.

67. Ellul, "Paradox of Anarchism and Christianity," 5.

invariably consider themselves the incarnation of authority."[68] He scoffed at the idea that a revolution could actually replace the current social order. The means required to generate the force needed to overthrow the existing power structures could only be attained through employing the same practices that the revolutionary would be trying to supersede. Illustrating this point, Ellul said:

> What is more, we are forced to believe that every other revolution is now impossible, because, in order to succeed, a revolution would be obliged to use the methods of the present world. For instance, in order to set men free we would need the adhesion of numbers of men, that is to say, the use of methods of propaganda to which we are accustomed, and then our politics would have to be addressed to the masses, because this alone would actually succeed, and it would be useless to try to accomplish a revolution without this basis.[69]

As a result, society stagnates, allowing the forces of *technique* to further their hold over contemporary humankind. He went on:

> This profound immobility, this incapacity for revolution—which is certainly the essential characteristic of our epoch—in opposition to the exasperated desire for this most necessary revolution, creates a formless kind of society. In spite of all the political struggles, which have never been so violent, in spite of apparent contradictions, there is a progress towards uniformity, an apparent alignment of all values, of all ideologies, based upon a few essential elements of civilization.[70]

Merton also saw that revolution had little hope of overturning the structures which buttressed contemporary society, holding humankind in their grip. In a letter to Dorothy Day, he indicated his frustration with resistance to the technological society, writing, "more and more drifting toward the derided and probably quite absurdist and defeatist position of a sort of Christian anarchist. This of course would be foolish, if I followed it to the end . . . But perhaps the most foolish would be to renounce all consideration of any alternative to the status quo, the giant machine."[71] As in Ellul's thinking, Merton suggested that revolution was not a method that could

68. Ibid.

69. Ellul, *Presence of the Kingdom*, 34–35.

70. Ibid.

71. Forrest, "Friendship of Letters," 60.

properly bring about social change or renewal. Rather, both men proposed a "third way."

The Third Way

What possible course of action is open to the individual living in the tech nological society? Is there any way to escape *technique's* influence? Merton and Ellul offer some thoughts on their answer to this question; answers which derive from their experiences living in a world of two armed camps arrayed against each other. Merton believed that through *kenosis* and *noia*, one can begin to escape from the bonds imposed on society by the twin pillars of spiritual malaise and the increasing demands of modern ization, secularization, and "progress." *Kenosis* refers to the self-emptying that one finds in the mystical traditions, and is an ego-shattering practice. The word "*kenosis*" comes from the Greek verb *kenoo*, meaning "to empty," and is translated in Philippians 2:7 as Christ having emptied himself of his divine nature in order to become fully human.[73] *Metanoia* is a Greek word for the concept of total personal transformation.[74] Emphasizing either of these practices and focusing on spiritual renewal through contemplation, one can begin to transcend the mass, identify the true self and begin the journey on the path to true freedom. In order to establish oneself on this path to freedom, Merton and Ellul proposed an approach that they referred to as "the third way." While their proposed third way was not a specific rec ommendation meant to provide a solution to the problems posed by tech nology in contemporary society, it does offer a method of transcendence, and in a sense is offered in order to liberate those who choose to follow it from *technique's* all-encompassing grasp. Langdon Winner lamented the lack of solutions to problems that beset contemporary society, stating:

> Specific ills in industrial civilization are said to be rooted very deeply in human aggressiveness, the machine mentality, the es sence of the subject/object split, the obsession of the West with *la technique*, rational thought, the workings of the second law of thermodynamics, or in some similarly intractable source. Thus, over many generations critics of industrialism and modern

72. Nouwen, *Thomas Merton: Contemplative Critic*, 83.

73. Gruden, *Systematic Theology*, 550.

74. Dekar, "What the Machine Produces," 219. Ellul does not discuss the concepts of *kenosis* and *metanoia*, and they are thus not elaborated upon further in this study.

techniques have been unable to propose cures for the host of difficulties they so vividly describe.[75]

The "third way" is an attempt to offer some kind of escape from these problems, if nothing else. Merton added these thoughts in a letter to his friend Czeslaw Milosz: "It seems to me, as you point out, and as other writers like yourself say or imply (Koestler, Camus, etc.) there *has to be* a third position, a position of integrity, which refuses subjection to the pressures of the two massive groups ranged against each other in the world."[76] In this passage, Merton presented the capitalist and communist systems from which the third way offers a respite. Both of these systems were manifestations of all of the forces of *technique*, including propaganda and advertising, and so by escaping these twin systems, one can by implication begin to evade *technique's* pervasive grasp.

Ellul asserted that the third way demanded actions that were inconsistent with the expectations that society had for individuals, and stated, "It is in the building of a new daily life, in the discovery of things, acts, situations utterly different from those that society would fasten on us, that this subjectivity can express itself."[77] Under the crushing burden of propaganda and advertising, it is difficult to build this kind of life. The political and economic systems in place in both East and West also served to limit the building of a life that Ellul described in the above passage. However, he also added:

> The liberation that is granted us must therefore reach all of the forms that the enslavement of sin could have taken on. It will therefore be a freedom with regard to the state (which does not at all imply a liberal state), with regard to labor (which no longer has the significance of constraint and penalty), with regard to money (it is in this liberation and because the Word of God reaches us that it is required of us to decide between Mammon and the Eternal), with regard to all sociological, political, familial conformities: that is, the necessities the world imposes upon us.[78]

As explained earlier, Ellul identified the necessities imposed by the world as the burdens which must be overcome in order to achieve freedom. In fact,

75. Winner, *Whale and the Reactor*, 67.

76. Faggen, *Striving towards Being*, 4. The next chapter will present Merton's engagement with Camus' literature.

77. Ellul, "Between Chaos and Paralysis," 749.

78. Ellul, *Sources and Trajectories*, 119.

simply struggling against the necessities is itself a manifestation of free dom. He identified the state, labor, and money as some of these necessities. Merton added to this discussion with his assertions that transcending the necessities imposed by the world requires not a revolt against the system itself, but a "depoliticization" of existing political institutions as a "step to wards true egalitarianism."[79] This act could lead to a transcendence of the polarizing systems that plagued contemporary society, and is indicative of the third way approach.

Ellul addressed the third way directly, commenting, "Christian ethics goes beyond the established options of good and evil. Whenever history and eschatology intersect in the apocalyptic moment, where the freedom of God intersects with human freedom, there the future is opened up and something new is made possible. It is at the point of tension where the necessity of the world confronts the freedom of the individual Christian that a 'third way' is opened up."[80] It is interesting to note that while both Merton and Ellul proposed a third way, further reflection upon the nature of this path indicates that it is unlikely to be followed by very many people. Transcending the self, desiring to escape from the crowd, recognizing that propaganda is manifest in nearly every facet of life, one could ques tion whether or not Merton or Ellul themselves can be considered to have followed this path. Referring to the possibility of confronting *technique* one author submits, "Ellul believes the truth of Christian revelation must confront the sociological world dominated by *technique*. The truth that confronts *technique* is an alien truth to this world. While alien, the truth, nevertheless, *is capable in some unfathomable way to contradict the way of servitude*. This way of contradiction, however, is rarely (if ever) realized in human history."[81] The "alien truth" referred to in this passage can be equated to Merton and Ellul's idea of freedom, while the way of contradic tion equates roughly to their conception of the third way.

Can Christians offer hope to the world? Ellul believed that "as we face this question the first thing to do, it seems to me, is to reject both false ways of posing [the question] and false answers to it."[82] Although "just how Ellul proposes that the Christian is to cope with this ambiguity of daily life, as guided by grace in the forgiving work of God in Christ, glad and

79. Inchausti, *Merton's American Prophecy*, 91.
80. Fasching, *Thought of Jacques Ellul*, 143.
81. Wauzzinski, *Discerning Prometheus*, 69–70.
82. Ellul, "Between Chaos and Paralysis," 747.

free, yet perplexed and bound by the pressing hard choices of this political existence, the reader is invited to pursue for himself."[83] This may be as close to a prescription that one will find in all of Ellul's work.

There is a political component to the third way as well in that it is an attempt to escape the left-right paradigm. Ellul specifically sought, along with his friend Bernard Charbonneau, to find a new path, one that "did not pay homage to the social-structural elements to which either of the traditional groups did. That is, Ellul did not have great faith in the market or the state, largely because of the intrusion of *technique* into both venues."[84] For the Christian who accepts the Word of God and chooses freedom, the third way is the logical path. Casting aside the dictates of commonly held opinion, ignoring the propaganda continually broadcast through the media, and even choosing to accept or reject church dogma, the free Christian follows his own conscience. In so doing, he takes a step away from the technological society. The third way, according to Ellul,

> is beyond the established options of good and evil. It is the invention of the new and unexpected. It is the unrestricted freedom which Paul describes when he says that everything is permitted or lawful. Therefore there need be no uniformity of opinion or action among Christians. The Christian may be a monarchist or a communist, a conscientious objector or a militarist. He or she may interpret the scriptures literally or may demythologize them, as long as each option is an expression of freedom in Christ.[85]

Merton would also equate this third way to a position of pure freedom. In a series of essays later published under the title *Thomas Merton's Dark Path* (1981), Merton explained the third way, which in reality is no way at all. Robert Inchausti summarizes this book's thesis:

> A monk's true subjectivity, his interior I, had no projects: it sought to accomplish nothing, not even contemplation. It sought only to *be* and to move according to the secret dynamics of being itself, following, not its own desires, but the promptings of a "superior Freedom." This superior freedom was the sense of emotional fulfillment that comes from doing the Will of God in the moment by being present to His presence. At first glance this may not seem like a third "political" position at all, but it begins to describe the

---

83. Beach, introduction to Ellul, *To Will and to Do*, viii.

84. Moore, "Environmental Issues," 328.

85. Fasching, *Thought of Jacques Ellul*, 143.

> dynamics of the "moving line" that constitutes a life lived in accord with conscience.[86]

Merton's exposure to and adoption of Eastern thought, particularly Zen Buddhism, is evident in this passage. Like the third way in politics, Merton believed that Buddhism was also a way—not a religion or a philosophy. Merton attributed Zen Buddhism's popularity in the West to the "wide spread dissatisfaction with the spiritual sterility of mass society, dominated by technology and propaganda, in which there is no room left for personal spontaneity."[87] For both Merton and Ellul, the third way represented a choice to transcend the technological determinism prevalent in mid-twentieth-century society.

There is, however, a point of significant disagreement between Merton and Ellul on this third way and its applicability to humankind in general. Ellul asserted that only Christians could transcend *technique* through this path of self-discovery and radical self-creation, stating, "The good news of the gospel affirms precisely that in Christ and through Christ we are free (provided that we live in faith!). 'It is for freedom that Christ has set you free.' To the Christian is given a freedom which he (and he only!) can challenge all slaveries of whatever kind and escape them himself. But here again we have a truth and a possibility of life which Christians do not appropriate."[88] Merton's ecumenical spirit and penchant for engaging faith traditions outside of his own would necessitate his disagreement with the idea that Christians alone could find a third way. He would, however, agree with Ellul's contention that

> the Christians (and that means starting out from the individual) can open the way for freedom to enter the world; and alas, we see that Christians are of all men the most conformist, the most compliant, the most bound by habit, the least free. In their conceptions of morality and virtue, of church work, of respectability, they are sunk in dogmatisms. This being so, how will it be possible to traverse the difficult era we live in and to come out elsewhere?[89]

Returning to self-transcendence as a requisite first step on the path to freedom, Ellul went on to demonstrate that it is also necessary to transcend the

86. Inchausti, *Merton's American Prophecy*, 90.

87. Rice, *Man in the Sycamore Tree*, 13.

88. Ellul, "Between Chaos and Paralysis," 750.

89. Ibid.

false self in order to discover one's true nature; to literally create oneself in order to transcend the very self that has been fashioned for us by *technique*. He added, "What is needed is the creation of a new style of life, and that this cannot be accomplished save by starting with the individual's discovery of himself. Every individual must become a creator of his own life—and that is an undertaking which will require a terrible effort . . . A person must not use his free time to 'distract' or 'cultivate' himself, but to create his own life."[90]

Ellul demonstrated his affinity for Kierkegaard with the comment that, regarding the discovery of our own true nature, "Kierkegaard, it seems to me, alone can show us how to start."[91] This mindset complements the search for a way that allows one to begin to transcend the force of *technique*. Again it is evident that while Ellul did not incorporate any Buddhist elements into his thinking, he and Merton are arriving at a similar destination regarding the third position. Referring again to the year in which Ellul formulated much of his political outlook: "In 1944, at the Liberation . . . we were going to move from Resistance to Revolution. But when we said that—and I would like to point out that Camus first used it in 1943 in combat groups—we did not mean a Communist, Stalinist, Soviet revolution. We meant a fundamental revolution of society, and we made great plans for transforming the press, the media, and the economic structures."[92] Here again Camus is mentioned, as well as some thoughts regarding the nature of revolution in Ellul's thinking. This revolution is not a violent clash between ideologically motivated armed camps, but a revolt against the determinative powers that dominate society. He stated, "If we are to question our society in so radical a fashion, we must adopt a point of view essentially different from that [of] society's—one that we cannot arrive at by starting from our human wisdom."[93]

Ellul had demonstrated that politics, like every other human endeavor, has given way to *technique*. Merton has also expressed that it is interior renewal, not political upheaval or revolution that is the first step towards realizing our God-given gift of freedom. The next chapter will expand upon these ideas and will further elaborate their critique of the technological society, although not through any particular theological, sociological, or

90. Ibid., 749.
91. Ibid.
92. Ellul, *Perspectives on Our Age*, 22.
93. Ellul, "Between Chaos and Paralysis," 749.

political lens. Chapter 6 examines their literary output in the form of po etry, and in Merton's case, his reading of other contemporary authors who have contributed to his particular critique. It will also examine the sanctity of the Word—both the divine Word through which Revelation entered his tory, and the human word as the mechanism through which the truth of the Revelation is made known.

6   Literature

This chapter serves three purposes. First, it examines Merton and Ellul on the subject of the Word—the revealed Word of God (Ellul) and the written word as the most reliable source of truth (Merton). According to both thinkers, contemporary society has denigrated the word, suffocating it under a deluge of images. Second, the chapter illustrates Merton's agreement with Ellul's *technique* through an examination of Merton's commentary on French author Albert Camus (1913–1960) and Romanian playwright Eugène Ionesco (1909–1994). An examination of Merton's *Prometheus* and a comparison of some of Ellul's and Merton's poetry will conclude the chapter.

SANCTITY OF THE WORD

Ellul and Merton held similar opinions regarding language in contemporary society. It was Ellul's belief that "the only opposition to the ideological bourgeois order comes from the world of art, the novel, painting, poetry, the theater, and philosophy."[1] He paid homage to the spoken word, which he believed revealed God's gift of freedom to the world. He found this in part in the creation account of Genesis 1, stating, "In the third verse we encounter the first act: 'Elohim speaks,' and this is repeated throughout the creation account. It is another important revelation about God, namely, that he creates by means of his word: a word that is at the same time distinct from God and in a sense is God himself."[2] This passage demonstrates Ellul's belief that God's spoken word is directly identifiable with God himself. The Word also introduces the potential for human freedom into the world.

---

1. Paul, "New Metamorphoses," 14.
2. Vanderburg, "How the Science versus Religion Debate," 433.

Contemporary society, captivated by *technique*, has lost the ability to un derstand this divine Word. It is more difficult to attain freedom in light of the fact that the visual image has overwhelmed the Word eclipsing divine revelation with human creativity that while in itself is something good, has the potential of distracting humans from nurturing a spiritual relationship with God. Ellul has identified this phenomenon as one of contemporary society's most pressing concerns. Ellul repeatedly "warned us that our modern addiction to images is a kind of terrorist time bomb ominously ticking away in the comfortable hotel of democratic society."[3] His task was to not only appeal to the sensibilities of those immersed in visual imagery, but quite simply to save the spoken and the written word from irrelevance. Among the many forces responsible for the subjugation of the word are propaganda and advertising. Ellul places the word on a pedestal, noting, "Anyone wishing to save humanity today must first of all save the word." For Ellul, the word maintains an importance far beyond the mere ability to communicate ideas between people. It is the means through which God revealed himself to humanity, "therefore . . . when God speaks the whole movement of history begins, and thanks to that Word there is communica tion, reciprocity, and exchanges with people who also speak . . . I believe that this tells us that from now on a relationship is established, and that because this is a relationship of the Word it offers freedom to the listener." The divine Word, according to Ellul scholar Willem Vanderburg, is the entity that establishes human freedom. Ellul emphasized this idea in the statement, "God is a God who speaks, the inverse of silent idols: And like all speech, which binds even while liberating, God, bound to humanity, is only so bound by the word."[6] The centrality of the Word in the Bible and revelation are evident in Ellul's belief that "offered as prolegomena are the central affirmations of the Bible: God is speech, and its fulfillment: the Word made flesh."[7] In Ellul's theology, the divine Word, which preceded the fall, established freedom for humanity.

It is not only the divine word itself, but the human word that Ellul de fends. He stated that "the human word is a response to the Word of God."

3. Hanks, introduction to Ellul, *Humiliation of the Word*, vii.

4. Ibid.

5. Vanderburg, *Jacques Ellul on Freedom*, 22.

6. Aubert, review of Vahanian, *Dieu Anonyme*, 5.

7. Ibid.

8. Ellul, *What I Believe*, 23.

In addition, human words carry other important meanings, and as such, "we believe . . . in certain words, such as the good, or freedom, or justice, which we do not define plainly or consistently but to which we cling firmly no matter what their content."[9] The word is not merely a signifier, attached to a single meaning, but rather, through poetry and literature can take on additional, metaphoric meaning. Ellul added that "the word (I am speaking of poetry), with reference to the real, can bring out what is hidden in it."[10] While the human word can operate in this manner, God's word remains fixed. This is another avenue through which Karl Barth's influence on both Ellul and Merton can be seen, as Barth stated:

> He [God] speaks the one undialectical word. He utters the Amen which settles matters—which does not stand in need of further supplementation. He dissolves the disturbing "and." His theology, his knowledge and speaking about himself, is no *theologia viatorum*. It is undialectical theology. But we are men. That is the simplest and most decisive reason for the exclusive possibility of dialectical theology. It must, however, be true that the proper, the final, the decisive word be left to God.[11]

The idea that the word and denigration of language has suffered under contemporary society's barrage of visual images is a belief shared by both Ellul and Merton.

Merton believed that contemporary society had lost the ability to infer ideas through literature, relegating the written word to secondary status when compared to the visual image. In *Cables to the Ace* (1968), Merton employed a literary style similar to that used by fellow Catholic author Flannery O'Connor, who had stated that "for those who are blind, or almost so, you have to write with large figures."[12] Merton's essays in *Cables* are meant to shake up the reader, allegedly overwhelmed by image-laden, colorful magazines and not used to actually reading a text. He wrote, "Listening is obsolete. So is silence. Each one travels alone in a small blue capsule of indignation. (Some of the better informed have declared war on language.)"[13] He wanted to shock the reader out of the stupor in which he believed the average person spent the majority of his or her day. Bombarded

9. Ibid., 3.
10. Ibid., 24.
11. Barth, *Die Christliche Dogmatic*, 456–57; cited in Mueller, *Karl Barth*, 26.
12. Kramer, *Thomas Merton*, 128.
13. Merton, *Cables to the Ace*, 3.

by propaganda and advertising, deluded by constant appeals to the false self, it is Merton's sincere belief that society had lost its ability to appreciate and understand literature, even simple reading. Mass entertainment had replaced actual thought.

In her novel *The Violent Bear It Away* (1960), Flannery O'Connor wrote, "A society strictly guided by intellect will not have the resources to constrain technology as individual creativity and authentic experience were conceded to experts and their technocratic systems."[14] Merton attempted to appeal to this society not only with *Cables to the Ace*, but with much of his other poetry, as he realized that we live in a world where "language has become so contorted that it is extremely difficult to honor the truth." Regarding this idea, Merton indicated:

> Man needs "massive lessons of irony and refusal." Being surrounded as he is by noises, noises which "are never values," it is almost as if he has forgotten proper ways to use language. It was with such ideas in mind that Merton wrote the concluding sentence of the second poem in *Cables*: "The sayings of the Saints are put away in air-conditioned archives"; and a similar idea is developed in many of the poems which follow. Contemporary man has forgotten how to look, listen, read, even to speak.[16]

Merton's frustration with contemporary society and with the inability of the common members of society to employ dialogue and literature increased throughout the 1960s. Both *Cables to the Ace* and *Raids on the Unspeakable* (1966) attest to this. His disappointment is evident in the introduction to *Cables*:

> Why not more pictures? Why not more rhythms, melody, etc.? All suitable questions to be answered some other time. The realm of the spirit is two doors down the hall. There you can obtain more soul than you are ready to cope with, Buster . . . Go shake hands with the comics if you demand a preface. My attitudes are common and my ironies are no less usual than the bright pages of your favorite magazine . . . The soaps, the smells, the liquors, the insurance, the third, dull, gin-soaked cheer: what more do you want, Rabble?[17]

14. O'Connor, quoted in Thompson, *Between Science and Religion*, 120.

15. Kramer, *Thomas Merton*, 128.

16. Ibid.

17. Merton, *Cables to the Ace*, 1.

One detects an increasing frustration in Merton's attitude towards his fellow citizens in much of his later literature. Even in the early 1940s, as Merton composed a number of poems such as "The Tower of Babel," he had already determined to address "the corruption of language and truth," and this idea is "central to the Babel works."[18] A certain dialectic is evident in Merton's entrance into the monastery, a place of purported silence, yet one from which he continued to engage with language, speech, and dialogue for the rest of his life.

Protestant theologian Carl Henry (1913–2003) addressed a number of issues relating to the divine Word and the reliability of the human word as a means for transmitting its meaning. Henry stated that "even churches may be culpable of distorting verbal substances and meaning and of contributing to a modern distrust of words as bearers of truth."[19] Henry also noted that, in a manner similar to Merton's adoption of a radical form of literature and poetry meant to "shock" the reader, "a number of the clergy have disowned preaching entirely as a means of communicating the Gospel, and prefer liturgy or drama or nonverbal witness."[20] Clearly the idea that the human word had lost its efficacy as a reliable device through which Revelation could be made known was not only espoused by the Roman Catholic Merton.

As the 1960s progressed, Merton followed the deliberations of the Second Vatican Council as closely as he could from his hermitage in Kentucky. He believed that "the council's primary task was to proclaim the gospel of love and hope to modern man in his own language without distorting the message. Since the message is not bound to any specific culture or age, the council should free itself from its medieval and baroque language without identifying it too closely or firmly with the present confused, technological society; it should make its eternal truths speak to current problems and questions."[21] Again demonstrating the importance of language, Merton beseeched church leaders to speak to contemporary society clearly and effectively, a task that he seemed to admit might be difficult against the background of the technological society.

Ellul and Merton were not alone in their appraisal of society's lack of ability to discern the truth through literature and the written word. Czech

---

18. O'Sullivan, "Thomas Merton and the Towers of Babel," 30.

19. Henry, *God, Revelation and Authority*, 358.

20. Ibid.

21. Baker, *Thomas Merton: Social Critic*, 82.

novelist Milan Kundera (1929–present) has argued that people in contem porary society are caught up in an age of "self-deception," and diagnosed contemporary ills as "the modernization of stupidity."[22] Paraphrasing Kun dera, Merton scholar Robert Inchausti summarizes Kundera's influence on Merton's thinking with respect to this phenomenon: "In the old world . . . stupidity was simple ignorance, illiteracy: one didn't know anything, but one could learn. In the modern world, stupidity has evolved into a new more virulent form: the nonthought of received ideas. There is just as much ignorance today as ever, but individuals hide it behind phrases acquired through superficial contact with the mass media, opinion makers, and the schools."[23] Kundera's quote illustrates a number of the concepts that have been discussed regarding both Merton's and Ellul's diagnosis of some of the more pronounced ills besetting contemporary society. Having fallen prey to the powerful forces of media and propaganda, people became less likely to think for themselves, instead following the crowd, stumbling along in the temples of the false self.

Merton's critique intensified as he continued to include topics such as the Cold War and the prospect of nuclear holocaust in his thinking. In light of these twin calamities, he assessed the situation Kundera identifies—the general expanse of ignorance—as truly catastrophic events. Merton wrote:

> It is frightening to realize that the façade of Christianity which still generally survives has perhaps little or nothing behind it, and that what was once called "Christian society" is little more than a materialistic neo-paganism with a Christian veneer. And where the Christian veneer has been stripped off we see laid bare the aw ful vacuity of the mass-mind, without morality, without identity, without compassion, without sense . . . Here spiritual religion has yielded to the tribal-totalitarian war dance and to the idolatrous cult of the machine.[24]

This passage identifies a number of the ideas presented thus far to include the mass man, propaganda and advertising manifest in the comment on materialist society, and the notion that Merton agrees with Kundera's as sessment of the contemporary intellect.

Both Merton and Ellul believed that television was a technology greatly responsible for furthering the "nonthought of received ideas" cited

22. Kundera, *Art of the Novel*, 163.

23. Inchausti, *Merton's American Prophecy*, 147.

24. Merton, "Religion and the Bomb," 9.

above. Kundera offers the novel as antidote to this situation—a situation made worse by the television. Writing to his friend the Polish poet Czeslaw Milosz (1911–2004), Merton commented on the goals of those who advertise through the use of television: "If in every man is a sage and an idiot, whoever flatters the idiot wins."[25] Ellul holds the image-oriented person in some degree of contempt as well, and stated that "experience tends to show that a person who thinks by images becomes less and less capable of thinking by reasoning and vice versa. The intellectual process based on images is contradictory to the intellectual process of reasoning that is related to the word."[26] *Technique*'s continued advance, and its manifestation through propaganda, advertising, and the media as explained in chapter 4 is the culprit behind this increase in visual imagery as substitute for reasoned thought. Tying together language, the word, freedom, and Camus' notion of the absurd, Merton proclaimed that language should be used "to awaken in man the lucid anguish in which alone he is truly conscious of his condition and therefore able to revolt against the absurd. Then he will affirm, over against its 'unreasonable silence,' the human love and solidarity and devotion to life which give meaning to his own existence."[27] In Merton's view, language gives us the ability to "awaken us to an awareness of our own condition" and allows us "to assert our humanity over and against the forces that oppose it."[28] Foremost among these forces is *technique*. Ellul would agree with Merton's assessment that language offers us this valuable weapon that if properly employed provides humankind the first step on the path towards attaining the divine gift of freedom.

Finally, Merton's view of language in twentieth-century America focused not only on its degradation as a means for discerning the truth, but on its having been co-opted by the state. While it is unlikely that Merton was a fan of the comedian Lenny Bruce (1925–1966), he praised Bruce's efforts to rescue language from its capture by those who would wield it in the form of propaganda designed to entrench the Cold War power structures. Of Bruce and language, Merton wrote:

> Once again, the use of language to extol freedom, democracy, and equal rights, while at the same time denying them, causes words to turn sour and rot in the minds of those who use them. In such

25. Faggen, *Striving towards Being*, 106.
26. Ellul, *Humiliation of the Word*, 258.
27. Hart, *Literary Essays of Thomas Merton*, 275.
28. Inchausti, *Merton's American Prophecy*, 135.

a context, the effort of someone such as Lenny Bruce to restore to language some of its authentic impact was a service despairingly offered to a public that could not fully appreciate it. One might argue that the language of this disconcerting and perhaps prophetic comedian was often less obscene than the "decent" but horrifying platitudes of those who persecuted him.[29]

Merton did not often explicitly address Ellul's writing or ideas in his own work. However, one can find an implicit concurrence with many of Ellul's fundamental ideas through examining Merton's literary output. One can surmise Merton's general assent to a number of Ellul's ideas through three specific avenues. These areas are first, Merton's engagement with Al bert Camus' writing; second, Merton's relationship to the work of Eugène Ionesco; and finally, Merton's own *Cables to the Ace* (1968) and *Raids on the Unspeakable* (1966). Exploration of these three avenues will take place within the context of an idea that both men passionately believed—namely that the written and spoken word had been buried in contemporary society under an onslaught of visual imagery. Ellul did, however, enjoy literature that dealt with the philosophy of the absurd, which, he wrote, "gives rise to a plentiful literature (novels and plays) which is both striking and passion ate. Thus we have the plays of Camus . . . then those of Ionesco."[30] Merton would turn to Camus and Ionesco in his quest to find meaning in the tech nological wilderness.

Merton's Literary Criticism

There are a number of similarities between Thomas Merton, Jacques Ellul and Albert Camus regarding the human condition in contemporary soci ety. One similarity in their approach is in understanding the significance of Karl Marx and Christianity. As with both Merton and Ellul, Camus believed that "in coming to terms with the Christian faith . . . one has come to terms with Marxism and with the underlying reasons for the ills of the twentieth century."[31] Crucial to Merton's formulation of the third way of integrity (discussed in chapter 5) is Camus' notion of "the absurd." Camus, who also maintained a friendship with Czeslaw Milosz, "became a major focal point of Merton's attempt to find a universal ground for faith in a world whose

29. Merton, "War and the Crisis of Language," 242.

30. Ellul, *Technological Bluff*, 200–201.

31. Brée, *Camus*, 49.

moral predicament made estrangement a viable but precarious path."[32] Regarding Merton's examination of these predicaments, Robert Inchausti wrote that

> Merton's own method for probing different perspectives was to inhabit them. In one of his most celebrated poems, "Chant to be Used in Processions Around a Site with Furnaces"—he explores in the first person singular the point of view of a concentration camp commandant. The narrator describes his work as an executioner, how the children were pacified, repeating the refrain, "I made improvements!"[33]

Merton displayed his utter contempt for the idea of unquestioned progress and technique run amok in poems such as these. In this particular poem, he is "bringing to language the self-justifications used by those who would carry forward the 'philosophy' of the apparatchiks."[34] The poem concludes with an absolute barrage against the Cold War mentality of the average American citizen: "Do not think yourself better because you burn up friends and enemies with long range missiles without ever seeing what you have done."[35] Merton employed the written word, in the form of poetry, as a weapon against those who had unquestionably accepted technological progress and who worshipped at the altar of ever-increasing efficiency.

Although they wrote in the 1960s, Merton and Ellul cannot be simply lumped together with the postmodernists, who as a group have considered the Christian metanarrative to be no longer either authoritative or relevant. Ellul denied the postmodern acceptance of the death of Christianity, nor did he seek to present any of his worldview in a manner consistent with the prevailing trends in the social sciences such as structuralism or essentialism. Merton likewise cut against the grain regarding the social science paradigms of the 1950s and 1960s. In fact, "Merton's ideas are totally antithetical to recent theoretical trends in the humanities and social sciences. His work is contextual, specific, unflinchingly existential."[36] Merton demonstrated his dislike of dogmatic systems in his comments on existentialism. Having explored Merton's thoughts on the visible, institutional church's alliance with the forces of *technique*, one can see that he did not

32. Faggen, *Striving towards Being*, xi.

33. Merton, "Chant to Be Used around a Site with Furnaces."

34. Inchausti, *Merton's American Prophecy*, 97.

35. Ibid.

36. Ibid.

hold back in his criticism of the appearance of this phenomenon in other intellectual structures. He stated, "Existentialism is an experience and an attitude, rather than a system of thought. As soon as it begins to present itself as a system, it denies and destroys itself."[37] It is perhaps no irony that Merton presents a great deal of his thinking on stultified systems in and Zen Masters, in which he attempted to claim existentialism as a "way that lies beyond the systems-oriented thinking that presents itself not only through technique but in so many other areas of modern life." He stated:

> Genuine existentialism is, like Zen Buddhism and like apophatic Christian mysticism, hidden in life itself. It cannot be distilled out in verbal formulas. Above all, the journalistic clichés about existential nihilism, pessimism, anarchism, and so on, are totally irrelevant, even though they may have some foundation in certain existentialist writings. It is my contention that these writings cannot fairly be taken as representative of genuine existentialism.[38]

While Merton would not have considered himself an existentialist, his thoughts on existentialism are similar to Camus'. Thomas Merton's accusations against the institutional church can be summed up in one short passage from of Camus' The Stranger (1942), an existentially-themed work:

> "Why do you call me sir?" said the prison chaplain, "why don't you call me Father?"
> "You are not my Father," said the condemned prisoner, "you are with the others."[39]

It is these "others," and those within the hierarchy of the visible church that are the target of Merton's critique. Even the condemned prisoner recognized that the institution charged with furthering the Gospel message in the world has compromised itself through a fatal alliance with the technological society. Merton noted a similar theme in Camus' The Plague In this story, the chaplain, Paneloux,

> represents in some sense the French clergy under the Nazis. But he also represents the Church as she confronts man in his moral and metaphysical estrangement—his "lostness" in an absurd world. What will she offer him? Can she give him anything more than a

37. Merton, Mystics and Zen Masters, 258.
38. Ibid.
39. Merton, Albert Camus and the Church, 150.

predesignated answer and a consoling rite? Does she ask anything more of him than conformity and resignation?[40]

In a sense, Merton's commentary on Camus and his engagement with his thought brings the most light to bear on Merton's concurrence with Ellul's worldview. However, Merton cannot be labeled a follower of Camus. For "if there is to be a choice between faith and the absurd, [Camus'] stoic conscience will, in the end, dictate the choice of the absurd" when the absurd is defined as the "gap between the actual shape of life and intelligent truth."[41] While Camus' choice of the absurd in itself demonstrates a type of "third way," Merton chose the path of faith, and so did Ellul.

Merton's "The Rain and the Rhinoceros" is an essay that appeared in *Raids on the Unspeakable* (1966). The book's intent was to address the challenges of the technological society "not in formal answers or accurate definitions, but in difficult insights at a moment of human crisis."[42] *Raids* is a literary onslaught against the technological society. Using metaphor and symbolism, it can be seen as "homage to creativity itself and as an aid to wisdom, which Merton took to mean the understanding of reality."[43] Similar to Ellul's theological methodology, Merton "attempts to deal with the repetitive, Spenglerian quagmire of history by viewing Christianity in its dynamic encounter with history rather than a set of abstract formulations of religious belief."[44] Using the essay as a weapon to confront the many ideas that have been covered thus far in this study, especially the notion of *technique* and the unquestioned acceptance of the idea of progress, Merton spared few contemporary societal institutions from his critique. The idea behind *Rain and the Rhinoceros* is taken from Eugène Ionesco's play entitled *Rhinoceros*. A commentary on the human condition in twentieth-century society, Ionesco's *Rhinoceros* illustrates the absurdity of a life made tolerable only through self-delusion. Merton drew on this theme and juxtaposed rain as an outside element that is meant to jar the reader away from the mechanical, technological world in which this self-delusion is continuously re-created. Merton began *Rain and the Rhinoceros* with:

---

40. Ibid., 152.
41. Ibid., 156–57.
42. Merton, *Raids on the Unspeakable*, 2.
43. Labrie, "Merton on the Unspeakable," 3.
44. Ibid.

> The rain I am in is not like the rain of cities. It fills the woods with an immense and confused sound. It covers the flat roof of the cabin and its porch with insistent and controlled rhythms. And I listen, because it reminds me again and again that the whole world runs by rhythms I have not yet learned to recognize, rhythms that are not those of the engineer.[45]

In this passage, Merton touched on many previously mentioned themes. His love of nature that he acquired in his youthful travels, the contrast be tween the serenity of nature and the man-made noise and confusion of the city, and technology's insidious advance, metaphorically compared to the engineer evaluating and attempting to understand and control everything, even rain. Describing the woods that enclosed his hermitage, he said:

> Here I am not alien. The trees I know, the night I know, the rain I know. I close my eyes and instantly sink into the whole rainy world of which I am a part . . . for I am not alien to it. I am alien to the noises of cities, of people, to the greed of machinery that does not sleep, the hum of power that eats up the night.[46]

Echoing Ellul's observation that technology's advance is furthered by pro viding solutions to the very ills that technology created in the first place, he went on to say, "I can have no confidence in places where the air is not first fouled and then cleansed, where the water is first made deadly and then made safe with other poisons."[47] The entire poem is designed to compel the reader to see beyond the false self and to awaken from the daze brought on by the forces which propel the technological society forward. Like a Zen master slapping the student who fails to grasp the true nature of reality, Merton "moves as the wind moves . . . like a thief in the night, his *Raids on the Unspeakable* leaves us few clues, save our own reawakened awareness of God."[48] He compared himself to Thoreau, adding, "Thoreau sat in his cabin and criticized the railways. I sit in mine and wonder about a world that has, well, progressed."[49] Expressing ideas similar to those that Merton addressed in *Raids*, Ellul shared his thoughts on progress, explicitly stating that "to say what I do not believe is simple. I do not believe in progress, or religion,

45. Merton, *Raids on the Unspeakable*, 9.

46. Ibid., 10.

47. Ibid., 10–11.

48. Finley, *Merton's Palace of Nowhere*, 16.

49. Merton, *Raids on the Unspeakable*, 12.

or politics, or science as the final answer."[50] It is important to note that Ellul does not believe in non-progress either. He simply believes, unlike the vast majority of his contemporaries, that progress is not the final answer to humankind's predicament, and that for as many benefits as it confers, there are pitfalls as well.

In order to discern Ellul's methodology for distinguishing between what he believed and what he did not, he offered:

> I would not say that if I do not believe in progress it is because I believe in nonprogress [*sic*]. The relation is more intimate and less logical. The two things depend on the taking of positions to a higher, more definite, and more decisive hierarchical degree or degree of abstraction . . . In what becomes didactically separate there is a need to retie the bonds, to bring the themes together again, to play the subtle game of multiple relations . . . Yet only the reader can do what is required, and to do so is not just a game or a matter of curiosity, but the only path to understanding.[51]

This path to understanding is precisely what Merton offered. Seeking to take matters to the higher plane, as Ellul suggests in the above passage, required "the artist and the intellectual to elude the web of collective thought. Paradoxically, the innocence of the artist for Merton was not solely a moral quality but a cognitive one as well, by which the artist was called upon to avoid the usual pitfalls of conventional thought."[52] Taking the idea of progress even further, Ellul stated that Christians do not "progress" towards the kingdom of God.[53] Referring to the Book of Ecclesiastes, he wrote: "Thus, according to Qoheleth, the human race does not progress. We may develop more perfect instruments, pull more strings, engage in more activities. But we *are* nothing more . . . What is the effective cost of each step 'forward?'"[54] These reflections follow the ideas presented in chapter 2 on "being versus doing." Ellul did not believe that by "doing" the right thing, the Kingdom will be drawn closer. He criticized the idea of progress, the idea that drives Western society forward. Complementing his assertions on self-transcendence, Merton explained that simply being in a state of solitude is not sufficient for either discovering ones true identity, or for escaping from the

50. Ellul, *What I Believe*, 2.

51. Ibid.

52. Labrie, "Merton on the Unspeakable," 9.

53. Ellul, *Reason for Being*, 65.

54. Ibid., 64.

collective mass. One that is "willingly enclosed by the laws of collective existence . . . has no more identity than an unborn child in the womb" and "is not yet conscious . . . [and] is alien to his own truth."[55] In another example of a dialectical approach, one must engage with society in order to transcend the grasp that it maintains over the false self, as Merton wrote in *Raids*, "Because we live in a womb of collective illusion, our freedom remains abortive. Our capacities for joy, peace, and truth are never liberated. They can never be used. We are prisoners of a process, a dialectic of false promises and real deceptions ending in futility."[56] Propaganda and the mass media further this collective illusion, a topic that both Merton and Ellul address in their writing and their poetry.

In order to transcend society's expectations, Merton quoted Ionesco's thoughts on the importance of useless acts, stating that "the universal and modern man is the man in a rush (i.e., a rhinoceros), a man who has no time, who is a prisoner of necessity, who cannot understand that *might be perhaps without usefulness*; nor does he understand that, at bottom, it is the useful that may be a useless and back-breaking burden. If one does not understand the usefulness of the useless and the uselessness of the useful, one cannot understand art. And a country where art is not understood is a country of slaves and robots."[57] Ellul noted that "a gratuitous, ineffective and useless act is the first sign of our freedom and perhaps the last," he explained that "this is freedom: man's freedom within God's freedom; man's freedom as a reflection of God's freedom; man's freedom exclusively received in Christ; man's freedom which is free obedience to God and which finds unique expression in childlike acts, in prayer and witness . . . within the tragic acts of politics and religion.[58] Merton and Ellul both emphasize "useless acts" as a means of sidestepping contemporary society's fixation with efficiency and calculation.

Ellul's engagement with Ionesco was limited. He explained that Huxley pointed out that the mixture of mundane chatter and intellectual chatter leads to wordlessness—and that "Eugene Ionesco's reputation as a playwright is based on this situation."[59] However, it is Merton's engagement

---

55. Merton, *Raids on the Unspeakable*, 14–15.

56. Ibid., 16–17.

57. Ionesco, *Notes et Contre Notes*, 21.

58. Ellul, *Politics of God and the Politics of Man*, 200.

59. Ellul, *Humiliation of the Word*, 156.

with Ionesco's plays that illustrates the extent to which Merton had appropriated much of Ellul's worldview regarding technology and freedom.

Thomas Merton used the Greek Promethean myth as a metaphor for contemporary humankind's predicament. Karl Barth also referred to Prometheus in a passage that bears resemblance to Merton's framing of the myth: "In religion this final passion becomes conscious and recognizable as experience and event. Can there be any affirmation of passion that outstrips the passion with which Prometheus robs Zeus of his fire and uses it for his own advantage? And yet, is it not perfectly obvious that such stolen fire is not the all-consuming fire of God, but only a furnace from which a very peculiar kind of smoke pours forth?"[60] According to Merton, "what Prometheus wants is not the glory of God but his own perfection" because "he has forgotten the terrible paradox that the only way we become perfect is by leaving ourselves, and, in a certain sense, forgetting our own perfection, to follow Christ."[61] Merton employed this literary device to emphasize the idea of self-transcendence. He went on to assert that the Old Testament story of Cain in Genesis 4 "turned out to be Prometheus in a fable that tells us much about the mentality of the Renaissance—and about our own."[62] Noting that Cain represented for Ellul the builder of the first city, and in so doing set humankind on the path to separation from God and God's Word, Merton continued with, "It is curiously significant that modern and 'progressive' man should consider himself somehow called upon to vindicate Cain with [Prometheus] whom he has been pleased to make the symbol of his own technological genius and of his cosmic aspirations."[63] Ellul's references to Cain regarding the building of the first city were another metaphor for man's technological hubris.

Continuing with the Promethean myth, Merton compared Prometheus to Christ:

> No one was ever less like Prometheus than Christ on His Cross. For Prometheus thought he had to ascend into heaven and steal what God had already decreed to give him. But Christ, Who had in Himself all the riches of God and all the poverty of Prometheus, came down with the fire Prometheus needed, hidden in His Heart. And He had Himself put to death next to the thief Prometheus in

60. Barth, *Epistle to the Romans*, 236.
61. Merton, *New Man*, 23.
62. Merton, *Behavior of Titans*, 11.
63. Ibid.

order to show him that in reality God cannot seek to keep any-thing good to Himself alone.[64]

Regarding freedom, Merton also added, "We must remember that the truth of Christian teaching culminates in the paradox that all that belongs to me is at the same time fully mine and fully God's"[65] These thoughts provide a link between some of Merton's thoughts on freedom and his literary output, in this case his work on Prometheus. Merton's literature was an extension of his sociological critique.

In contrast to the idea of self-transcendence presented in chapter Merton explained the Promethean attributes of one that sought to affirm the false self rather than attempt to identify one's own true nature. Comparing the prodigal son from the Gospel of Luke 15:11–32 to Prometheus, Merton stated:

> The prodigal has not stolen anything, but he thinks that to "find himself," he must segregate whatever can be classified as "his" and exploit it for his own self-affirmation. His selfishness and his withdrawal are like theft of fire. His sojourn with the swine corresponds to the punishment of Prometheus devoured by the vulture. The prodigal's self-fulfillment, though not spectacular, is still Promethean.[66]

Merton concluded his essay on Prometheus by tying the idea of the true and false self into the story. He wrote:

> Grace is given to us for the precise purpose of enabling us to dis-cover and actualize our deepest and truest self. Unless we discover this deep self, which is hidden with Christ in God, we will never really know ourselves as persons. Nor will we know God. For it is by the door of this deep self that we enter into the spiritual knowl-edge of God. (And indeed, if we seek our true selves it is not in order to contemplate ourselves, but to pass beyond ourselves and find Him.)[67]

This summary ties together a number of ideas that have been presented thus far in this study concerning Merton's thinking on the topic of free dom. The necessity to transcend the self is not proposed in order that we

---

64. Merton *Behavior of Titans*, 22.
65. Merton, *New Man*, 25.
66. Ibid.
67. Ibid., 30.

might have some other notion of the self to contemplate—one that is more "wholesome" or desirable, having achieved this "transcendence." Instead, one transcends the false self—the self that we present to others and that society reinforces through advertising, media, and propaganda—in order to discover God and to achieve the gift of freedom that God has given, and given freely. A final thought from Merton emphasizes the role that Prometheus plays in advancing this argument. "Here again we return to the Promethean tragedy and its inescapable dilemma," Merton wrote, adding, "Prometheus does not want freedom as a gift" but that "he wants to prove himself mature by the conquest of the jealous, secret fathers hidden in the clouds of Olympus."[68] Finally bringing the idea that God's Word represents the "gift" of freedom and not something that one had to steal, Merton wrote:

> The union of the Christian with God is the exact opposite of a Promethean exploit, because the Christian is not trying to steal something from God that God does not want him to have. On the contrary, he is striving with his whole heart to fulfill the will of God and lay hands upon that which God created him to receive. And what is that? It is nothing else but a participation in the life, and wisdom, and joy and peace of God Himself. This is greater than any other gift, higher than any other power. It is supreme freedom, the most perfect fulfillment.[69]

Representative of humankind's desire to push the idea of "progress" as far as it can go, and to allow the force of *technique* to determine the shape of our destiny, the Promethean myth succinctly summarizes Merton's sociological critique.

COMPARATIVE POETRY

Merton and Ellul both believed that the written and spoken word had lost its meaning in a world engulfed in *technique* and awash in visual imagery. They also believed that literature presented an effective means for transmitting their thoughts regarding the human condition, and Merton composed a number of poems that were a part of his critique. For him, poetry was part of his "distinctive mode of cultural criticism" and was expressed "at least as effectively . . . as in his prose."[70] Poetry was a part of Merton's arsenal, while

---

68. Ibid., 31.
69. Ibid., 34.
70. Schneiders, "Merton, Friend of God and Prophet," 81.

Ellul wrote poetry as an escape, a diversion from his constant writing and publishing.

Merton's poem "Figures for an Apocalypse" contains a segment titled "In the Ruins of New York." Presenting a view of the human city that parallels much of Ellul's thinking, Merton certainly is not hoping for or attempting to predict the actual destruction of New York—a city in which he spent a great deal of his life, and in which the poem itself was published. He was rather portraying the city in a manner similar to Ellul's *Meaning of the City*—the lair in which man seeks to build his own world apart from and away from God. Portions of the poem include:

> How are they down, how have they fallen down
> Those great strong towers of ice and steel,
> And melted by what terror and what miracle?
> What fires and light tore down,
> With the white anger of their sudden accusation,
> Those towers of silver and steel?
> ....
> The ashes of leveled towers still curl with tufts of smoke.
> ....
> This was a city
> That dressed herself in paper money.
> She lived four hundred years
> With nickels running in her veins.
> She loved the waters of the seven purple seas,
> And burned on her own green harbor
> Higher and whiter than ever any Tyre.
> She was as callous as a taxi;
> Her high-heeled eyes were sometimes blue as gin,
> And she nailed them, all the days of her life,
> Through the hearts of her six million poor.
> Now she has died in the terrors of a sudden contemplation
> Drowned in the waters of her own, her poisoned well.[71]

Merton's portrayal of New York finds a parallel in Ellul's assertion that Cain built the first city, motivated by a desire to replace the God-given natural

---

71. Merton, "Figures for an Apocalypse."

world with one of his own making. Ellul stated, "Cain has built a city. For God's Eden he substitutes his own, for the goal given to his life by God, he substitutes a goal chosen by himself—just as he substituted his own security for God's. Such is the act by which Cain takes his destiny on his own shoulders, refusing the hand of God in his life."[72] It is this city that Merton believes will collapse, and he uses New York as a metaphor for this idea. Having neglected God and sought to build the Garden of Eden in some earthly realm, both Merton and Ellul believe that man's attempt to live outside of God's realm, rejecting the gift of freedom and in its place worshipping *technique* and progress, will ultimately lead to failure. Ellul composed a number of small poems that portray a similar idea—that humanity's striving for progress is not the panacea that it is often uncritically portrayed. Ellul frequently includes references to environmental degradation and the vanity inherent in our continued quest for progress and *technique's* spread. His work entitled *Oratorio* addresses many of the themes that he spent his life thinking about, to include "nature, technology, death, God, man isolation, and freedom."[73] There are portions of Ellul's *Oratorio* that compare in their focus with Merton's "In the Ruins of New York." Drawn from the third part of *Oratorio*, which is a four-part work patterned on the four horsemen of the apocalypse, these stanzas include:

> *Ah! Quand seront comblés les fossés de ton ame*
> *assainis les marais et construits les remparts*
> *répandus dans la plaine et bunkers et silos—*
> *Élève cette Tour d'où to comptes tes biens!*[74]

> Ah! When will the gaps in your soul be filled
> the swamps drained and the ramparts constructed and
> scattered across the plain with bunkers and silos—
> Erect that tower where you count your wealth![75]

> *Les monceaux de scories restants seuls de ta rage*
> *et seul libre, le vent qui disperse tes biens . . .*
> *Devant tant de richese—regarde donc les mains*

---

72. Ellul, *Meaning of the City*, 5.
73. Lynch, "Poetry of Jacques Ellul," 11.
74. Ellul, *Oratorio*, 47.
75. Lynch, "Poetry of Jacques Ellul," 12.

qui se tendant en vain—reflétant ton image[76]

Only the slag heaps of your rage remain
and, solely free, the wind that scatters your goods …
Before so much wealth—look at your hands
that grasp in vain—reflecting your image[77]

Contemple l'esclavage où tu mist a fortune
Les fleuves avortés les conduits forcées
Et les monts déboisés qui pleurent leur absence
Les filons épuisés et les poches vidées[78]

Consider the slavery in which you place your fortune
The aborted rivers, the forced canals
And the deforested mountains that weep their lack
The exhausted veins and empty pockets.[79]

These three passages capture much of the same critique that Merton ex
pressed in "The Ruins of New York." Directed against humankind's attempt
to not only build a city, but to disregard God's creation in the quest for
progress and gain, Ellul uses poetry in a manner similar to Merton, al
though he wrote these poems only to be published after his death.

Ellul and Merton both specifically referenced the machine in their
poetry. From Ellul:

Mais te voici maintenant soudé à tes machines
et rien ne peut plus dégager de leur destin
La Machine
     elle fonctione—
     elle fonctione de nuit, de jour
Tu te fatigues, tut e crispes tu te tends tut te trompes—
Tu la suis.[80]

---

76. Ellul, *Oratorio*, 47.

77. Lynch, "Poetry of Jacques Ellul," 12.

78. Ellul, *Oratorio*, 47.

79. Lynch, "Poetry of Jacques Ellul," 12.

80. Ellul, *Oratorio*, 48.

But here you are now fused with your machines
And nothing can extricate you from your destiny
The machine
    It operates—
    It operates by night, by day
You grow weary, you grow tense, you strain, you fool yourself—
You follow it.[81]

Merton composed a poem titled "Exploits of a Machine Age," a portion of which mirrors Ellul's thoughts on the power of the machine:

To the protected work
They fled, to the unsafe machinery
They lived by. "It will go better this time,"
We have arranged, at last,
To succeed. Better luck
This time.[82]

Finally referring again to environmental degradation, an issue of great importance to both thinkers, Ellul wrote:

L'homme a dit: "Je produis"—Les richesses écloses
au terme du travail des générations
ont répondu sans frien au viol total des choses—
Detruite la Nature, et l'homme en est caution![83]

Man said: "I produce"—The riches budding
at the end of the toil of generations
responded unchecked to the absolute rape of things
Nature destroyed, and man is the guarantee![84]

Consistent with their upbringings in natural environments and their concern with technological progress destroying the natural world in order that progress might continue to advance unchecked, the natural world was a

81. Lynch, "Poetry of Jacques Ellul," 12.
82. Merton, "Exploits of a Machine Age," 237.
83. Ellul, *Oratorio*, 47.
84. Lynch, "Poetry of Jacques Ellul," 12.

common motif for both men as they composed not only their sociological critiques, but their literature as well.

Other topics which have provided the focus for this study are also found in their poetry. In a passage from his poem titled "The Tower of Ba bel" (1942), Merton illustrates some of his thoughts on propaganda. There are a number of avenues through which this work can be viewed, among them being some of the concepts that previous chapters dealt with in detail. For example, the poem represents "a personal metaphor for Merton in his struggle to integrate his own perceived true and false self. Merton formu lated a theory of spiritual development around the concept of the true/false self. The theory is integral to the Babel works as it links strongly to the themes of truth and illusion within those same works."[85] While propaganda was already discussed in chapter 4, this short stanza reveals a great deal of his thinking on this particular topic. Written in the first years of World War Two, propaganda is obviously a topic of concern. He not only describes the nature of propaganda, but also in the final verses, he shares additional thoughts on the role of the visible church in contemporary society:

> Call propaganda to the stand!
>
> CLERK: Do you swear to conceal the truth, the whole truth and to confuse nothing but the issue?
>
> PROPAGANDA: I do.
>
> LEADER: What is your name?
>
> PROPAGANDA: Legion.
>
> LEADER: Where do you live?
>
> PROPAGANDA: In the heads of the people.
>
> LEADER: What do the people look like?
>
> PROPAGANDA: Zombies.
>
> LEADER: How long have they looked like zombies?
>
> PROPAGANDA: Since we got inside.
>
> LEADER: How did you get inside?
>
> PROPAGANDA: By shots in the arm, by beatings over the head, noises in the ear and all the right kind of medicines.
>
> LEADER: Who destroyed the Tower?

85. O'Sullivan, "Thomas Merton and the Towers of Babel," 13.

PROPAGANDA: The religious warmongers, the clergy, the free-masons, the Pope, the millionaires, the Elders of Zion, the Young Men's Christian Association, the Jesuits and the Legion of Mary.

LEADER: You are a faithful guardian of the Mammoth Democracy, you shall be decorated with the order of the Tower and you shall possess exclusive freedom of speech and worship in every part of the world. Go forth and form the minds of the young. [*Turning to* CLERK] Call Falsehood to the stand.[86]

Describing the building of the Tower of Babel, and its eventual destruction, Merton shares additional thoughts on the city as bulwark against God's will, and humankind's desire to separate themselves from that will. In a later stanza of the poem he wrote:

By the power of its own curse. Cursed by God
Because its builders cursed themselves,
They hated peace, refused the blessing.
They hated to be themselves, hated to be men.
Wanting to be gods, they were made less than themselves.
They might have become gods
If they had designed to remain men.
CHORUS: In one hour, O Babylon,
In one night hour, after so many years,
After so much blood, and so much power,
In one small hour, you lie destroyed.[87]

Revealing their disdain for the technological society in their literature and poetry, both Merton and Ellul offer a pessimistic outlook. Even with their third way proposed as a methodology for transcending *technique's* grip, they continued to critique contemporary society throughout their lives.

In the final analysis, Jacques Ellul offers the harsher and more consistent sociological critique, essentially offering us almost no way out of our predicament. Having spent the majority of his life explaining that the forces of *technique* determined society, and then providing a point-by-point explanation of the ways in which the many aspects of our existence were shaped by this powerful force, he concluded, consistent with the Protestant as opposed to the Catholic viewpoint on such matters, that the technological

86. Merton, "Tower of Babel," 258–59.
87. Ibid., 270.

society could not be so easily transcended. His assessment of *technique* more of an autopsy of contemporary society than any kind of remedy for escaping the grip that it holds on all of us. Some power from outside of the technical system offered the only hope for actually transcending the system. This idea, drawn from the Reformed Protestant tradition, is what one would expect from Ellul.[88] Concerning the completion of the edifice of technical society, he said, "It will not be a universal concentration camp, be cause it will be guilty of no atrocity. It will not be insane, because everything will be ordered . . . we shall have nothing more to lose, and nothing to win . . . we shall be rewarded with everything our hearts ever desired . . . and the supreme luxury of the society of technical necessity will be to grant the bonus of useless revolt and of an acquiescent smile."[89] The Catholic Merton was less severe in his overall appraisal and possibly a bit more lighthearted in the final analysis, allowing for the possibility that human action could lead to humankind's transcending the bonds of *technique*. He saw, "as one might expect a Catholic to see, the new creation constantly appearing in the simple events of nature and human relationships, bearing indelible witness to the grace of God."[90] In the last year of his life, while composing *Cables to the Ace*, he referred to a midget in a stanza of one of his poems, perhaps using the word "midget" to describe his fellow citizens, immersed as they were in the illusion of freedom. He wrote, "'Hats off,' cried the midget. 'Hats off to the human condition!'"[91] A fitting declaration to his contemporaries who were being propelled along in the herd, part of the mass of contempo rary society struggling not only to find their true selves, but even to come to the simple realization that such an act was, in Merton's and Ellul's thinking, a necessary first step on the road to freedom.

---

88. Davenport, "Jacques Ellul and Thomas Merton," 10.

89. Ellul, *Technological Society*, 427.

90. Davenport, "Jacques Ellul and Thomas Merton," 10.

91. Merton, *Cables to the Ace*, 18.

7 Conclusion

Having examined Thomas Merton and Jacques Ellul, what can we conclude about their respective views on the impact that technology has
had on the human condition? Both men believe that technology has the
latent ability to curtail humanity's attainment of freedom, individually and
collectively. Their Christocentric view of the nature of freedom demands
that individuals set aside a blind faith in technology's redemptive power,
frequently expressed in the idea of "progress." Although certain distinctions are apparent when evaluating their critiques through the lens of their
particular faith traditions, the conclusions that they both reach regarding
the impact of technology on the human condition are remarkable similar.

Merton agrees with Ellul's theory that *technique* is the greatest threat
to freedom. *Technique* is manifested in every human endeavor as it seeks
to push the limits of efficiency ever further. This study examined facets of
contemporary society that are most affected by *technique* and the conse-
quent impact that this has had on humanity's ability to attain freedom as
conceptualized in the worldviews of both Merton and Ellul.

There are a number of biographical similarities in the upbringing
of Merton and Ellul that account for the development of their particular
worldviews. Beginning with their births in France in the early twentieth
century to parents of four different nationalities other than French, their
young lives display some remarkable similarities. Their childhood in
non-religious households by artistic parents led them both to come to the
Christian faith through conversions around their twentieth year. Both had
parents that were artists and both considered themselves to have had an
extraordinarily "free" and memorable childhood. Although Merton was
not an only child, he, like Ellul, considered himself to be somewhat of a re-
cluse that enjoyed solitude, contemplation, and reading. They thus provide
examples of a Kierkegaardian maxim that one must "become" a Christian if

one is truly going to live the faith as opposed to being reared in the customs and traditions of the large mass of practicing believers for whom the faith is an outward manifestation of consent to various ideas.

In addition, they both experienced nature and freedom in their youths. These experiences led to a love of nature and fond memories of the natural, untrammeled world. Ellul's provincial upbringing in southwestern France and Merton's many travels throughout the East Coast of the United States, Bermuda, England and France, as well as other countries provided numerous opportunities to interact with the natural environment. Both thinkers held to the idea that it was not in the natural environment that individuals sought to distance themselves from God, but in the city. The city is a contemporary example of *technique* and its deleterious effect on humanity's search for freedom.

It is in a particular definition of freedom that both Merton and El lul approach the subject of technology. One attains freedom through an acceptance of God's grace and a willingness to follow Jesus Christ, living in accordance with the Gospel message. This view of freedom follows a radically different trajectory from that which most Western philosophers have proposed.

Merton and Ellul are not opposed to technology *per se*. Rather, they direct their critique at the uncritical acceptance of technology as a panacea to many contemporary societal shortcomings. This study traced the genesis of this line of thinking through an examination of some of their shared life experiences as well as some of the intellectual antecedents upon which they both relied. Comparing their thought in a number of areas demonstrated that there are many commonalities in their thinking regarding technol ogy's impact on the human condition in contemporary society. Having developed a particular outlook and having situated technology's role in their thinking on the human condition in the twentieth century, this study examined three avenues for evaluating technology's impact on freedom. The first perspective was the theological, followed by the sociological and concluding with an examination of the immanent political perspective. Each of these three avenues presented an intellectual antecedent to their thought, and then proceeded to identify commonalities in their thinking on a point-by-point basis. A sixth chapter provided a look at their thinking on the status of the Word in contemporary society—both the divine Word through which Revelation was made known to man and the human Word.

Within this chapter was also a comparison of both men's writing, including their poetry.

Beginning with the transcendent perspective of their theological worldview, the study considered the influence that Swiss theologian Karl Barth had on their theology. While Barth influenced Ellul to a greater extent than he did Merton, Barth provided both men with an appreciation of the importance of the divine Word as the source of human freedom. In Ellul's case, Barth also revealed the dialectical method—a method that Ellul would employ with great effect in presenting his entire life's work. The theological perspective also considered both Ellul and Merton on the role of the visible and the invisible church. Both men, Ellul a Protestant and Merton, a Roman Catholic, believed that the visible church—the institutional, hierarchical, and physical structures that compose the church in the world, has aligned itself with the forces of *technique* at the expense of focusing solely on promulgating the Gospel message, which is the source of freedom. The invisible church refers to the practices of the faithful, an adherence to and acceptance of the Gospel message, whether individually or in small groups. The path to true freedom is most often found within the invisible church. This is not to imply that Merton and Ellul disparage the visible church *per se*, but they do criticize the visible church for its tendency to pursue efficiency, growth, and expansion for the purposes of its own increased power and prestige.

The next chapter examined their sociological perspective. Presenting Søren Kierkegaard and Aldous Huxley as antecedents, this chapter introduced Merton and Ellul on a number of topics that they believe are significant barriers to attaining freedom. Self-transcendence is an important and crucial first step in attaining freedom, and the chapter began with a look at this idea. Technology serves to further the desires manifest in the false self, hindering our ability to break through the egocentricity that characterizes the members of the crowd. The idea that one must discover the true self is a recurring theme throughout Merton's work. His entry into the monastery in 1941 epitomizes that search, and he dedicated his life and his work to helping others along this path, whether layman or ecclesiastic. Ellul also emphasizes self-transcendence, although not as often or as emphatically. For both thinkers, in order to prepare oneself to follow the Gospel message that introduces the gift of freedom, one must transcend the false self. This occurs through prayer and contemplation—a topic covered in chapter 3. While Merton would stress the mystical elements of contemplation and would eventually turn towards the East in an attempt to understand this mystery, Ellul maintained that mysticism did not offer a true path towards acceptance of the Gospel message. Despite this avowed rejection of mysticism, Merton and Ellul demonstrate an affinity in their thinking on the nature and purpose of prayer, and Ellul even models some of his poetry after the mystical traditions established by Christian mystics such as St. John of the Cross, as shown in chapter 6. In addition, they both rely on the apophatic tradition in describing the God that imparts the gift of freedom. The technological society reinforces and strengthens the false self in many insidious ways, driving those who wish to discover the true self to greater efforts. Both men commented on the insidious nature of propaganda and advertising, and both referred to the twin phenomena of leveling and the mass man. Presented in the nineteenth century by Kierkegaard, both Merton and Ellul refer to these ideas in their writing.

Kierkegaard introduced the idea of "leveling" in the mid-nineteenth century. The Danish philosopher influenced many later thinkers to include both Merton and Ellul. The leveling process created the "mass man," a person caught up in the crowd, especially vulnerable to propaganda. An insidious phenomenon, propaganda institutionalizes Milan Kundera's "nonthought of received ideas." Violence is a part of the human condition, but technique and contemporary technology have exacerbated its effects. While propaganda can serve to further incite the passions that lead to violence and war, Ellul also asserts that the city is a focal point for war.

Ellul notes that propaganda is not necessarily the portrayal of false information as true information, but rather is a methodology for encouraging thought and action along predetermined lines for a predetermined objective. The state might determine these objectives, or even the institutional church, but whatever the case, the mass man is the consumer of propaganda, whether living in the Communist or the Capitalist world.

The Cold War provided a backdrop against which both men were able to express their views on non-violence. It was also at this time, the late 1950s, and early 1960s that Merton's views on *technique's* insidious impact on contemporary society begin to resemble the criticism that Ellul had laid out in *The Technological Society*. Merton's thoughts on America's involvement in Vietnam demonstrate that he had begun to accept Ellul's thinking on the insidious and catastrophic impact that *technique* and the pursuit of efficiency for its own sake was having on the American mindset. He attributed the war effort directly to this phenomenon.

Politically, both men were attracted to Karl Marx, although with varying degrees of enthusiasm. Merton became a communist for a short time while a student at Columbia University. Ellul never joined the party, but both men would later renounce Marxism as a political ideology while still maintaining an affinity for Marx's analysis of the human condition as well as his dialectical methods. Examining Marx and his diagnosis of society's ills led both men to conclude that the systems in place in the US and in the USSR were fundamentally the same—they had both succumbed to *technique* and the worship of progress and efficiency regardless of the consequences. One of the consequences was the possibility of nuclear holocaust. These ideas and the stances that both men took in resisting the propaganda directed at their societies, designed to instill the idea that the enemy must be vanquished at all costs, is reflected in their literature and in their poetry. Chapter 6 compared their literary efforts, which for Merton was a part of his arsenal directed at the technological society, while Ellul wrote as an escape and for personal enjoyment. Regardless of his motives, there are a number of similarities in their style and their poems in many cases reflect similar themes. Of interest in examining Merton's literary criticism, especially his thoughts on Albert Camus and Eugène Ionesco, is the realization that through his reflections on these authors, he indirectly demonstrates his concurrence with Ellul's thoughts on the human condition in the technological society.

Studying Merton and Ellul together has shown that both consider a variety of threats manifest in technology that inhibit humanity's attainment of freedom. They both assert that in order to become truly free, one must transcend the false self. The technological society has put in place a number of obstacles to this objective, to include propaganda, advertising, and the construction of the city, which reinforces the false self and replaces the divine milieu with one of humankind's own making.

Although beyond the scope of this study, there are a number of other avenues for further inquiry relating to similarities between Merton and Ellul. This study abandoned some tangential investigations in order to maintain a balanced approach to the present topic. An examination of both men's thinking and reflection on the non-violence practiced by Mohandas Gandhi was not included, nor was their relationship with the work of American theologian Reinhold Niebuhr. Both of these topics would make interesting studies for those wishing to pursue Merton, Ellul, or both and their relationship to other twentieth-century thinkers in the field of religion and political theory.

Some other areas for further study also emerged. Chapter 3 duced the concept of the sacralization of technology. Additional research on this topic might situate other philosophers and theologians into this debate in order to determine whether this phenomenon is identified by only a small coterie of individuals such as Merton and Ellul, or if it is a more widely shared opinion. If the latter, then are there additional consequences not identified in this paper, for example, might there *technique* also offer a number of positive consequences?

Chapter 5 introduced the Catholic Worker movement and the eco nomic theory of distributism. Mentioned in this section was British journalist and social critic, and Christian apologist G. K. Chesterton. An interesting dissertation topic would be to trace his thoughts on technol ogy and its impact on the human condition, focusing on distributism as a means of transcendence. An anthology of his war letters written for the *Illustrated London News* throughout the First World War also would be a valuable endeavor.

Integrating the perspectives offered by both Merton and Ellul into the panoply of philosophers currently associated with the field of political the ology would be a welcome addition to this emerging discipline. Both men offer a political and theological critique worthy of consideration by those involved in political theology. Whether considering their ideas individually or in tandem, they both have something useful to add to the dialogue.

Finally, there is the question of twenty-first-century thinkers who have continued down the intellectual path traveled by Merton and Ellul. Is there anyone today taking up the clarion call, asserting that *technique* has created its own environment and its own milieu in which one is trapped, unaware that our desires, goals, aspirations, even our own thoughts have been man ufactured for us by the machine? The milieu in which the technological society operates makes Plato's cave seem like a warm and welcoming place, since contemporary society, forged by *technique*, offers almost no chance of escape—no chance to see the light. The very few who have gone on to ac cept the third way of integrity have little hope of being understood by those leveled souls feeding on the preconceived notions that the mass so blindly confuses with thought and with knowledge. The situation is bleak, but for Ellul and Merton the third way at least offers an escape. While they were not interested in attracting followers, it was their hope that others would use their thought as a springboard for further reflection on the human condition. Is there a field of work focusing specifically on the technological society, or has *technique* so thoroughly vanquished humankind that we no longer recognize it, and cannot see past the pitfalls that both Ellul and Merton spent so much of their lives uncovering? Will mass man continue blindly accepting the desires that the system has manufactured for the false selves that make up the leveled mass of humanity? Is there anyone that has carried forth the mantle of defiance? Is there anyone left who will resist the machine?

This study has demonstrated that although many questions remain for contemporary readers and society, Thomas Merton and Jacques Ellul individually and collectively addressed the challenges of technology and the humanities consciously and conscientiously to the best of their abilities. For others that may add to the dialogue, their thoughts provide a foundation from which to begin.

Appendix

Suggested Reading

Both Thomas Merton and Jacques Ellul have been the subject of graduate-level dissertations, many of which were written during their lifetimes. Their thinking has been evaluated through a number of different avenues, and their thought has been compared and contrasted with other intellectuals of their time. However, no full-length study has specifically compared Merton and Ellul. Many of the following books, articles, and dissertations were consulted in preparing this book. Readers may find them of interest when looking for avenues for further reading on either Merton or Ellul, or on technology and society in general.

The Merton Seasonal and *The Merton Annual* have published numerous articles and reviews on Merton's thought, writing, and poetry. The 2000 edition of the *Annual* contains two articles that outline Merton's technological worldview. The first is "The Restoration of Balance: Thomas Merton's Technological Critique" by Phillip M. Thompson. Thompson provides a clear and concise overview of Merton's letters, poetry and writing that focuses on the technological advances that Merton experienced firsthand as the twentieth century progressed. Thompson portrays Merton as one who resisted the unquestioned acceptance of progress, stating that "[Merton's] was a voice of prophetic resistance, advancing an alternative vision to the regnant techno-scientific paradigm of the modern world."[1] Merton's thinking is also contrasted with ideas from Michel Foucault, Hannah Arendt, and Aldo Leopold, in addition to other luminaries that contributed to the debate on technology in the middle of the twentieth century.

---

1. Thompson, "Restoration of Balance," 63.

Also from the 2000 edition of *The Merton Annual* is John Wu's "Tech nological Perspectives: Thomas Merton and the One-Eyed Giant." Wu provides one of the few published comparisons between Merton and Ellul. In this particular article, he examines the impact that they both believed that *technique* has had on the human condition. Wu states specifically that "though undocumented, one could also make the case that [Merton's] reading of Ellul's broadly pungent and dark view of technology and the technician played a part in moderating and finally crystallizing Merton's own position."[2]

Claire Hoertz Badaraco's "The Influence of 'Beat' Generation Poetry on the Work of Thomas Merton" appeared in the 2002 edition of *The Mer ton Annual.* This piece looks at Merton's engagement with various schools of poetry such as Objectivism and the Imagists. Hoertz presents the Thomas Merton that was fully engaged with the world. Examining Merton's engage ment with the secular intelligentsia, even if in many cases he disagreed ve hemently with the approaches taken and the conclusions reached by some of the leading Beat poets, allows one to place Merton in the panoply of cultural critics as well as religious figures. In doing so, Hoertz presents a number of Merton's thoughts and comments on topics such as advertising and propaganda—both important elements that overlap with Jacques El lul's thinking.

"Thomas Merton and the Textuality of the Self: An Experiment in Postmodern Spirituality" by Robert Webster appeared in the University of Chicago's *Journal of Religion* in July 1998. Webster presents the bold thesis that "Merton provides the postmodern age with a text for reading." ster's presentation through this particular lens will allow for a comparison of Merton and Ellul *vis a vis* the postmodernist movement.

Of tremendous benefit to any examination of Merton and technology is Robert Inchausti's *Thomas Merton's American Prophesy* (1998). Inchausti presents Merton's thought in a concise, readable format and in so doing he captures many of the themes relating to Merton's views on technology's impact on freedom. Inchausti is also the author of another invaluable work, *Subversive Orthodoxy: Outlaws, Revolutionaries, and Other Christians in Disguise* (2005). This book presents Merton and Ellul as well as Dorothy Day and other significant figures in the guise of radicals setting themselves

2. Wu, "Technological Perspectives," 89.
3. Webster, "Merton and the Textuality of the Self," 389.

apart from society in order to save it. Inchausti's two books proved to be of enormous value to this study.

Living the Word, Resisting the World (2002), by Andrew Goddard, is subtitled *The Life and Thought of Jacques Ellul*. This comprehensive account of Ellul's writing is an expansion of Goddard's 1995 doctoral dissertation. Widely recognized as one of the most thorough treatments of Ellul's entire corpus, this book focuses specifically on his treatment of law, violence, the state, and politics. Goddard provides an account of some of the formative experiences that led to Ellul's more mature thought on not only these four subjects, but on the development of his theological approach as well as the sociological approach emphasizing *technique*. While most authors and scholars tend to concentrate on the theological or the sociological exclusively, Goddard manages to fuse the two and to examine the points at which they intersect. In addition, Goddard looks at the impact that Ellul's association with the Personalist Movement of the 1930s had on his later thinking. This work "integrates matters too often separated in works on Ellul: his life and his theoretical stances . . . his 'dialogue' with Karl Barth at different stages of his life, and, especially, his sociological and theological writings."[4] It is an indispensable book for any Ellul study.

Marwa Dawn's *Sources and Trajectories: Eight Early Articles by Jacques Ellul* (1997) presents an important addition to the English language corpus on Ellul. Spanning his thoughts on Christianity to his sociological analysis of *technique*, Dawn has selected a range of articles that will provide the general reader with an introduction to Ellul's complex worldview, while at the same time filling some gaps that the Ellul student might encounter when following his thinking along one of his two main trajectories.

Ellul conducted a series of interviews with Madeleine Garrigou-Lagrange, and these sessions were later compiled into *In Season, Out of Season: An Introduction to the Thought of Jacques Ellul* (1982). The chapters that comprise this short work cover the entire spectrum of Ellul's thought— from the sociological to the theological. There is an enormous amount of information that helps illuminate some of the highlights of his entire body of work without having to reference a particular work from within the Ellul panoply.

Russell E. Willis's Emory University doctoral dissertation, "Toward a Theological Ethics of Technology: An Analysis in Dialogue with Jacques Ellul, James Gustafson, and Philosophy of Technology" (1990), provides

---

4. Hanks, review of Goddard, *Living the Word*, 19.

an insight into Ellul's ethical concerns regarding technology. Willis seeks to further Ellul's theological ethics, answering the question of how technology, the concept of *technique*, and more importantly, Ellul's entire corpus, can be seen as an attempt to define a technological ethics. Willis's claim that "self-limitation" is the basis for crafting a technological and theological ethic can be compared to Merton's recommended avenues for achieving libera tion from the homogenized, leveled, mass society. A number of prominent philosophers' definitions of technology are presented in this dissertation, to include Carl Mitcham and Ian Barbour.

Katherine Temple's doctoral dissertation "The Task of Jacques Ellul: A Proclamation of Biblical Faith as Requisite for Understanding the Modern Project" (1976) explores both the sociological and the theological tracks of Ellul's thought. Temple proposes that *technique*, one of the central concepts of Ellul's entire body of work, is not the enemy of man *per se*. Rather, man accepts *technique*, and the technological society arose as a result of man having given it his complete allegiance.

Also of tremendous benefit to this book was the doctoral disserta tion written by Colleen Ann O'Sullivan of Australian Catholic University titled "Thomas Merton and the Towers of Babel" (2006). An exploration of Merton's poetry, specifically focusing on the poem "Tower of Babel," this work helped frame the discussion in chapter 6 on Merton's literary output in general. Sullivan's study deserves careful reading by any scholar writing on Merton today.

Calvin Troup discusses Ellul's contributions to the field of literary the ory and criticism in "Include the Iconoclast: The Voice of Jacques Ellul in Contemporary Theory and Criticism" (1998). Troup explains that Ellul has come out radically against postmodern and post structural theory, claim ing that they are both simply subsets of *technique*. He also illustrates Ellul's *Humiliation of the Word* as one of the only texts in which Ellul crosses the boundary between his body of work on Christianity and the Christian rev elation and the other body of work which almost exclusively remains in the realm of sociology, dealing with the phenomenon of *technique*.

Randy Kluver's *Contributions of Jacques Ellul's "Propaganda" to Teach ing and Research in Rhetorical Theory* (1995) makes the case that Ellul's oft-cited study of the nature of modern propaganda should be included in the pantheon of literature with which students of rhetorical theory should become familiar. Kluver states that as a thinker who has had an enormous impact in the fields of sociology, philosophy, and critical theory, Ellul should be included with others such as Marcuse and McLuhan in any survey of rhetorical theory and criticism. Kluver cites *Propaganda* as a major contributor to our understanding of the relevance of propaganda's impact on social life and politics.

The Ellul Forum has been published quarterly since 1988. Its purpose is to analyze and apply Ellul's thought to aspects of today's society. It is important to note that the editors do not consider Ellul's writing to be a canon of sacred literature. Rather, all of Ellul's writing should be considered as the beginning of a conversation. In that spirit, a number of articles appearing in *The Ellul Forum* are pertinent to this particular study. Gene Davenport's *Jacques Ellul and Thomas Merton on Technique* (July 1991) is an excellent overview of the similarities that Ellul and Merton demonstrate in their critique of modern civilization. Davenport draws out the idea that for both Ellul and Merton, the products that modern technology has furnished are only the most visible manifestation of the technical phenomenon. He also notes that Merton, like Ellul, believes that the technical phenomenon has reached a point in which humans serve the technical process rather than vice versa.

Also in the July 1991 edition of *The Ellul Forum* is Jeff Dietrich's *Jacques Ellul and the Catholic Worker of the Next Century*. This survey provides some interesting parallels between Ellul's thinking and some of the Catholic philosophers that most influenced Merton, such as Pierre Teilhard de Chardin. Although Ellul comes to us from the Protestant tradition, his expansive reading and synthesizing of ideas regarding Christianity comes to us through having evaluated religious thinkers from across the entire Christian spectrum.

Another article from *The Ellul Forum* comes from Phillip M. Thompson. *Jacques Ellul's Influence on the Cultural Critique of Thomas Merton* (July 2000) discusses in detail some of the antecedents to Merton's thinking regarding the impact of technology, regulation, machines, and the attendant changes in our mentality and our outlook which have a direct, and for the most part, a degenerative impact, on what Merton would consider the authentic expression of faith and belief.

Continuing the exploration of Merton in *The Ellul Forum*, the entire July 1998 edition is devoted to Thomas Merton's critique of technological civilization. This edition provides a tremendous amount of material that will help shed not only some light on Merton's own thinking on this subject, but will point to a number of similarities between Merton and Ellul and some of the intellectual antecedents to their thinking. Christopher J. Kelly's "Contemptus Mundi: Thomas Merton's Critique of Technological Civilization" is one such article in the July 1998 edition. Kelly presents the thesis that "Merton's experience of the *via negativa*, as reflected in his book *The Sign of Jonas*, led him into a post-modern framework from which came his critique of society."[5]

Gerald Walters' and Kenneth Hudson's *Technology and Society* is a compilation of papers presented at the first Bath Conference in the United Kingdom. The express aim of this conference was to "state the most urgent problems in broad terms, ranging widely from questions of ethics and the new opportunities for leisure of a technological society, to more specific problems of social, political and economic organization."[6] papers presented at the conference, one titled "The Christian Tradition and the modern Predicament" by Kenneth Grayston stands out as particularly relevant to this dissertation.

Carl Mitcham's *Thinking through Technology: The Path between En gineering and Philosophy* (1994) provides a vantage point from which one can begin to conceptualize the debate concerning the role of technology in modern society. Mitcham hopes to provide "a critical introduction to the philosophy of technology."[7] The approach that Mitcham employs to differentiate two distinct viewpoints on the philosophy of technology is to examine this phenomenon through two separate lenses. The first is the humanities philosophy of technology, which is followed by the engineer ing philosophy of technology. Within the section of the book dealing with the humanities philosophy of technology, Mitcham elaborates at length on Jacques Ellul's contribution to the debate on technology's impact on the human condition, a debate which Mitcham describes as having essentially begun in America in 1963 at a workshop sponsored by the Catholic Uni versity of America titled "Philosophy in a Technological Culture."[8] Accord ing to Mitcham, Ellul asserted that technology was the "autonomous and defining characteristic of modern society."[9] Mitcham goes on to compare and contrast a number of the leading thinkers who have contributed to the debate on technology, to include German Philosopher Martin Heidegger,

---

5. Kelly, "Contemptus Mundi," 3.

6. Walters and Hudson, *Technology and Society*, 2.

7. Mitcham, *Thinking through Technology*, ix.

8. Ibid.

9. Ibid.

the Spanish philosopher Ortega y Gasset, the American philosopher and urban planner Lewis Mumford and of course French philosopher Jacques Ellul.

Phillip M. Thompson's *Between Science and Religion: The Engagement of Catholic Intellectuals with Science and Technology in the Twentieth Century* (2009) presents the reader with four Catholic intellectuals and their contribution to the continuing debate between Rome and the modern world. Of the four, the chapter on Thomas Merton and his contemplative response to the challenges posed by technology was important in situating Merton's thoughts on the topic with not only Ellul but with Mumford and other intellectuals. Thompson's excellent *Returning to Reality: Thomas Merton's Wisdom for a Technological Age* is one of the best primers on Merton's thought on the topic of technology.

Ian Barbour's *Religion and Science* (1997) provides an overview of the relationship between theology and technology. Focusing on the interaction between science and religion, Barbour helps to situate Ellul and Merton within the greater philosophical debate on theology's role in a technological society.

Finally, Albert Borgmann's *Power Failure: Christianity in the Culture of Technology* (2003) provides some interesting avenues for further inquiry, and for the further study of the relationship not only between Merton and Ellul on technology and freedom, but between technology and the human condition in general. Borgmann describes technology as an invisible culture, and many of his ideas, presented in the early twenty first century, are similar to those proposed by Merton and Ellul almost a half century ago.

Bibliography

Adams, Daniel J. *Thomas Merton's Shared Contemplation: A Protestant Perspective*. Kalamazoo, MI: Cistercian, 1979.

Adams, Geoffrey. *Political Ecumenism: Catholics Jews and Protestants in DeGaulle's Free France: 1940–1945*. Quebec: McGill-Queens University Press, 2006.

Aubert, Phillipe. Review of *Dieu Anonyme; ou, la Peur des Mots*, by Gabriel Vahanian. *Ellul Forum* 5 (1990) 5–6.

Bacevich, Andrew J. *The Imperial Tense*. Chicago: Dee, 2003.

———. "Selling Our Souls: Of Idolatry and iPhones." *Commonweal* (2011) 11–13.

Badaraco, Claire Hoertz. "The Influence of 'Beat' Generation Poetry on the Work of Thomas Merton." *Merton Annual* 15 (2002) 121–35.

Bailey, Raymond. *Thomas Merton on Mysticism*. Garden City, NY: Image, 1987.

Baker, James Thomas. *Thomas Merton: Social Critic*. Lexington: University of Kentucky Press, 1971.

Barth, Karl. *Die Christliche Dogmatic im Entwurf*. Vol. 1, *Die Lehre vom Worte Gottes, Prologomena zur christlichen Dogmatic*. Munich: Kaiser, 1927.

———. *The Epistle to the Romans*. Translated by Edwyn C. Hoskyns. London: Oxford University Press, 1933.

———. *Ethics*. Translated by Geoffrey W. Bromiley. New York: Seabury, 1981.

———. *God Here and Now*. Translated by Paul M. Van Buren. New York: Routledge Classics, 2003.

———. *The Word of God and the Word of Man*. Translated by Douglas Horton. New York: Harper & Row, 1957.

Barth, Karl, and Eduard Thurneysen. *Revolutionary Theology in the Making: Barth-Thurneysen Correspondence, 1914–1925*. Translated by James D. Smart. Richmond, VA: John Knox, 1928.

Berger, Rose Marie. "Personal, Prolific, Provocative." *Merton Seasonal* 34 (2009) 29–32.

Berry, Wendell. "A Citizen's Response." In *The Imperial Tense*, edited by Andrew Bacevich, 229–38. Chicago: Dee, 2003.

Bochen, Christine M. "Sowing Seeds of Contemplation and Compassion: Merton's Emerging Social Consciousness." *Merton Seasonal* 35 (2010) 17–27.

Bochen, Christine M., and William Shannon, eds. *Thomas Merton: A Life in Letters—The Essential Collection*. San Francisco: HarperOne, 2008.

Borgmann, Albert. *Power Failure: Christianity in the Culture of Technology*. Grand Rapids: Brazos, 2003.

Brée, Germaine. *Camus: A Collection of Critical Essays*. Englewood Cliffs, NJ: Prentice Hall, 1962.

Bretall, Robert. *A Kierkegaard Anthology*. Princeton: Princeton University Press,

Bromiley, Geoffrey W. *Introduction to the Theology of Karl Barth*. Grand Rapids: Eerdmans, 1979.

Burke, John David. "Jacques Ellul: Theologian and Social Critic." PhD diss., Washington State University, 1980.

Busch, Eberhard. *Karl Barth: His Life from Letters and Autobiographical Texts*. Philadelphia, Fortress, 1975.

Clancy, William. "Karl Barth and Thomas Merton: Grace as Demand." *Worldview* (1969) 11–12.

Clenendin, Daniel B. *Theological Method in Jacques Ellul*. London: University Press of America, 1987.

Clooney, Francis X. "Karl Barth, Thomas Merton: 40 Years Later." *America*, 5 December 2008. http://americamagazine.org/content/all-things/karl-barth-thomas-merton-40-years-later.

Coates, A. J. *The Ethics of War*. Manchester, UK: Manchester University Press, 1997

Cooney, Anthony. *Distributism*. London: Third Way, 2001.

Cornell, Thomas C., et al., eds. *A Penny a Copy: Readings from "The Catholic Worker*. Maryknoll: Orbis, 1995.

Cotgrove, Stephen. "Technology, Rationality and Domination." *Social Studies of Science* 5 (975) 55–78.

Crawford, Matthew B. *Shop Class as Soulcraft: An Inquiry into the Value of Work* York: Penguin, 2009.

Creegan, Nicola Hoggard. Review of *The Technological Bluff*, by Jacques Ellul. *Ellul Forum* 7 (1991) 2–3.

Cunningham, Lawrence. *Thomas Merton and the Monastic Vision*. Grand Rapids: Eerdmans, 1999.

Davenport, Gene. "Jacques Ellul and Thomas Merton on Technique." *Ellul Forum* 10–12.

Dekar, Paul. "What the Machine Produces and What the Machine Destroys: Thomas Merton on Technology." *Merton Annual* 17 (2004) 216–34.

Dietrich, Jeff. "Jacques Ellul and the Catholic Worker of the Next Century." *Ellul Forum* 7 (1991) 5–9.

Douglas, James W. *JFK and the Unspeakable*. New York: Touchstone, 2008.

———. "On Transcending Technique." In *Introducing Jacques Ellul*, edited by James Holloway, 139–47. Grand Rapids, Eerdmans 1970.

Elie, Paul. *The Life You Save May Be Your Own*. New York: Farrar, Straus & Giroux,

Ellul, Jacques. "Be Reconciled." Translated by Joyce Main Hanks. *Ellul Forum* 2–3.

———. "The Betrayal by Technology: A Portrait of Jacques Ellul." Transcript of an interview by Jan van Boeckel. 1992. http://www.archive.org/details/JacquesEllul-TheBetrayalByTechnology-EnglishTranscript.

———. "Between Chaos and Paralysis." *Christian Century* 85 (1968) 747–50.

———. *A Critique of the New Commonplaces*. Translated by Helen Weaver. New York: Knopf, 1968.

———. "Delineating the Ideologies of Science." *Graduate Faculty Philosophy Journal* (1987) 251–67.

———. *The Ethics of Freedom.* Translated by Geoffrey W. Bromiley. Grand Rapids: Eerdmans, 1976.

———. *The Humiliation of the Word.* Translated by Joyce Main Hanks. Grand Rapids: Eerdmans, 1985.

———. *In Season, Out of Season.* Translated by Lani K. Niles. San Francisco: Harper & Row, 1982.

———. "Karl Barth and Us." *Sojourners* (1978) 22–24.

———. "Mirror of These Ten Years." *Christian Century* 87 (1970) 200–204.

———. *Money and Power.* Translated by LaVonne Neff. Downers Grove: InterVarsity, 1984.

———. *The New Demons.* Translated by C. Edward Hopkin. New York: Seabury, 1975.

———. *Oratorio.* Bordeaux: Opales, 1997.

———. "The Paradox of Anarchism and Christianity." *Ellul Forum* 3 (1989) 5–6.

———. *Perspectives on Our Age.* Edited by William H. Vanderburg. Translated by Joachim Neugroschel. New York: Seabury, 1981.

———. *The Political Illusion.* Translated by Konrad Kellen. New York: Knopf, 1967.

———. *Prayer and Modern Man.* Translated by C. Edward Hopkin. New York: Seabury, 1970.

———. *The Presence of the Kingdom.* Translated by Olive Wyon. London: SCM, 1951.

———. *Propaganda: The Formation of Men's Attitudes.* Translated by Konrad Kellen and Jean Lerner. New York: Vintage, 1965.

———. *Reason for Being.* Translated by Joyce Main Hanks. Grand Rapids: Eerdmans, 1990.

———. *Sources & Trajectories.* Translated by Marva J. Dawn. Grand Rapids: Eerdmans, 1997.

———. *The Subversion of Christianity.* Translated by Geoffrey W. Bromiley. Grand Rapids: Eerdmans, 1986.

———. "Technique and the Opening Chapters of Genesis." In *Theology and Technology*, edited by Carl Mitcham and Jim Grote, 123–37. Lanham, MD: University of America Press, 1984.

———. *The Technological Bluff.* Translated by Geoffrey W. Bromiley. Grand Rapids: Eerdmans, 1990.

———. *The Technological Society.* Translated by John Wilkerson. New York: Vintage, 1964.

———. *The Technological System.* Translated by Joachim Neugroschel. New York: Continuum, 1980.

———. "Technology and the Gospel." *International Review of Mission* 66 (1977) 109–17.

———. *To Will and to Do.* Translated by C. Edward Hopkin. Boston: Pilgrim, 1969.

———. *Violence; Reflections from a Christian Perspective.* Translated by Cecelia Gaul Kings. New York: Seabury, 1969.

———. *What I Believe.* Translated by Geoffrey W. Bromiley. Grand Rapids: Eerdmans, 1989.

Ellul, Jacques, and Patrick Troude-Chastenet. *Jacques Ellul on Politics, Technology, and Christianity.* Translated by Joan Mendes-France. Eugene, OR: Wipf & Stock, 2005.

Farrell, James J. "Thomas Merton and the Religion of the Bomb." *Religion and American Culture: A Journal of Interpretation* 5 (1995) 77–98.

Faggen, Robert. *Striving towards Being: The Letters of Thomas Merton and Czeslaw Milosz.* New York: Farrar, Strauss & Giroux, 1997.

Fasching, Darrell J. "In This Issue: Jacques Ellul as a Theologian for Catholics." *Ellul Forum* 7 (1991) 1.

———. *The Thought of Jacques Ellul: A Systematic Exposition*. New York: Mellen,

Fiala, Andrew. *The Just War Myth*. New York: Rowman & Littlefield, 2008.

Finley, James. *Merton's Palace of Nowhere*. Notre Dame: Ave Maria, 1978.

Forest, Jim. "A Friendship of Letters: On the Correspondence between Thomas Merton and Dorothy Day." *Touchstone* 25 (2011) 58–63.

Fox, Richard Wrightman. *Reinhold Niebuhr: A Biography*. San Francisco: Harper & Row, 1985.

Furlong, Monica. *Merton: A Biography*. San Francisco: Harper & Row, 1980.

Gaddis, John Lewis. *The Cold War: A New History*. New York: Penguin, 2005.

Gill, David W. "The Dialectic of Theology and Sociology in Jacques Ellul." Paper presented at the American Academy of Religion Annual Meeting, Chicago, November

———. "Jacques Ellul's Ethics: Legacy and Promise." *Ellul Forum* 39 (2007) 3–9.

———. *The Word of God in the Ethics of Jacques Ellul*. Metuchen, NJ: Scarecrow,

Gilson, Etienne. *The Spirit of Medieval Philosophy*. Translated by A. H. C. Downes. New York: Scribner, 1936.

Goddard, Andrew. "Ellul on Scripture and Idolatry." *Ellul Forum* 36 (1995) 6–9.

———. "Ellul on Violence and Just War." *Ellul Forum* 32 (2003) 3–7.

———. *Living the Word, Resisting the World*. Cumbria, UK: Paternoster, 2002.

Grant, George. Review of *The Technological Society*, by Jacques Ellul. In vol. 3 of *Collected Works of George Grant*, edited by Arthur Davis and Henry Roper, 416–17. Toronto: Toronto University Press, 2005.

Grayston, Donald. "The Making of a Spiritual Classic: Thomas Merton's Seeds of Contemplation and New Seeds of Contemplation." *Studies in Religion/Sciences Religeuses* 3 (1974) 339–56.

Green, Clifford, ed. *Karl Barth: Theologian of Freedom*. Minneapolis: Fortress, 1991

Gruden, Wayne. *Systematic Theology: An Introduction to Biblical Doctrine*. Grand Rapids: Zondervan, 1994.

Gustafson, James M. "Theology Confronts Technology and the Life Sciences." *Commonweal* (1978) 386–92.

Hanks, Joyce. *The Reception of Jacques Ellul's Critique of Technology: An Annotated Bibliography of Writings on His Life and Thought*. New York: Mellen, 2007.

———. Review of *Living the Word, Resisting the World*, by Andrew Goddard. *Ellul Forum* 20 (1998) 19–20.

Hart, Brother Patrick, *The Literary Essays of Thomas Merton*. New York: New Directions, 1984.

———, ed. *The Message of Thomas Merton*. Kalamazoo, MI: Cistercian, 1981.

Henry, Carl F. H. *God, Revelation and Authority*. Vol. 3, *God Who Speaks and Shows* Waco, TX: Word, 1979.

Hollinger, Dennis P. *Choosing the Good: Christian Ethics in a Complex World* Rapids: Baker, 2002.

Horne, Alistair. *A Savage War of Peace: Algeria, 1954–1962*. London: MacMillan,

Huxley, Aldous. *Ends & Means*. London: Chatto & Windus, 1940.

———. *The Perennial Philosophy*. New York: Harper & Row, 1944.

Inchausti, Robert. *Subversive Orthodoxy: Outlaws, Revolutionaries, and Other Christians in Disguise*. Grand Rapids: Brazos, 2005.

―――. *Thomas Merton's American Prophecy*. New York: State University of New York Press, 1998.

Ionesco, Eugène. *Notes et Contre Notes*. Paris: Gallimard, 1975.

―――. *Rhinoceros*. New York: Calder, 1960.

James, William. *The Varieties of Religious Experience*. New York: New American Library of World Literature, 1958.

Kant, Immanuel. *Religion within the Limits of Reason Alone*. Translated by Theodore M. Greene and Hoyt H. Hudson. New York: Harper & Brothers, 1960.

Karnow, Stanley. *Vietnam: A History*. New York: Penguin, 1997.

Kelly, Christopher J. "Thomas Merton's Critique of Technological Civilization." *Ellul Forum* 21 (1998) 3–13.

Kierkegaard, Søren. *The Present Age*. Translated by Alexander Dru. New York: Harper & Row, 1962.

Kilner, John F. "Physician-Assisted Suicide: Today, Yesterday and Tomorrow." In *Suicide: A Christian Response*, edited by Timothy J. Demy and Gary P. Stewart, 129–41. Grand Rapids: Kregel, 1998.

Kline, Francis. "In the Company of Prophets? Merton's Engagement with the World." *Merton Annual* 12 (1999) 117–28.

Kramer, Victor. *Thomas Merton: Monk and Artist*. Boston: Twayne, 1984.

Kluver, Randy. "Contributions of Jacques Ellul's 'Propaganda' to Teaching and Research in Rhetorical Theory." Paper presented at the 81st Annual Meeting of the Speech Communication Association, San Antonio, November 1995.

Konyndyk, Kenneth J. "Violence." In *Jacques Ellul: Interpretive Essays*, edited by Clifford G. Christians & Jay M. Van Hook, 251–69. Chicago: University of Illinois Press, 1981.

Kuhns, William. *The Post-Industrial Prophets: Interpretations of Technology*. New York: Harper & Row, 1971.

Kundera, Milan. *The Art of the Novel*. New York: Harper & Row, 1988.

Labrie, Ross. *The Art of Thomas Merton*. Fort Worth: Texas Christian University Press, 1979.

―――. "Thomas Merton on Marx and Marxism." *Merton Seasonal* 35 (2010) 3–14.

―――. "Thomas Merton on the Unspeakable." *Merton Seasonal* 36 (2011) 3–11.

Leclerq, Dom Jean. *The Love of Learning and the Desire for God*. Translated by Catherine Misrahi. New York: Fordham University Press, 1961.

Lee, David. "Taking Merton to Work." *Merton Seasonal* 34 (2009) 31–35.

Lester, Julius. "The Revolution: Revisited." In *Introducing Jacques Ellul*, edited by James Holloway, 91–123. Grand Rapids: Eerdmans 1970.

Lilla, Mark. "The Persistence of Political Theology." *Current History* 107 (2008): 41–46.

Lipski, Alexander. *Thomas Merton and Asia*. Kalamazoo, MI: Cistercian, 1983.

Lovekin, David. *Technique, Discourse and Consciousness: An Introduction to the Philosophy of Jacques Ellul*. Cranbury, NJ: Associated Press, 1991.

Lynch, James. "The Poetry of Jacques Ellul." *Ellul Forum* 22 (1999) 11–14.

Marcuse, Herbert. *One Dimensional Man*. Boston: Beacon, 1964.

Marlin, Randall. *Propaganda & the Ethics of Persuasion*. Peterborough, Ontario: Broadview, 2002.

Massa, Mark. "Young Man Merton: Erik Erikson, the Mountains of Purgatory, and the Post-War 'Catholic Revival.'" *U.S. Catholic Historian* 15 (1997) 107–25.

Matheson, T. J. "Marcuse, Ellul, and the Science Fiction Film: Negative Responses to Technology." *Science-Fiction Studies* 19 (1992) 326–39.

Menninger, David C. "Jacques Ellul: A Tempered Profile." *Review of Politics* 37 235–46.

———. "Marx in the Social Thought of Jacques Ellul." In *Jacques Ellul: Interpretive Essays* edited by Clifford G. Christians and Jay M. Van Hook, 17–32. Chicago: University of Illinois Press, 1981.

———. "Political Dislocation in a Technical Universe." *Review of Politics* 42 (1980

———. "Politics or Technique? A Defense of Jacques Ellul." *Polity* 14 (1981) 110

Merton, Thomas. "Albert Camus and the Church." In *A Penny a Copy*, edited by Thomas C. Cornell et al., 150–63. Maryknoll: Orbis, 1995.

———. "The Angel and the Machine." *Merton Seasonal* 22 (1997) 3–6.

———. *The Ascent to Truth*. New York: Harcourt, Brace, 1951.

———. *The Behavior of Titans*. New York: New Directions, 1961.

———. *Cables to the Ace*. Silver City, NM: Unicorn, 1968.

———. "Chant to Be Used around a Site with Furnaces." In *The Collected Poems of Thomas Merton*. New York: New Directions, 1977.

———. *The Cold War Letters*. Edited by William H. Shannon and Christine M. Bochen. Maryknoll: Orbis, 2008.

———. *The Collected Poems of Thomas Merton*. New York: New Directions, 1977

———. *Conjectures of a Guilty Bystander*. Garden City, NY: Doubleday, 1966.

———. *Dancing in the Waters of Life*. Edited by Robert E. Daggy. San Francisco: HarperCollins, 1997.

———. *Disputed Questions*. New York: Harcourt Brace Jovanovich, 1960.

———. *Emblems of a Season of Fury*. New York: New Directions, 1961.

———. "Figures for an Apocalypse." In *Collected Poems of Thomas Merton*. New York: New Directions, 1977.

———. *The Geography of Lograire*. New York: New Directions, 1968.

———. *The Inner Experience: Notes on Contemplation*. Edited by William Shannon. San Francisco: HarperCollins, 2003.

———. *The Literary Essays of Thomas Merton*. Edited by Patrick Hart. New York: New Directions, 1960.

———. *Love and Living*. Edited by Naomi Burton Stone and Patrick Hart. New York: Farrar, Straus & Giroux, 1979.

———. *Mystics and Zen Masters*. New York: Noonday, 1961.

———. *The New Man*. New York: Farrar, Straus & Giroux, 1961.

———. *New Seeds of Contemplation*. New York: New Directions, 1961.

———. *Raids on the Unspeakable*. New York: New Directions, 1966.

———. "Religion and the Bomb." *Jubilee* 10 (1962) 7–13.

———. Review of *Camus: Journal of the Plague Years*, by Albert Camus. In *Review* 75 (1967) 717–30.

———. Review of *The Technological Society*, by Jacques Ellul. In *Commonweal* 81 357.

———. *The Secular Journal of Thomas Merton*. New York: Farrar, Straus & Giroux,

———. *Seeds of Contemplation*. New York: New Directions, 1949.

———. *Seeds of Destruction*. New York: Farrar, Straus, and Giroux, 1961.

———. *The Seven Storey Mountain*. New York: Harcourt, Brace, 1948.

———. *The Silent Life*. New York: Farrar, Strauss & Giroux, 1957.

———. *Thomas Merton: A Vow of Conversation*. Edited by Naomi Burton Stone. New York: Farrar, Strauss & Giroux, 1988.

———. "The Tower of Babel." In *The Collected Poems of Thomas Merton*. New York: New Directions, 1977.

———. *Turning toward the World*. Edited by Victor A. Kramer. San Francisco: HarperCollins, 1996.

———. "War and the Crisis of Language." In *The Nonviolent Alternative*. Edited by Gordon C. Zahn. Rev. ed. *Thomas Merton on Peace*. New York: Farrar, Straus & Giroux, 1980.

———. *Zen and the Birds of Appetite*. New York: New Directions, 1968.

Mill, John Stewart. *The Collected Works of John Stuart Mill*. Vol. 10, *Essays on Ethics, Religion and Society*. Edited by John M. Robson. Originally published 1833. http://oll.libertyfund.org/index.php?option=com_staticxt&staticfile=show. php%3Ftitle=241&Itemid=27.

Miller, Duane Russell. "The Effect of Technology upon Humanization in the Thought of Lewis Mumford and Jacques Ellul." PhD diss., Boston University, 1970.

Mitcham, Carl. "Jacques Ellul and his Contribution to Theology." *Cross Currents* 35 (2005) 1–8.

———. *Thinking through Technology: The Path between Engineering and Philosophy*. Chicago: University of Chicago Press, 1994.

Mitcham, Carl, and Jim Grote, eds. "Technology as a Theological Problem in the Christian Tradition." In *Theology and Technology: Essays in Christian Analysis and Exegesis*. Lanham, MD: University Press of America, 1984.

Moore, Rick Clifton. "Environmental Issues and the Watchdog Role of the Media: How Ellul's Theory Complicates Liberal Democracy." *Bulletin of Science, Technology & Society* 21 (2001) 325–33.

Mueller, David L. *Karl Barth*. Waco, TX: Word, 1972.

Mumford, Lewis. *Myth of the Machine*. Vol. 1, *Technics and Human Development*. New York: Harcourt Brace Jovanovich, 1967.

Musto, Ronald. *The Catholic Peace Tradition*. Maryknoll: Orbis, 1986.

Nielsen, Kai. "Technology as Ideology." In *Research in Philosophy & Technology*, edited by Paul Durbin, 131–48. Greenwich, CT: JAI, 1978.

Nouwen, Henri M. *Thomas Merton: Contemplative Critic*. San Francisco: Harper & Row, 1972.

O'Connell, Patrick F. "Communism." In *The Thomas Merton Encyclopedia*, by William H. Shannon et al., 71–73. Maryknoll: Orbis, 2002.

O'Grady, Colm. *A Survey of the Theology of Karl Barth*. New York: Corpus, 1968.

O'Sullivan, Colleen Ann. "Thomas Merton and the Towers of Babel." PhD diss., Australian Catholic University, 2006.

Padovano, Anthony T. *The Human Journey: Thomas Merton, Symbol of a Century*. Garden City, NY: Image, 1984.

Paul, Gerard. "New Metamorphoses of Bourgeois Society." *Ellul Forum* 33 (2004) 12–17.

Pearce, Joseph. *Literary Converts*. San Francisco: Ignatius, 2000.

Pennington, M. Basil. *Toward an Integrated Humanity: Thomas Merton's Journey*. Kalamazoo, MI: Cistercian, 1987.

———. *Thomas Merton, My Brother*. London: Cistercian Abbey of Spencer, 1996.

Pope Leo XIII. *On the Condition of the Working Classes (Rerum Novarum)*. 15 May 1891. Papal Archive. The Holy See.

Porquet, Jean-Luc. *Jacques Ellul: l'homme qui avait presque tout prevu*. Paris: Le Cherche Midi, 2003.

Porter, J. S. *Thomas Merton: Hermit at the Heart of Things*. Ottawa: Novalis, 2008

Potter, Vincent G. "Karl Barth and the Ontological Argument." *Journal of Religion* (1965) 309–25.

Pramuk, Christopher. *Sophia: The Hidden Christ of Thomas Merton*. Collegeville: Liturgical, 2009.

Punzo, Vincent. "Jacques Ellul on the Technical System and the Challenge of Christian Hope." *Proceedings of the American Catholic Philosophical Association* 70 17–31.

Real, Michael R. "Mass Communication and Propaganda in Technological Societies." In *Jacques Ellul: Interpretive Essays*, edited by Clifford G. Christians and Jay M. Van Hook, 108–25. Chicago: University of Illinois Press, 1981.

Reardon, Patrick Henry. "A Many-Storied Monastic: A Critical Memoir of Thomas Merton at Gethsemani Abbey." *Touchstone* 25 (2011) 50–57.

Reed, Gerard. "Thomas Merton's Concept of Sanctification." *Wesleyan Theological Journal* 18 (1983) 90–99.

Rice, Edward. *The Man in the Sycamore Tree*. New York: Doubleday, 1972.

Richardson, Hedy Louise. "Hope in an Age of Despair: The Social Thought of Wendell Berry and Jacques Ellul." EdD diss., Pennsylvania State University, 1997.

Scheske, Eric. "The Conservative Convert: The Life and Faith of Russell Kirk." *Touchstone* 16 (2003). http://www.touchstonemag.com/archives/article.php?id=16-05-041

Schneiders, Sandra. "Merton, Friend of God and Prophet." *Merton Annual* 7 (1994

Scott, Peter, and Walter T. Cavanaugh, eds. *The Blackwell Companion to Political Theology* Malden, MA: Blackwell, 2004.

Scruggs, Ryan. "Faith Seeking Understanding: Thomas Merton's Interest in Karl Barth." MA diss., McGill University, 2009.

Shannon, William H. "Can One Be a Contemplative in a Technological Society?" *Seasonal* 22 (1997) 12–20.

———, ed. *Thomas Merton: Witness to Freedom*. San Francisco: Harcourt, Brace,

———. *Thomas Merton's Paradise Journey: Writing on Contemplation*. Turnbridge Wells, UK: Burns & Oates, 1981.

Shannon, William H., et al. *The Thomas Merton Encyclopedia*. Maryknoll: Orbis,

Silva, Sergio. "Notes on the Catholic Church and Technology." *Ellul Forum* 5 (1990

Son, Wha-Chul. "Reading Jacques Ellul's *The Technological Bluff* in Context." *Bulletin of Science, Technology & Society* 24 (2004) 518–33.

Süssman, Cornelia, and Irving Süssman. *Thomas Merton*. New York: Image, 1980

Teaghan, John F. "A Dark and Empty Way: Thomas Merton and the Apophatic Tradition." *Journal of Religion* 58 (1978) 263–87.

Temple, Katherine C. "Born Again Catholic Workers." Interview by Jeff Dietrich. *Forum* 7 (1991) 7–9.

———. "Jacques Ellul: A Catholic Worker Vision of the Culture." *Ellul Forum* 6–7.

———. "The Task of Jacques Ellul: A Proclamation of Biblical Faith as Requisite for Understanding the Modern Project." PhD diss., McMaster University, 1976

Thompson, Phillip M. *Between Science and Religion: The Engagement of Catholic Intellectuals with Science and Technology in the Twentieth Century*. New York: Lexington, 2009.

———. "Jacques Ellul's Influence on the Cultural Critique of Thomas Merton." *Forum* 25 (2000) 10–16.

———. "The Restoration of Balance: Thomas Merton's Technological Critique." *Merton Annual* 13 (2000) 63–79.

———. *Returning to Reality: Thomas Merton's Wisdom for a Technological World.* Eugene, OR: Cascade, 2012.

Troude-Chastenet, Patrick. "Jacques Ellul: On Religion, Technology and Politics." *Ellul Forum* 22 (1999) 3–10.

Troup, Calvin. "Include the Iconoclast: The Voice of Jacques Ellul in Contemporary Theory and Criticism." *Journal of Communication and Religion* 21 (1998) 22–46.

Tucker, Robert C., ed. *The Marx-Engels Reader.* New York: Norton, 1965.

Vahanian, Gabriel. "Technology, Politics, and the Christian Faith." In *Introducing Jacques Ellul,* edited by James Holloway, 51–63. Grand Rapids: Eerdmans, 1970.

Vanderburg, Willem H. "The Essential Connection between the Two Parts of the Work of Jacques Ellul." *Bulletin of Science, Technology & Society* 24 (2004) 534–47.

———. "How the Science versus Religion Debate Has Missed the Point of Genesis 1 and 2: Jacques Ellul (1912–1994)." *Bulletin of Science, Technology & Society* 30 (2010) 430–45.

———. "The Iconoclasm of Jacques Ellul." *Bulletin of Science, Technology & Society* 18 (1998) 76–86.

Walters, Gerald, and Hudson, Kenneth. *Technology and Society.* Bath: Bath University Press, 1966.

Wauzzinski, Robert A. *Discerning Prometheus: The Cry for Wisdom in Our Technological Society.* London: Associated University Presses, 2001.

Weber, Joseph C. "Feuerbach, Barth, and Theological Methodology." *Journal of Religion* 46 (1966) 24–36.

Webster, Robert. "Thomas Merton and the Textuality of Self: An Experiment in Postmodern Spirituality." *Journal of Religion* 78 (1998) 387–404.

Weil, Simone. *Oppression and Liberty.* Translated by Arthur Wills and John Petrie. Amherst: University of Massachusetts Press, 1955.

Wentworth, Sue Fisher. "On the Lookout for the Unexpected: Ellul as Combative Contemplative." *Ellul Forum* 52 (2013). http://ellul.org/?p=385.

Williams, Rowan. "Not Being Serious: Thomas Merton and Karl Barth." Archbishop of Canterbury website, 10 December 2008. http://rowanwilliams. archbishopofcanterbury.org/articles.php/1205/not-being-serious-thomas-merton-and-karl-barth.

Willis, Russell Edward. "Toward a Theological Ethics of Technology: An Analysis in Dialogue with Jacques Ellul, James Gustafson, and Philosophy of Technology." PhD diss., Emory University, 1990.

Winner, Langdon. *Autonomous Technology.* Cambridge: MIT Press, 1977.

———. *The Whale and the Reactor.* Chicago: University of Chicago Press, 1986.

Wu, John, Jr. "Technological Perspectives: Thomas Merton and the One Eyed Giant." *Merton Annual* 13 (2000) 80–104.

Zwick, Mark, and Louise Zwick. *The Catholic Worker Movement: Intellectual and Spiritual Origins.* Mahwah, NJ: Paulist, 2005.

--

12991018R00118

Made in the USA
San Bernardino, CA
04 July 2014